SIMPLER

THE FUTURE of GOVERNMENT

CASS R. SUNSTEIN

SIMON & SCHUSTER

New York   London   Toronto   Sydney   New Delhi

Simon & Schuster
1230 Avenue of the Americas
New York, NY 10020

First Simon & Schuster hardcover edition April 2013

SIMON & SCHUSTER and colophon are registered
trademarks of Simon & Schuster, Inc.

For information about special discounts for bulk purchases,
please contact Simon & Schuster Special Sales at
1-866-506-1949 or business@simonandschuster.com.

The Simon & Schuster Speakers Bureau can bring authors to your live event.
For more information or to book an event contact the Simon & Schuster Speakers
Bureau at 1-866-248-3049 or visit our website at www.simonspeakers.com.

Designed by Akasha Archer

Manufactured in the United States of America

10 9 8 7 6 5 4 3 2 1

Library of Congress Cataloging-in-Publication Data

Sunstein, Cass R.
    Simpler : the future of government / Cass R. Sunstein.
        pages   cm
    1. United States—Politics and government—2009–   2. United States—Economic
policy—2009–   I. Title.
    E907.S86   2013
    973.932—dc23   2012048234

ISBN 978-1-4767-2659-5
ISBN 978-1-4767-2661-8 (ebook)

For Samantha Power and Richard Thaler

[E]ach agency shall identify and consider regulatory approaches that reduce burdens and maintain flexibility and freedom of choice for the public. These approaches include warnings, appropriate default rules, and disclosure requirements as well as provision of information to the public in a form that is clear and intelligible.

Executive Order 13563, "Improving Regulation and Regulatory Review"

Over and over the old scouts will say, "The guy has a great body," or "This guy may be the best body in the draft." And every time they do, Billy will say, "We're not selling jeans here," and deposit yet another highly touted player, beloved by the scouts, onto his shit list.

Michael Lewis, *Moneyball*

CONTENTS

INTRODUCTION

The Cockpit of the Regulatory State

This is a book about making things simpler. In particular, it is about how governments can be much better, and do much better, if they make people's lives easier and get rid of unnecessary complexity. Think, for a moment, about the best computers and tablets. They have all sorts of complicated machinery—machinery that is so complicated, in fact, that it would have been barely imaginable just a decade before. But for users, they are simple and intuitive. They don't require manuals. You can work with them on the basis of what you already know. Government should be a lot more like that.

I am not saying that government should be much smaller. I do believe that in some domains, smaller is better, and government should shrink. But that is not my topic here. To have a simpler government, you need to have a government. The term *user-friendly* isn't exactly user-friendly, but simplicity is friendly, and complexity is not. True, complexity has its place, but in the future, governments, whatever their size, have to get simpler. To understand how I came to these views, to see what progress we have already made, and to know what the future has in store, we need to step back a bit.

In 2008, I had my first date (or maybe predate interview) with my now-wife, Samantha Power. Offering a little test (in case it really was a date), she asked me, "If you could have any job in the world, other than law professor, what would it be?" As I later learned, she was hoping to hear that I would play in the E Street Band with Bruce Springsteen or start at shortstop for the Boston Red Sox. Instead I said, apparently with a dreamy, faraway, what-could-possibly-be-better look, "Ohhhh, OIRA."

Her answer: "What the heck is OIRA?" (She might have used a four-letter word other than "heck.") Miraculously, I got a second date.

OIRA (pronounced o-eye-rah) is Washington-speak for a little office with a big impact: the White House Office of Information and Regulatory Affairs. OIRA was created in 1980 by the Paperwork Reduction Act. (Yes, there is such a thing.) Under the Paperwork Reduction Act, no federal agency is allowed to collect information from the American people, or to make you fill out a form, unless OIRA allows it to do so. In 1981, President Ronald Reagan gave OIRA an even more important role, which is to oversee federal regulation. By executive order, President Reagan also said, in a controversial and crucial provision, that "regulatory action shall not be undertaken unless the potential benefits to society for the regulation outweigh the potential costs to society." He charged OIRA with responsibility for ensuring compliance with that edict.

In that very year, I happened to be working as a young lawyer in the Department of Justice. By a stroke of luck, I was heavily involved in the legal work that established what has turned out to be OIRA's enduring role. I was even able to participate in the drafting of the all-important cost-benefit provision. For nearly three decades, heading OIRA had been my dream job.

From 2009 to 2012, I ended up as administrator of OIRA. In that position, I helped to oversee the issuance of nearly two thousand rules from federal agencies. Under President Obama's direction, I promoted simplification, including the use of plain language, reductions in red tape, readable summaries of complex rules, and the elimination of costly, unjustified requirements. I argued in favor of the use of "nudges"—simple, low-cost, freedom-preserving approaches, drawing directly from behavioral economics, that promise to save money, to improve people's health, and to lengthen their lives. Also under President Obama's direction, I promoted a disciplined emphasis on costs and benefits, in an effort to ensure that the actions of government are based on facts and evidence, not intuitions, anecdotes, dogmas, or the views of powerful interest groups.

In this book I describe the large-scale transformation in American government that took place while I was OIRA administrator. I explore initiatives designed to increase simplicity—some now in effect, others on the horizon, still others for the distant future. As we will see, initiatives of this kind can be used not only by governments all over the world but by countless private organizations as well, including businesses large and small, and indeed by all of us in our daily lives. Each of us can benefit from simplicity, and all of us can make things simpler.

The Cockpit

The OIRA administrator is often described as the nation's "regulatory czar." That is a wild overstatement. The president leads the executive branch, and the United States has no czars (really). But the term does give a clue to the influence and range of the office. OIRA is the cockpit of the regulatory state.

The office oversees federal regulations involving clean air and water, food safety, financial stability, national security, health care, energy, agriculture, workplace safety, sex and race discrimination, highway safety, immigration, education, crime, disability rights, and much more. As a general rule, no significant rule can be issued by any of the nation's Cabinet departments— including the Department of Transportation, the Department of Treasury, the Department of State, and the Environmental Protection Agency— unless OIRA says so.

Of course, OIRA does not work on its own. On the contrary, the OIRA administrator works for the president, and many others in the Executive Office of the President have important roles. For example, the OIRA administrator works under the director of the Office of Management and Budget, a Cabinet member whose principal concern is usually the budget, but who may have something to say about rules. In addition, the chairs of the National Economic Council and the Domestic Policy Council (both with offices in the West Wing of the White House) might have a strong view about federal regulations. Their positions count.

On scientific issues, the head of the Office of Science and Technology Policy is central. On economic matters, the Council of Economic Advisers has a lot of technical expertise and is indispensable to federal rulemaking. The Office of the Vice President may have important information to add. The White House is managed by the president's chief of staff, and under any president, the chief of staff is immensely important, because he is in charge of ensuring fidelity to the president's priorities. OIRA is part of a team, not a free agent, and the unambiguous leader of the team is the president.

Nonetheless, OIRA's authority to slow down or even to halt regulations— to say no to members of the president's Cabinet—gives the administrator a major role in shaping their content. Suppose, for example, that OIRA believes that there is a better way to save lives on the highway. Perhaps a new approach would be more lenient, more stringent, simpler, or just different. If that is what OIRA thinks, it has a real opportunity to work with the Department of Transportation to explore that possibility. And if OIRA thinks that a rule—involving, for example, clean water—should not go forward, it is possible that the rule will not see the light of day. (After I had been in the job for a few years, a Cabinet member showed up at my office and told my chief of staff, "I work for Cass Sunstein." Of course that wasn't true—but still.)

OIRA also has a big role in shaping the president's agenda. With the support of the president and other high-level officials, it can help move the government in different directions. It can refuse to approve complex or expensive rules. It can certainly nudge. It can protect small businesses, perhaps by encouraging agencies to exempt them from expensive rules. It can promote new rules to protect human rights and food safety, to prevent sexual violence, or to produce big increases in the fuel economy of cars. It can support efforts to protect against terrorist attacks. It can ask agencies to deregulate—to eliminate outmoded and costly regulatory requirements. It can promote efforts to prevent distracted driving, to prohibit discrimination on the basis of sexual orientation, or to use electronic health records (potentially saving both money and lives). In multiple ways, it can help save lives.

As it happens, I have known President Obama for many years, ever since 1991, when he started to teach at the University of Chicago Law School (my professional home for over a quarter of a century). A year or so before that, a friend of mine on the Chicago faculty said that we should consider hiring a sensational *Harvard Law Review* editor with whom he had been working. I remember the conversation well, in part because of the young editor's unusual name. Chicago ended up hiring Barack Obama, who became a colleague and a friend. Blessed by that bit of good fortune, I was privileged to get my dream job.

Regulatory Moneyball, Not Sewer Talk

Here is a possible approach to regulatory issues, one that can be tempting to some government officials: Ask which groups favor or oppose a proposed rule, who would be satisfied and who distressed, and whether a particular approach could be chosen that would please some without displeasing others. These questions are not exactly irrelevant; public officials need to answer them. But they are far from the most important matters. On the rare occasions when members of my staff pointed out the views of interest groups, I responded (I hope with humor, but also with a point), "That's sewer talk. Get your mind out of the gutter."

As OIRA administrator, I sought to focus instead on these questions: What do we actually know about the likely effects of proposed rules? What would be their human consequences? What are the costs and benefits? How can government avoid reliance on guesses and hunches? What do we know about what existing rules are actually doing for—or to—the American people? How can we make things simpler?

Science is often indispensable to answering these questions, and scientific experts, inside and outside the federal government, are indispensable too. To resolve disputes about the likely effects of rules, economists are essential. Some of the most helpful insights come from cutting-edge social science, including behavioral economics, which attempts to study how people actually act, rather than how standard economic theory supposes that they act. We have started to incorporate the resulting findings, and we need to do far more.

The plea for empirical foundations may seem obvious, a little like a plea for sense rather than nonsense, or for a day of sunshine rather than brutal cold. If so, think for a moment about *Moneyball*, the best-selling book (and Oscar-nominated film) about Billy Beane, who worked with his statistics-obsessed assistant, Paul DePodesta, to bring the Oakland Athletics into the top tier of baseball teams. In a short time, Beane and DePodesta transformed baseball itself, by substituting empirical data for long-standing dogmas, intuitions, and anecdote-driven judgments.

Consider this exchange:

"The guy's an athlete, Bill," the old scout says. "There's a lot of upside there."

"He can't hit," says Billy.

"He's not that bad a hitter," says the old scout.

"Yeah, what happens when he doesn't know a fastball is coming?" says Billy.

"He's a tools guy," says the old scout. . . .

"But can he hit?" asks Billy.

"He can hit," says the old scout, unconvincingly.

Paul reads the player's college batting statistics. They contain a conspicuous lack of extra base hits and walks.

"My only question," says Billy, "if he's that good a hitter why doesn't he hit better?" . . .

Over and over the old scouts will say, "The guy has a great body," or "This guy may be the best body in the draft." And every time they do, Billy will say, "We're not selling jeans here," and deposit yet another highly touted player, beloved by the scouts, onto his shit list.[1]

Too much of the time, those thinking about regulation have been a lot like old baseball scouts in the era before Billy Beane. Scouts said that someone is "a tools guy" or that he "has a great body." Those seeking or resisting regulation say, "The public is very worried," or "Polls show that the majority of people strongly favor protection against air pollution," or "The industry has strong views," or "The environmental groups will go nuts," or "A powerful senator is very upset," or "If an accident occurs, there will be hell to pay." In government, I heard one or more of these claims every week.

None of these points addresses the right question, which is what policies and regulations will actually achieve. As we shall see, we keep developing better tools for answering that question. All over the world, regulatory systems need their own Billy Beanes and Paul DePodestas, carefully assessing what rules will do before the fact and testing them after the fact, and occasionally depositing some highly touted rules, beloved by regulators, onto the shit list.

We're not selling jeans here.

Doing, Not Doing, Undoing

Between 2009 and 2012, a lot of new rules were established. As we will see, they are saving both lives and money. (Admittedly, some of them are pretty complex.) But a lot of potential rules, favored by one or another influential group, never saw the light of day. And at the same time that new rules were being issued, a number of existing rules were streamlined, simplified, or eliminated.

Insisting on careful analysis of costs and benefits, we issued historic rules to increase the fuel economy of cars and trucks, in the process saving consumers billions of dollars, increasing energy security, and making the air a lot cleaner. (It is a parenthetical benefit, but a big benefit nonetheless, that people will have to spend a lot less time going to gas stations; that makes life a bit simpler.) We took unprecedented steps to increase safety on the highways and to combat distracted driving. We adopted rules to allow HIV-positive people to come into our nation. We issued many new safeguards for airline passengers—among other things, banning more-than-three-hour delays on the tarmac and requiring airlines to disclose hidden fees, to pay higher penalties for overbooking flights, and to provide adequate food and water after a two-hour tarmac delay.

We made refrigerators, dishwashers, clothes washers, and other appliances far more energy-efficient. We imposed strict limits on air pollution from power plants, saving thousands of lives annually as a result. We promoted numerous steps to improve nutrition in schools and to reduce childhood obesity. We increased cigarette taxes and required graphic health warnings to be placed on cigarette packages. We took strong steps to combat discrimination on the basis of disability, sex, and sexual orientation.

While doing all this, we refused to issue a large number of rules favored by progressive groups, generally on the theory that they could not be justified, especially in an economically difficult time. Indeed, the Obama administration issued fewer regulations in its first four years than did the Reagan, George H. W. Bush, Clinton, and George W. Bush administrations in their first four years. We closely monitored the number and the cost of rules, and when we declined to proceed, it was often to reduce cumulative burdens and to ensure against undue complexity in the system. In a highly controversial but unquestionably correct decision, the president himself told the Environmental Protection Agency that he did not support finalizing an air pollution rule that would reduce ozone emissions.

Wherever the law allowed, we insisted on careful consideration of benefits and costs. We focused on economic growth and job creation, and we sought to ensure that regulation did not compromise either of those goals. We recognized (and this is a critical point, sometimes overlooked by progressive groups) that when high costs are imposed on the private sector, it is not only some abstraction called "business" that pays the bill. Consumers may pay too, in the form of higher prices—and higher prices are especially hard on people who don't have a lot of money to spend. Workers may be harmed as well, through lower wages and hours and possibly fewer jobs. High costs on large businesses can hurt many people. Small businesses create a lot of jobs, and when they are faced with excessive regulatory burdens, the economy and numerous human beings are going to suffer.

We were not only interested in issuing smart regulations. We were focused on deregulation too. For now and for the future, sensible deregulation is a high priority; it should be a continuing part of modern government, and it is a crucial part of Regulatory Moneyball. To that end, we initiated a historic "regulatory lookback," designed to scrutinize rules on the books to see what could be streamlined, simplified, or removed. The lookback has already eliminated a large number of costly and pointless rules and requirements, in the process saving billions of dollars and taking away tens of millions of hours in annual paperwork burdens. I expect that these numbers will be a lot larger before long.

In fact "retrospective analysis" of existing rules, meant to assess what is working and what is not, has become a standard part of American government. This development is attracting worldwide attention, and it probably counts as the most important innovation in regulatory policy since President Reagan first created the OIRA process more than three decades ago. It is a central feature of a simpler government.

No matter who occupies the White House in the coming decades, much of the transformation will endure. It will endure in large part because it has no obvious political tilt. To be sure, many regulations split people along political lines. But many do not, and Democrats and Republicans, liberals and conservatives, left and right—all should be able to support careful analysis of costs and benefits and continuing scrutiny of rules on the books.

The transformation is hardly complete. To simplify the system, to protect safety and health, and to promote economic prosperity, we need to do much more.

Nudges and Choice Architecture

I have referred to the use of nudges as a regulatory tool. For many years, I have worked (with my friend and colleague, the funny and brilliantly creative economist Richard Thaler) on that topic.[2] Nudges consist of approaches that do not force anyone to do anything and that maintain freedom of choice, but that have the potential to make people healthier, wealthier, and happier. Consider, for example, a requirement that automobile companies disclose the fuel economy of new cars, or an educational campaign to combat texting while driving, or an effort to encourage employers to enroll employees automatically in savings plans. Nudges are often the height of simplicity. Thaler even has a mantra: *Make It Easy*.

Those who favor nudges recognize the importance of freedom of choice. They respect free markets and private liberty. They allow people to go their own way. At the same time, they emphasize that people may err and that, in some cases, most of us can use a little help. They insist that choices are made against a background, created by private and public institutions. Nudges are everywhere, whether we see them or not.

Good nudges should be taken as a crucial part of simplification and Regulatory Moneyball. They are based on an accurate, rather than fanciful, understanding of how human beings think and act. They are subject to careful empirical testing. What matters is whether they work. The best nudges have high benefits and low costs.

Choice architecture is the social environment against which we make our decisions. It is not possible to dispense with a social environment, and hence choice architecture is an inevitable (though often invisible) part of our lives. A bookstore has a choice architecture (which books do you see first?); so does a website that sells books (how big are the onscreen covers?). Choice architecture can be found when we turn on a computer; when we enter a restaurant, a hospital, or a grocery store; when we select a mortgage, a car, a health care plan, or a credit card; when we visit our favorite websites; and when we apply for a driver's license or a building permit or Social Security benefits. For all of us, a key question is whether the relevant choice architecture is helpful and simple or harmful, complex, and exploitative. Good nudges improve choice architecture.

In my years in the Obama administration, the new policies, many of them nudges, included the following:

- Creative efforts *to ease people's choices*, making it far easier for them to attend college, to save for retirement, to get nutritious meals at school, and to obtain health insurance.
- *Disclosure requirements*, designed to protect students, consumers, and investors by ensuring that they "know before they owe."
- A general emphasis on promoting *freedom of choice*, promoting regulatory approaches that maximize that form of freedom.
- *Private-public partnerships*, designed to reduce deaths and diseases from smoking, distracted driving, and obesity.
- A strict emphasis on *measuring costs and benefits*, with an insistence that the benefits must justify the costs.
- An emphasis on the importance of *human dignity*, relevant to rules designed to reduce prison rape and forbidding discrimination on the basis of disability and sexual orientation.
- The *lookback* at rules on the books, designed to eliminate or to streamline hundreds of requirements that no longer make sense (if they ever did).
- Efforts to promote *international regulatory cooperation* by eliminating pointless divergences in regulatory requirements across national boundaries.

Simplifications

Some people, especially those who are not enthusiastic about President Obama, are likely to find my emphasis on simplification a bit puzzling, perhaps even surreal. They might ask, "Hasn't the Obama administration opted for more regulation, and more complexity, at every turn? Isn't the Affordable Care Act intolerably complicated, and indeed a bit of a mess?" Maybe the critics will agree that Wall Street reform has some virtues, to protect consumers and to reduce the risk of another financial meltdown, but surely (they will insist) simplicity isn't among those virtues. We are speaking, after all, of laws that run to thousands of pages. Simplification is the goal of those who favor free markets and laissez-faire, who want to scale back government and return decisions to the private sector. How can a former Obama administration official presume, or dare, to write a book about simplification?

To provide an answer, we need to make a distinction. Some people want a radical and wholesale reduction in the functions of the federal government. They would like to return the United States to something like, or at least closer to, what it was before Franklin Delano Roosevelt's New Deal. Most Americans vigorously disagree with them (as do I). But let me be very clear: This book is not meant to address the question whether we should return to the days of Herbert Hoover, or dramatically reduce government's functions, in order to promote simplification or for any other reason. That is not my goal, and while it is an important topic, I do not explore it here. My goal is instead to suggest that *without a massive reduction in its current functions*, government can be far more effective, far less confusing, far less counterproductive, and far more helpful if it opts, wherever it can, for greater simplicity. If this is a less revolutionary goal than a return to Hoover, we shall nonetheless see that it is revolutionary in its own way.

There is another understanding of simplification, one that also accepts government's current functions. On this understanding, what we need is fewer rules and more discretion. Here is the basic claim: Too much of the time, the government tells people exactly what to do and exactly how to do it. It issues highly prescriptive requirements for schools, teachers, hospitals, and employers, at an absurd level of detail, rather than just describing its general goal and letting human beings use their own creativity and initiative to get there. In a nutshell: Fewer rules and more common sense.

In many contexts, this suggestion is entirely right, and it needs to be heeded. In the Obama administration, we took it seriously, avoiding inflexible requirements and using public-private partnerships in such areas as childhood obesity, distracted driving, and consumer protection. In a historic executive order, which now operates as a kind of mini-constitution for the regulatory state, President Obama directed agencies to select flexible "performance standards" rather than rigid "design standards." Time and again, we sought to identify ways to enable those in the private sector to choose their own route to promote social goals. This approach reduces costs. It promotes freedom. And there is far more to do in this vein.

But the preference for "common sense," and the critique of unduly specific rules, should be taken with many grains of salt. As OIRA administrator, I often heard the following plea from the private sector: "Please, tell us what you want us to do!" On many occasion, companies said that they were prepared to comply with the rules, and to do so in good faith, but they needed to know what, specifically, compliance entailed. They did not want ambiguity or vagueness, even if it seemed to be an invitation to use common sense. One reason is that they did not want to run legal risks; specificity could inform them how to be on the right side of the line. Another reason is that sometimes they did not know what, exactly, they ought to do, and details would be extremely helpful. Common sense just wasn't enough. And from the standpoint of government itself, a grant of discretion to the private sector could also be a problem, because people might choose approaches that would undermine important goals, such as workplace safety and clean air.

Think again about the best tablets and computers. They don't leave people at sea, asking them to use common sense to figure out what to do next. They are easy to use because the rules are clear and easy to understand and follow. Even three-year-olds can do that. (I have one, and he can.)

Of course, companies often sought, and seek, greater discretion rather than less. Undue specificity can be a real problem, in part because it is connected with undue complexity and might create bureaucratic nightmares. We can therefore identify two fallacies. The first is that the future of government lies in fewer rules and more discretion. The second is that the future of government lies in more rules and less discretion.

To make progress on this question, we need to avoid abstractions and chest-thumping. The context matters. If government can reduce costs and increase flexibility by granting discretion, and if it can do so without creating uncertainty, evasion, or confusion, it should grant discretion. If government can reduce costs and increase simplicity by producing clear rules, and if it can do so without creating expensive and pointless rigidity, it should opt for clear rules. The project of simplification will call for an increase in discretion in some domains and an increase in clear requirements in others.

Politics

What about politics? You might well ask.

It is impossible to work in Washington without having an acute sense, every day, of political polarization. Here's one of the worst parts. It is easy to find cases in which some Republicans concluded that if President Obama was for something, they were against it, not because they thought that it was a bad idea (in fact they might even like it), but only because President Obama was for it. Strong evidence, discussed in chapter 4, suggests that people will often follow their political party even if their own independent view suggests that their party is wrong. A number of conservatives and Republicans, including members of Congress, privately praised our efforts at simplification and even told me that they much liked nudges. But they wouldn't say so publicly.

There is a serious problem here for actual governance, and for Democrats and Republicans alike. Any president knows that if he supports a particular policy, a lot of people will oppose it immediately, and that if the administration maintains a discreet silence, some of its preferred policies might, ironically, get enacted.

Most of the ideas in this book can be supported by people of diverse political affiliations. Prime Minister David Cameron of the United Kingdom is a Conservative, and he has been keenly interested in the kinds of initiatives explored here. He is a big fan of nudging. In fact I have worked closely with my counterparts in the United Kingdom, mostly in the Conservative Party, who have been entirely focused on careful empirical analysis, simplification, removal of red tape, and nudging. Advised by Thaler, Prime Minister Cameron has gone so far as to create a Behavioural Insights Team, located in his Cabinet Office and directly focused on careful empirical analysis and on nudges. The team is informally called the "Nudge Unit." The official website states that its "work draws on insights from the growing body of academic research in the fields of behavioural economics and psychology which show how often subtle changes to the way in which decisions are framed can have big impacts." The team has used these insights to spur important new initiatives in numerous areas, including smoking cessation, energy efficiency, organ donation, consumer protection, and compliance strategies in general. It is saving a lot of money and making a lot of progress.

In fact nudging is an increasingly international phenomenon. Nudges are being used by private and public organizations in South Korea, Australia, Denmark, Germany, and many other nations.

Simplification is hardly part of a partisan agenda. It has broad appeal, especially in a period of economic difficulty, in which reduced complexity is important for business in general, for small business in particular, and for many of us in our daily lives. Nudging can also be used to promote a wide range of goals, including those that are shared by people with diverse political views. And because nudges avoid mandates and bans, they are particularly appealing to the many conservatives who seek to maintain flexibility and freedom of choice.

Insofar as I focus here on cost-benefit analysis and the need to rethink and scale back existing regulatory requirements, we already have compelling evidence of the possibility of transcending standard political divisions. Cost-benefit analysis has been supported for over three decades and by five presidents, both Republican and Democratic. It is clearly here to stay. Indeed, it is part of the informal constitution of the American regulatory state, and it too is attracting support all over the world. To be sure, some regulations split people along political lines. But many do not, and Democrats and Republicans, liberals and conservatives, left and right—all should be able to support careful analysis of costs and benefits and continuing scrutiny of rules on the books.

Let's return to our main theme. In a period of great economic difficulty, recent policies signal the arrival of a fresh approach to government, one that is uniquely well-suited to democracies that seek to achieve prosperity in the global economy of the twenty-first century. While a lot was done between 2009 and 2012, it was merely a start. All large institutions, including governments, can do a lot more to make things more automatic and to enlist simplicity, seeking to match their products and services to what people find natural and intuitive. One of the main goals of this book is to identify enduring lessons not only for governments but for the private sector as well, including schools, hospitals, and businesses both large and small.

1

THE MOST DANGEROUS MAN IN AMERICA

In a difficult economic period, what is the proper role of government? How should public officials proceed when they seek to stabilize the financial system, reduce air pollution, protect consumers and investors, safeguard national security, reform health care, and increase energy independence? Might creative approaches put money in people's pockets, and maybe even save lives, without squelching innovation and competitiveness? Is it possible to protect public safety and health while promoting economic growth and increasing employment? Will it help if government is open and transparent and tells the public what it knows and what it does not know?

These questions have produced a lot of debate over the past half-century. The debates are most prominent during elections and amid protest movements, but they occur every day. They can be found in corporate boardrooms, Washington think tanks, universities, and high schools, and over family dinners. For nearly three decades, I spent much of my professional life writing about them, mostly in obscure, technical publications in academic journals with such enticing names as *Journal of Risk and Uncertainty*, *Environmental and Resource Economics*, *Philosophy and Public Affairs*, and *Journal of Political Philosophy*.

One of my major claims has been that we need to go beyond sterile, tired, and rhetorical debates about "more" or "less" government and focus instead on identifying the best tools and on learning, with close attention to evidence, what really works. Nudges are especially promising in this regard. (In government, I saw the immense importance of selecting good tools but also learned that however sterile, tired, and rhetorical, the "more" or "less" debates continue to matter. They have a lot of life left. They might be immortal. They might be vampires. Possibly zombies.)

Along with many others, I have also focused on the importance of considering both costs and benefits. Following President Reagan, who was largely responsible for making cost-benefit analysis a regular feature of American government, I have contended that regulators need to focus on *net benefits*, that is, benefits minus costs. If an energy efficiency rule costs $50 million but has benefits of $150 million, it is probably a good idea, at least if we can trust those numbers. I have urged that a disciplined analysis of costs and benefits is indispensable to deciding what to do, and as a nudge to move public officials in the right directions.

Suppose that we are deciding whether to require trucking companies to install new safety equipment, airlines to give more rest time to pilots, farmers to reduce the risks of food safety problems, or power plants to impose new pollution controls. These decisions should not be resolved by focusing on a specific accident or incident that occurred two months earlier, or the supposed need for precaution, or the concerns and complaints of well-organized private groups, or the fear that if something bad happens in the next months, there will be hell to pay. Instead of exploring these less than productive issues, I suggested that we should try to catalogue the costs and benefits of alternative courses of action and choose the approach that would do the most good and the least harm.

One of my central points was that cost-benefit analysis and democratic self-government are mutually supporting. Openness about costs and benefits can inform democratic decisions. Without a clear sense of the likely consequences, sensible choices become far more difficult, even impossible. Indeed, efforts to catalogue costs and benefits, and to disclose that catalogue to officials and the public, are themselves a kind of choice architecture—choice architecture for choice architects—and they can greatly improve public decisions. And if a rule or requirement is too confusing or complex, people are likely to complain. In that way, public scrutiny can be a great friend of sense rather than nonsense, and of simplicity rather than obfuscation.

Knocking on Doors

In January 2008, I found myself alongside Obama's advisers Austan Goolsbee and Samantha Power, knocking on doors on a cold night in Des Moines, Iowa, for Senator Barack Obama. Needless to say, many people were knocking on doors in Iowa that month. Some besieged Iowans were less than receptive. They had to answer a lot of doorbells. A grim-faced older woman threatened to slam the door in my face. When I explained that I was there not to see her but instead her voting-age daughter, Ashley, she promptly yelled out to her daughter, *"Ashley, will you come slam the door in his face?"* (She did.)

Despite the slammed door, Senator Obama won the Iowa primary. After a lot more door-knocking, the Democratic nomination and the presidency were his.

Very soon after Election Day, I had a brief chat with the president-elect, congratulating him on his victory. In early December, Peter Orszag, the incoming director of the Office of Management and Budget, invited me to camp out in Washington to work with the transition. A very large team of people was crammed into a single building with small offices. The team included the president-elect, the vice-president-elect, and soon-to-be Cabinet members and high-level advisers. All of us were keenly aware that the nation was in the midst of the most difficult economic period since the Great Depression. The situation was already quite dire, indeed far worse than most Americans were aware—and we knew that it could soon get a lot worse.

Along with President Clinton's OIRA administrator, Sally Katzen, and her former special assistant, Michael Fitzpatrick, I focused solely on regulatory policy: How would the Obama administration deal with the legacy of the Bush administration? How could we correct its failures? What should we repeal? What should we keep? What should we add? What new directions would be best? Our little team attempted to answer these questions. We worked on a set of executive orders that, within the first few days of the Obama presidency, would require open government, prompt a rethinking of regulation, and generally help set the stage for much of what would come.

In early December, Peter Orszag told me that the president-elect wanted me to join the administration to direct OIRA. That was an easy offer to accept. I had lunch in the West Wing of the White House with Susan Dudley, President Bush's OIRA administrator, who said that she had "the best job in Washington." After she described the issues that she encountered in a given day—homeland security, air pollution, energy, highway safety, civil rights—it was clear that I would be immensely lucky to be able to follow her. In fact it would be the honor of a lifetime.

In light of the fact that the nation was facing a period of acute economic difficulty, I thought that OIRA's role was likely to be especially important. In December 2008 a full-scale depression did not seem out of the question. Stupid, complex, costly regulations, hurting businesses large and small, might make things a lot worse. But financial reform and health care reform were presidential priorities, and smart regulations could make things better and help to provide safeguards against future catastrophes, economic or otherwise. In many areas, ranging from highway safety and food safety to clean air, new regulations could save a lot of lives. At the time, I believed that a great deal could be done to transform the regulatory state, promoting simplification, adopting nudges, using new, state-of-the-art tools, avoiding unintended side effects, and making evidence and data, rather than sloganeering and dogmatism, the foundation of regulatory policy. In retrospect, those beliefs were right. But there was a lot about OIRA that I didn't know, and a lot that I thought I knew was just wrong.

With enthusiasm, I agreed to head OIRA. In early January, weeks before the inauguration, the White House announced that the president intended to nominate me. I expected a formal nomination within a few weeks, with confirmation shortly thereafter, so that I could start just about immediately. How naive I was.

Some progressive groups were quite unhappy with the president's decision, mostly because of my enthusiasm for cost-benefit analysis and my wariness about excessive and costly regulation. Many progressives feared, and said publicly, that I would be an obstacle to necessary safeguards for the public. In a column with a scary title, "How Anti-Regulation Is Obama's New Regulatory Czar?" Frank O'Donnell, president of Clean Air Watch, said that progressives "would've screamed" if a Republican president had selected someone with my views. He insisted that I "shouldn't get a pass just because [I] was nominated by Obama."

Moreover, any Democratic nominee for OIRA was bound to run into trouble with Republican senators. Republicans have long seen the OIRA administrator as the only safeguard against expensive, crazy, job-killing regulations. They would inevitably fear that under a Democratic president, this safeguard would be far too weak. (By 2011, the term "job-killing regulations" had become so pervasive in Washington that I wondered whether the word "regulation" had been excised from the English language and replaced with that term.)

The Life Audit

Before my nomination could be sent formally to the Senate, I was subjected to the nightmarish process known as vetting, which entails an extremely careful look, by the White House, at a potential nominee's background, including speeches, articles, books, personal life, and taxes. Think of this as a Life Audit by a team of people who have a far broader mandate than the Internal Revenue Service. Your whole life is an open book.

Unfortunately for my vetters, I have written countless speeches, well over four hundred articles, and a lot of books. The vetters had to sift through thousands of pages to ensure that I hadn't said anything that was inexplicable or beyond the pale. I didn't have copies of most of my speeches (I tend to speak from handwritten notes), and no one could be expected to wade through four hundred articles, so the vetting process was not a lot of fun. Nonetheless, a small, intrepid team did its best. While it found nothing obviously disqualifying, there were plenty of red flags. For example, I had written about animal rights, suggesting that lawyers should be able to represent abused animals to sue for violations of animal cruelty laws. I had also said, in oral remarks captured on video, that sport hunting should be banned. (Ouch. I know, I know, that's a bad idea. I know. I know.) Without endorsing the idea, I had discussed the possibility of a kind of fairness doctrine for the Internet, calling on politically opposed sites to link to each other. (Ouch again. I hadn't endorsed the idea, and actually I later repudiated it, but still, a bad one.) I had written about abortion, same-sex marriage, pornography, human cloning, and guns. For those who wanted to make trouble for a presidential nomination, I must have seemed a dream come true.

Going through all this material was grueling and miserable, but the tax issue turned out to be far more difficult. This was so not because of any anticipated problem, but because presidential nominees have to devote a lot of time and effort (and money) to a careful investigation to ensure that there was nothing troublesome from past years, or even decades. Tax issues had derailed a number of potential nominees of both parties, and my tax record was subject to close scrutiny.

Here's the problem: Over a period of decades the possibility of a tax glitch, or worse, is pretty high. Suppose, for example, that you have been paying taxes since 1980. Even if you're careful and honest, there's a chance that at some point, you did something wrong, or at least not quite right. If so, the IRS may well have asked you just to pay up, which isn't so bad—but you might have badly jeopardized your chances of Senate confirmation.

In my case, things looked essentially fine. But I didn't remember everything, and my tax accountant, then in his early eighties, faced a barrage of questioning from the White House, sometimes about tax decisions made more than a decade ago. As the scrutiny intensified, I started to worry, every day, that some notice would arrive from the IRS, destroying my prospects and embarrassing me publicly. As it happened, I was a bit late in making a payment to the District of Columbia for unemployment compensation for my son's nanny—fortunately, not a catastrophe.

Somehow I survived the scrutiny. I was finally nominated in late April.

The Most Dangerous Man in America

The vetting turned out to be just the start of the process. Like many presidential nominees, and indeed like many people in the public eye (even if briefly), I learned to live with a simple fact of life: *In the modern era, whatever might be thought will be said.*

Some progressive groups continued to be skeptical or actively hostile. For them, OIRA was not merely an obstacle but evil, a villain, the place where indispensable public protections went to die. They hoped for a fundamental transformation of its role, in which OIRA would let the Environmental Protection Agency and other Cabinet departments do as they wished and no longer carefully scrutinize health, safety, and environmental rules. That kind of transformation, they knew, was not something that I was likely to endorse. They expressed acute disappointment that the president had chosen someone who favored cost-benefit analysis and who promoted modest, low-cost approaches to regulation. As it turned out, nudges weren't wildly popular on the left, which often prefers firm mandates. (By the way, there is unquestionably a place for such mandates, as we will see.)

But the most serious problems emerged on the right. It was widely reported that I was a radical animal rights activist who would seek to ban hunting, forbid meat eating, ban conspiracy theories, outlaw marriage, eliminate free speech, and steal human organs. (Organ stealing, it turned out, is not entirely irrelevant to nudging. Really. I might discuss that later.) Some conservatives began to characterize me as an extremist, a socialist, a Marxist, a Trotskyite, a police state fascist, and some kind of Rothschild Zionist (I confess I have no idea what that is). Wild rumors spread about what I thought and planned to do—an irony, or perhaps destiny's joke, in light of the fact that I had finished a book on the topic of false rumors, and how they spread, just a few months before.[1]

Animals and animal rights turned out to be a major issue (though they occupied a very small fraction of my time and focus when I was an academic). As early as January 15, the Consumer Federation of America wrote that I had "a secret aim to push a radical animal-rights agenda in the White House." In its account, "Sunstein supports outlawing sport hunting, giving animals the legal right to file lawsuits, and using government regulations to phase out meat consumption. . . . Sunstein's work could spell the end of animal agriculture, retail sales of meat and dairy foods, hunting and fishing, biomedical research, pet ownership, zoos and aquariums, traveling circuses, and countless other things Americans take for granted." OMG (as they say).

There was much more. Fifteen conservation and sportsmen organizations sent a group letter to the Senate, asking it to block my nomination. The National Wild Turkey Federation appeared to see my defeat as a particularly high priority. The US Sportsmen's Alliance described me as a "rabid animal rightsist." The Sportsmen's Alliance emphasized the need for sportsmen "to 'take up their arms'" in order "to block this 'Czar,'" who would otherwise "be given the power to impose these views on all of us and destroy our collective heritage." On national television, former Governor Mike Huckabee invited me to south Arkansas, during the opening day of deer season, to see the "reaction" that I "would not enjoy" in light of my proposal to ban hunting. A representative headline from a blog post: "Regulatory 'Czar' Sunstein Defends Stealing Organs from Hopeless Patients." Another described me as a "Murderous Nutcase."

Fearing that I would insist on turning everyone in America into a vegetarian (though I am not one), the influential American Farm Bureau expressed its strong concerns to Congress. A public letter laid out the case against me. As I read it, my heart sank. Opposition from the Bureau is no light matter, and it could get a lot of attention in the US Senate. To address the Bureau's concerns, I met with members twice. They were earnest, decent, unfailingly courteous, informed, substantive, mildly suspicious, and nervous. Would I really try to stop people from eating meat? Would I impose all sorts of new restrictions on the beef industry? (Would my motto be "Put Cows First"?) Under the circumstances, I know, and knew, that these were natural questions for them to ask, but I had no interest in doing anything of the sort. In any case, the OIRA administrator must follow the law and the will of the president, and even if he were inclined to move in such directions, he would have no authority to do so. One of my main goals was to ensure that our regulatory system was compatible with the economic recovery, which would entail careful scrutiny of expensive new rules, including rules that would burden farmers, and serious efforts to reduce costs. The Bureau listened carefully and eventually supported my confirmation.

Notwithstanding that development, the die was cast. This would be an ugly and highly contentious process. Early on, I learned that a Republican senator had placed a hold on my confirmation; this hold was the equivalent of a filibuster, meaning that I could not get an up-or-down vote. (A single senator is entitled to do that, just by saying so.) The problem was that under Senate rules, we had a hard time identifying the senator—the hold was initially anonymous—and so I had no opportunity to meet with him and address his concerns.

After a few weeks, we were able to find out that Senator Pat Roberts of Kansas was responsible for the hold. Finally, he agreed to meet with me. He began the discussion by saying (knowingly and with a twinkle in his eye) that what we needed at OIRA was someone who believed in cost-benefit analysis. He was generous, funny, and kind. He said that he thought I was a good choice and would do a good job, but that of course he would vote against me. He asked me some questions about agriculture and farming, and in response to my answers he agreed to lift the hold. Maybe we were ready for a vote.

But a second hold immediately emerged. Here again we had a hard time identifying the senator who was responsible. It turned out to be Georgia's Saxby Chambliss, whose staff initially seemed hostile and angry (apparently because of agriculture issues) and refused to set up a meeting or even to talk seriously about my nomination. After repeated entreaties from the White House, Chambliss agreed to meet with me. The senator was quite courteous, but the meeting was tough. Whether or not the agricultural community was opposing me (and some segments of it continued to do so), he seemed very concerned that I was on a kind of wild mission against the meat and poultry industries. To me, this was truly surreal. Eventually Senator Chambliss lifted his hold, and we all thought that we could proceed to a vote.

Except not. Senator John Cornyn of Texas decided to put on a new hold, and so we had to meet with him as well. Of course, his schedule was full, and meeting with me was not exactly his top priority. Eventually he agreed to meet. He was not much focused on cows and vegetarianism, but he did press a number of questions about guns and the Second Amendment. My views on the Second Amendment are mainstream—I agree with the view that it creates an individual right to own guns—and he asked me to write him a formal letter to this effect. I did, and he was satisfied.

In the meantime, I learned that powerful Republican-leaning business organizations, including the US Chamber of Commerce and the National Association of Manufacturers, strongly supported my confirmation (on the ground that I favored cost-benefit analysis and would not be likely to rubber-stamp expensive regulations). They had been relatively quiet, in part on the ground that their support could create problems with Democrats and progressive groups. But they decided that it was time to make their views publicly known. Surely, then, we were ready for a vote.

Except not yet. During the confirmation process, the commentator and best-selling writer Glenn Beck, who then had a national television show on Fox, developed what appeared to be a kind of obsession with me. (I use the word advisedly; he has apparently discussed me on the air well over a hundred times.) He despised the idea of nudging. In his view, nudges are a form of manipulation, insidious, sneaky, scary, secret, slimy, smelly, shady. He decided, and said repeatedly on national television while pointing to a picture of me, that I was "the most dangerous man in America." Sometimes he prefaced "most dangerous" with "most evil," as in "most evil, most dangerous man in America." (Considering the fact that the nation has a large number of murderers, that is quite a statement.)

He provided a series of apparent exposés and conspiracy theories, with arrows pointing from one person's face to another person's face, culminating in the claim that the head of OIRA has "one of the most powerful jobs in the world." On several occasions he said that "first it's nudge, then it's shove, then it becomes shoot." He said that I control "everything through nudges."

In Orwell's *1984*, there is a brilliant, powerful, and frightening scene of the "Two Minutes Hate," in which party members must watch a film depicting national enemies. (As it happens, the leading enemy is named Goldstein.) At times, Beck's attacks on me, featuring my smiling face, were not entirely unlike those scenes. A new website was created, stopsunstein .com, filled with inflammatory quotations, some taken out of context to suggest that I endorsed views that I rejected and was merely describing.

I began to receive a lot of hate mail, including death threats, at my unlisted home address. One of them stated, "If I were you I would resign immediately. A well-paid individual, who is armed, knows where you live." And for reasons that remain mysterious to this day, I was still unable to get a vote in the Senate.

In the Meantime

The death threats and confirmation wars did not prevent me from working in government. From the first day of the Obama administration, I was privileged to serve as senior adviser in the Office of Management and Budget during some of the most challenging months in the nation's history. That position did not require confirmation, and while I had to be careful not to perform any of the functions of the OIRA administrator, there was a lot to be done.

In the position of senior adviser, I was able to participate in some high-level discussions involving the central issues of the time, including the future of the auto industry, open government, health care reform, regulation of the financial sector, and environmental protection. I was lucky enough to be present during some of the conversations in which President Obama decided to save General Motors and Chrysler. And I was able to spend a great deal of time in the discussions that led to the Dodd-Frank financial reform law. As we will see, key features of that law can be categorized as nudges.

With respect to OIRA itself, I could not run the operation or meet with those outside government, but I could certainly attend OIRA's staff meetings. One of my main goals was to learn as much as I could and to be in a position, when confirmed, to hit the ground running—to identify and implement the best possible reforms of the OIRA process, with the goal of ensuring that the administration would be able to deliver real safety and health benefits for the American people, and do so in a way that was compatible with economic growth and job creation.

In the meantime, the prospects for an up-or-down vote on my confirmation were increasingly dismal. Toward the close of summer, it looked as if the Republicans would take a hard line against many Obama nominees. With respect to OIRA, our best guess was that Republican senators had decided to apply a process of "rotating holds," so that any time a hold was lifted, another hold would be immediately put in place. For this reason, it was essentially meaningless, I suspect, that Senators Roberts, Chambliss, and Cornyn had lifted their holds. Later in the administration, Republicans routinely blocked up-or-down votes on Obama nominees. It didn't much matter who the nominees were; nomination by President Obama was enough to cause big trouble. But at this stage, this kind of organized effort was not yet usual.

Our only option was to seek to break the filibuster with a cloture vote, which requires sixty votes, and which would require the Senate, in the midst of really important business, to set aside thirty hours for discussion of yours truly. (Is it necessary to say that this too seemed surreal?) Senator Harry Reid, the majority leader, called me to say that he would ensure such a vote. The vote was scheduled for September 9, 2009. On that day, I was put on the phone with a number of fence-sitting senators to try to persuade them that I was not going to ban hunting, steal guns, or focus on rodents. Ultimately the Senate voted 63–35 in my favor, thus allowing an up-or-down vote.

Glenn Beck covered the vote live on national television, showing the proceedings on the Senate floor while telling his viewers ominously that if I was confirmed, they were "in danger." He added, "It is time to get everyone you know to call Capitol Hill [because Sunstein is] the most dangerous guy out there right now."

On September 10, the Senate voted for confirmation by a nail-biting margin of 57–40. Senator Bernie Sanders of Vermont, a socialist, voted against me on the ground that I was too far to the right. I had had a pleasant enough conversation with him on the day of the vote—on reflection, maybe not quite pleasant enough—in which he accused me, perhaps with a tinge of rage, of being biased in favor of big banks and wanting to prevent any regulation of them. I still have no idea where he got that.

Minutes after the favorable tally, the president invited me to the Oval Office for a congratulatory visit. Rahm Emanuel, the president's chief of staff at the time, was the first to greet me, saying with evident sarcasm, "Fifty-seven to forty! That's a landslide!"

It is hard to capture the true terribleness of the contemporary confirmation process: the Life Audit, the risk of a highly public humiliation, the repeated efforts to destroy one's reputation, the accusations, the falsehoods (and the disregard for the truth), the threats, the difficulty of engaging skeptics on the merits. What you learn, but what is almost impossible to appreciate, is that most of the attacks, however personal they seem, are not personal at all; they actually have nothing to do with the human being at whom they are aimed. But as an Obama Cabinet official told me when I asked one day how he was doing, "I have no complaints that you want to hear about." So let's move on.

Professors and Public Officials

From September 10, 2009, until August 10, 2012, I was privileged to head OIRA and thus to play a role in helping to oversee, in the most difficult economic period since the Great Depression, some of the most important domestic policy decisions made in the Obama administration. Beyond the day-to-day interactions about particular rules and decisions, I had a responsibility to think broadly about what we might do that would be new or different, and that might save money and lives, in a way that would promote, or be compatible with, the central goals of climbing out of a terrible economic hole and laying solid foundations for the future.

One of my goals in this book is to explore what was actually done during my time at OIRA—to outline a series of initiatives and changes that, in my view, count as a major reorientation in national regulatory policy. In the process, I offer some glimpses into the operations of the federal government at the highest levels, with the hope that the glimpses might be of general interest and correct some widespread misunderstandings. A little-known secret: While a lot of high-level decisions are portrayed as politically motivated, and while public officials are often accused of "caving" to one or another side, almost all of the time they are just trying to do the right thing. I have referred, for example, to the president's decision not to support finalizing the Environmental Protection Agency's ozone rule. That decision was made on the merits. Contrary to published reports, it was not motivated by politics.

If I did not know it before, I learned in my first week, and probably on my first day, that there is a huge difference between the role of an academic and the role of a public official. The difference is hard to overstate. As an academic, you are supposed to come up with original ideas. You tend to work individually or at most with a few collaborators. You need not—and probably should not—focus only on what is feasible. If an idea is interesting and fresh and makes people think, it might be okay to defend it even if, on reflection, the idea is lousy or a bit nuts. If you are clueless about government (and most academics, even in law and political science, are *completely* clueless about government), it might still be acceptable to venture an interesting, clueless idea, so long as it is really interesting. When I was in government, academic friends would sometimes call me with their latest thoughts, almost all of which were inventive and fascinating, but some of which were daft, and most of which would, as a practical matter, be dead on arrival.

A necessary qualification: Some public officials are dismissive of academics. Hearing an academic's name and proposals, they sometimes roll their eyes, and understandably so. In view of what officials have to do, and how quickly they have to do it, eye-rolling is the right response. But thoughts that seem daft, and would be dead on arrival, sometimes win the day before too long. In economics departments in the 1960s and 1970s, there was a lot of enthusiasm for cost-benefit analysis, even though it was not exactly popular in the halls of power in Washington. In 1981 President Reagan required cost-benefit analysis, and in 2011 President Obama cemented its role. A never-to-be-forgotten quotation from John Maynard Keynes: "The ideas of economists and political philosophers, both when they are right and when they are wrong, are more powerful than is commonly understood. Indeed the world is ruled by little else. Practical men, who believe themselves to be quite exempt from any intellectual influence, are usually the slaves of some defunct economist." In view of the immense influence of Keynes's thinking on practical men and women in government during the Great Recession, these words are especially apt.

In government, you are accountable to your boss, the president of the United States. An idea that is lousy or a bit nuts, or that is really not feasible, is not welcome, even if it makes people think. You must not strike out on your own. You cannot speak publicly without authorization, and what you say is constrained. You are part of a team with a clear leader, and whatever you initiate or proceed with has to be consistent with the judgments and goals of the team. Official documents have to go through a clearance process, which can be long and frustrating, but which is a crucial means of ensuring that the team is committed to it. (After a particularly frustrating clearance process, I pointed out to some of my government colleagues the remarkable coincidence that the word *clearance* contains the exact same number of letters as the word *excrement*. No one didn't know what I meant.)

After a month or two in the job, it is disastrous to be clueless about government. One of my early mistakes was not to invite two very busy, very important people to a certain meeting, on the theory that they were busy and important. Big mistake. They were surprised and offended, and they rightly complained to others. What is true for weddings is true for government as well: Not inviting people can be a terrible idea.

A public official who comes from academic life cannot possibly impose his academic views on the US government. The president is your boss, and you have the rare honor of trying to serve the American people. If OIRA were headed by a radical animal rights activist—as I am not, though I do care plenty about animal welfare—it would be wildly inappropriate for him or her to try to pursue an animal rights agenda. As an academic, I coauthored a paper on conspiracy theories—about how they arise, why people believe them, and what government might do to set the record straight if they are threatening to give rise to violence. In university circles, the paper was a bit of a snooze, but it became a lightning rod and was ridiculously mischaracterized in certain circles (especially, but not only, among those who believed that the United States had covered up its own participation in the 9/11 attacks). That paper was relevant to exactly nothing that I did in government.

In fact most of my academic writing was entirely irrelevant to my job. Most, but not all.

Before entering government, I believed in the immense importance of careful analysis of costs and benefits. That belief has not wavered for an instant. In fact I am even more committed to that belief today.

Before entering government, I believed in the importance of careful inspection of rules on the books, to see what is working and what is not, and to streamline, simplify, or fix what is not working. That belief became far stronger while I was a public official.

Before government service, I believed in the importance of engaging the public in the process of evaluating and reevaluating rules. Those outside government often know a lot more than public officials do. They may well have the best ideas about what should be accelerated, what should be changed, and what should be stopped in its tracks. My experience in government did not undermine this belief. On the contrary, it fortified it, not only or even mostly because democratic government requires consultation of the public (though that is true), but most fundamentally because policy decisions need to benefit from the dispersed knowledge of the public.

I believed in nudges before entering government. I believe in them today.

But What Does OIRA Actually Do?

I have said that OIRA is the cockpit of the regulatory state. What does that mean, in practice?

In a nutshell, OIRA's main job is to help oversee the issuance of federal regulations. Congress enacts a lot of laws—for example, the Clean

Air Act, the Occupational Safety and Health Act, the Affordable Care Act (sometimes known as Obamacare), Medicare, Medicaid, and countless others. Many provisions of these laws do not actually become implemented until agencies issue regulations. Sometimes Congress leaves big gaps, and it gives agencies a lot of discretion to decide how best to implement the laws that it enacts. In a key provision of the Clean Air Act, Congress told the Environmental Protection Agency to issue rules that are requisite to protect the public health, with "an adequate margin of safety"; the EPA has to figure out what that means. Congress directed the Occupational Safety and Health Administration to issue rules that are "necessary or appropriate" to protect worker safety; OSHA has to decide what those open-ended terms mean.

Sometimes Congress is more specific, but it still gives agencies room to maneuver, in the sense that they must make important judgments about public policy. And when Congress gives agencies authority to issue rules, it often allows them to decline to exercise that authority if they believe that it is best not to act. In short, Congress sets out the basic framework, but a lot of the most important action comes in implementation, as agencies decide on the content of regulations.

That's where OIRA comes in. Before executive agencies can propose or finalize significant rules, presidents have long required them to submit their drafts to OIRA for review. After receiving their drafts, OIRA's staff—career officials, who do not have any particular political allegiance—will read them carefully and also circulate them to many officials throughout the executive branch. A lot of White House offices might be interested. For example, the National Economic Council, whose director works right under the president, might have some thoughts and concerns, and the same is true of the Domestic Policy Council. The Office of Science and Technology Policy, part of the Executive Office of the president, might have views about the scientific judgments of an agency.

Outside the White House, there can be intense discussions among Cabinet departments about regulations. For example, the Department of Agriculture will know a great deal about how rules affect farmers, the Department of Transportation will know a great deal about how rules affect the transportation sector, and the Department of Energy will know a great deal about implications for the energy sector. The OIRA process enables their perspectives, concerns, and objections to be brought to bear on rules issued by other agencies. Part of OIRA's defining mission is to ensure that rulemaking agencies are able to receive the specialized information held by diverse people (often career officials) within the executive branch.

In fact I saw this as a main part of my job. Every day, OIRA had to ask: Has everyone who has expertise, or a point of view, been allowed to weigh in? The term "process foul"—government lingo—is used when someone has been wrongly excluded from internal discussions. A process foul is a very bad thing. You really don't want to commit one. And a lot of my job consisted of listening to people with different points of view and trying to come up with a solution that would satisfy the reasonable concerns of everyone involved.

Another defining OIRA mission is to promote a well-functioning system of public comment, including state and local governments, businesses large and small, and public interest groups. OIRA often works to ensure that important issues and alternatives are clearly and explicitly identified for public comment when rules are proposed. It works closely with agencies to ensure that public comments are adequately addressed in final rules, where appropriate by modifying relevant provisions in proposed rules. Indeed, a central function of OIRA is to operate as a guardian of a well-functioning administrative process, to ensure not only respect for law but also compliance with procedural ideals that may not always be strictly compulsory but that might be loosely organized under the rubric of "good government." Reducing complexity, increasing benefits, and minimizing costs are a big part of that function.

If OIRA or other agencies within the federal government have serious questions about a draft rule, OIRA will work with the drafting agencies to see if the questions have good answers. Sometimes they do, and agencies will proceed as they originally planned. Sometimes they do not, and agencies will alter their rules accordingly. An agency might conclude, for example, that it has taken an approach that is too complicated or confusing, or that it should exempt small businesses. In the overwhelming majority of cases, the discussion is substantive, technical, nonpolitical, and agreeable. Senior officials—including Cabinet heads—do get involved, but only in relatively rare cases when issues cannot be resolved at a lower level.

OIRA also plays a role in establishing the regulatory priorities of the executive branch. I have said that President Obama called for a government-wide regulatory lookback, designed to reassess rules now on the books (see chapter 8). OIRA helped to oversee the lookback process. If OIRA believes that greater simplicity is a good idea, it can insist on greater simplicity—and as we will see, I did exactly that. And if OIRA believes that a certain initiative would be a good idea, it might well contact an agency to say so. In all cases, OIRA works closely with other White House offices to ensure that executive agencies act consistently with law and with the president's priorities and commitments. A lot of my time was spent on those topics.

Is Regulation a Four-Letter Word?

No one chants, "What do we need? Regulation! When do we need it? Now!" No political banners say, "More regulation!"

True, people want safe food, clean air, and clean water. But in the abstract, regulation is never a popular idea. In a tough economic environment, it might seem like a recipe for disaster. Businesses large and small have long argued that they are subject to excessive red tape and government oversight—and in the context of a serious recession, that concern has been acute. In the United States, with its strong libertarian leanings, regulation is particularly vulnerable to political attack.

For many of those who oppose the Affordable Care Act and financial regulatory reform, two signature achievements of President Obama's first term, it seems clear that the Obama administration took the perverse approach of ramping up regulation, and thus jeopardizing economic growth and job creation, at precisely the time when regulation was likely to be most harmful. The critique of regulation as antithetical to prosperity and to greater employment has been especially passionate within some segments of the business community. At least to some extent, it has spread to the nation as a whole. What critics deem wrong with regulation in general might seem to be a problem with regulatory nudges as well.

There is some important truth in the general critique of regulation. As we shall see, I took it very much to heart in government. The goal of simplification builds on that critique. But we have to be careful. A market economy cannot exist without the basic rules of contract and property, let alone the rules of the criminal law. Those rules are a form of regulation. They are established and enforced by public officials. You cannot have free markets without rules of the road. As Friedrich Hayek, perhaps the greatest critic of socialism and excessive state authority, wrote, "In no system that could be rationally defended would the state just do nothing. An effective competitive system needs an intelligently designed and continually adjusted legal framework as much as any other." [2]

No one can sensibly object to regulation as such. Those who defend free competition and property rights need regulation, which makes markets and property possible. Those who most fiercely and noisily oppose "regulation" and "government intervention" are often the very people who most benefit from them.

The real objection must be to certain kinds of regulation. Some people oppose rules that go beyond what is strictly necessary for an "effective competitive system" and that reflect the use of public power, and above all national power, to achieve certain social goals, unless those goals involve the establishment of free market system itself.

Here too, though, we have to be careful. Should we rely entirely on the free market to protect the safety of food? To protect clean air? Even the most market-friendly economists recognize the existence of market failures, which can justify regulation. Suppose that food safety and clean air regulation can save large numbers of lives and do so at a low cost. Or suppose, even, that such regulation can save large numbers of lives and do so at a high cost. Ever since the Reagan administration, American presidents have focused on producing "net benefits," or benefits minus costs. If the net benefits are high, we have good reason to go forward, whatever our abstract misgivings about regulation.

In the Obama administration, we placed a great deal of emphasis both on cost-benefit analysis and on maximizing net benefits. Indeed the net benefits of our regulations, through the first three years, were more than twenty-five times those in the comparable period in the Bush administration, and more than six times those in the comparable period in the Clinton administration. Consider the following figure. [3]

Figure 1.1. Total annual net benefits of major rules through the third fiscal year
of the past three presidential administrations.

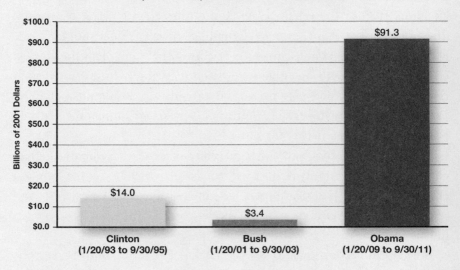

Source: Office of Management and Budget, *Draft 2012 Report to Congress on the Benefits and Costs of Federal Regulations and Unfunded Mandates on State, Local, and Tribal Entities*, 54, figure 2-1, www.whitehouse.gov/sites/default/files/omb/oira/draft_2012_cost_benefit _report.pdf.

The $91.3 billion in net benefits includes billions of dollars in savings for consumers, achieved by (among other things) fuel economy and energy efficiency rules; billions of dollars in savings for business large and small, achieved by cost-saving rules that include significant deregulation; and thousands of lives saved and accidents or illnesses prevented, achieved through rules cleaning the air and making the highways and the food supply safer. A 2010 rule from the Food and Drug Administration, for example, is preventing dozens of annual deaths from salmonella, as well as up to 79,000 annual illnesses.[4] The benefits of this rule dwarf the costs, and it is important to go forward with such rules.

In the last decade, the highest cost year, for federal regulations, was 2007, under President Bush. In President Obama's first three years, his administration did not hit that high, and indeed costs in those years were well in line with historical standards (notwithstanding the extremely high benefits). In a hard economic period, we were extremely careful to avoid imposing excessive costs. And I have every reason to believe that when the numbers are finalized for the entire first term, the net benefits will be far greater than $91.3 billion.

None of this means that those in the business community, and others, are wrong to complain about excessive regulation. In many areas, they are right. Regulation is often confusing, inconsistent, redundant, and excessive. We need to do a lot more to simplify it and to scale it back. I have noted that President Obama approved fewer rules in his first term than did President George W. Bush or indeed any other recent president in the same period; this is no accident. Nor is it accidental that the Obama administration did a great deal to eliminate and streamline existing regulations. Good choice architecture regulates the regulators; we need choice architecture for choice architects. (I will have much more to say about this.) But as we shall see, it is a big mistake to treat regulation, even national regulation, as a four-letter word.

All over the world, people are in the midst of an increasingly intense debate over the proper uses of government. The debate continues to be stuck in decreasingly helpful clichés and sound bites, emphasizing either the dangers of "more" government and the risk of "socialism" or the threats posed by "the big polluters" and "the banks." The real issues lie elsewhere. What is needed, not only in the United States but all over the world, is smart, innovative strategies and tools, focused above all on evidence and on what works and what doesn't.

In 2009–12, we made a start. There is much more to be done.

2 DON'T BLINK

Chocolates

Source: Salina Hainzl

When I joined the federal government in 2009, I shared a suite with Jeffrey Zients, who was at the time deputy director for management at the Office of Management and Budget. Jeff is an exceedingly generous person as well as a terrific manager. Early on, he placed a large bowl of chocolates in the common area in our suite in the Eisenhower Executive Office Building. The bowl was not only proximate but also highly visible. Whenever I entered or exited my office, there it was: a little mountain of delicious candy.

The occupants of our little suite, including Maggie Weiss (Jeff's assistant) and Jess Hertz (my counselor), ended up eating a lot of chocolate. At first we were grateful. As the chocolate accumulated in our stomachs, we remained grateful. Before long, however, we started to wish that the bowl of chocolates were elsewhere. As time passed, the irresistible bowl became a bit of a curse. (Okay, I started to hate it.)

Slightly desperate, I decided to remove the bowl from the common area and to put it into Jeff's office, about six feet away. Maggie and Jess applauded. Mission accomplished: We ate a lot less chocolate.

This was a bit of a puzzle. Being generous, Jeff really doesn't mind if people go into his office, even if their goal is to get chocolates. But the small change in location made all the difference. The bowl was no longer visible whenever I entered or exited my office. The mere fact that we had to go into Jeff's office, just a few feet away, discouraged Maggie, Jess, and me from spending too much of the day eating chocolate. (True, we snuck in from time to time, but within a few weeks, the bowl itself disappeared. Maybe Jeff found himself eating too much chocolate?)

In placing the chocolates in the shared space, Jeff acted as a choice architect, and those of us who ate a lot of chocolate were affected by his architecture. In relocating the bowl, I was engaged in some choice architecture of my own. We can understand choice architecture as the design of the social environment in a way that influences people's choices—for example, by affecting ease or accessibility, by providing information, or by making certain features of the situation salient and clear or instead invisible.

Choice architects can be found in the private and public sector. They design cafeterias and menus at restaurants (which may or may not include bright colors, loud music, eye-catching pictures, distinctive names, or calorie labels); these designs greatly affect how much, and what, people eat. Choice architects produce the forms that you have to fill out to get health insurance or financial aid for college, or to qualify for a mortgage or a school loan. They establish what you see when you check into a hotel, rent a car, go into a store, pay taxes, select a health insurance plan, or apply for a driver's license or for social security benefits. Parents, teachers, doctors, architects, and website managers are choice architects. In part because of his emphasis on what would be simple and automatic, Steve Jobs was one of history's all-time great choice architects.

Choice architects nudge people. They can promote complexity or simplicity; they might confuse people or make things easy. They decide that your dinner plates and glasses are large rather than small, that the first items you see in the grocery store are candy and nuts, that your favorite restaurant offers folk music, that your car has a rearview camera and a clear display of how many miles per gallon you are now getting, that your mortgage papers are long and complex, and that you see, or don't see, all of the extra fees associated with your airfare.

The word *nudge* of course can be used in many different ways. In ordinary language, it might refer to a wide range of actions, including fines and taxes. Let us understand nudges as *approaches that influence decisions while preserving freedom of choice.* (I will have more to say on the definitional question when we explore the nanny state in chapter 9.) On this understanding, all of the following count as nudges:

- An effort to inform consumers by ensuring that mortgages are made simpler, shorter, and clearer.
- An effort to provide clear, simple information about healthy diets, communicated in part through a widely disseminated new icon.
- A disclosure requirement imposed on providers of retirement plans, so that people can clearly see their projected monthly income in retirement.
- A default rule that automatically enrolls people in a health care plan.
- A default rule, designed to protect privacy, ensuring that unless people say otherwise, their movements online cannot be tracked.
- A default rule ensuring that unless people specifically direct otherwise, their organs will be available, under medically hopeless conditions, to others who need them.
- An effort to arrange items in a grocery store so that healthy foods are especially conspicuous.
- An effort to redesign school cafeterias so as to promote healthy choices and to reduce the risk of obesity.
- Graphic warnings on cigarette packages.
- An effort to inform consumers how their energy use compares with that of their neighbors.
- An effort to inform voters, before an election, how their voting record (in terms of frequency) compares to that of other people in their county or state.
- An effort to let voters know, on the day of an election, exactly how to get to the polls.
- A reminder, by telephone or text, that a consumer is about to go over his or her allotment of monthly minutes.

- An effort to work with the private sector to discourage texting while driving.
- An initiative by which governments or companies disclose information, in machine-readable formats, to enable people to track their energy usage and health care choices and expenditures, including through new apps.

By contrast, a threat of criminal punishment, imposed on those who do not buckle their seat belts, is not a nudge. An increase in a cigarette tax is not a nudge, because it alters economic incentives. A fine is not a nudge. A cap-and-trade system for greenhouse gases is not a nudge. If government requires people to make a (tax) payment for failing to purchase health insurance, it is not nudging. Of course economic incentives can be large or small, and as the incentive gets smaller, it approaches a nudge.

Nothing in my argument here suggests that government should restrict itself to nudges. If the goal is Regulatory Moneyball, nudges play a major role in regulation, but they are hardly the entire picture. When I was in government, we issued a lot of nudges, but we did much more. Like its predecessors, the Obama administration has supported a number of laws and issued a number of regulations that include prohibitions, requirements, and economic incentives. We prohibited federal employees and those transporting hazardous materials from texting while driving. To save consumers money, we required refrigerators, small motors, and clothes washers to be more energy-efficient. To reduce accidents and save lives, we required trucking manufacturers to install equipment to reduce the stopping distance of trucks. In chapter 7, I will have something to say about the circumstances in which mandates and bans are justified. For the moment, let me simply note that more flexible approaches have evident virtues and that they form a distinctive category.

To be sure, it is not entirely clear whether some initiatives count as nudges. What if government decides to require people to sign tax forms at the beginning, rather than at the end, on the theory that if they sign at the beginning, they will be less likely to cheat?[1] A step of this kind is an effort to alter choice architecture, and it can be seen as a nudge, in the sense that it is a small shift in the social environment that can make a big difference. But it does not preserve freedom of choice, so it does not exactly fit the definition.

Or what if the government proposes to prohibit companies from selling more than fifteen cigarettes in a package, or from selling soda in bottles that have more than sixteen ounces, but allows people to buy all the cigarettes or all the soda they want? Strictly speaking, such actions are not quite nudges, because they do alter economic incentives, but they certainly have nudge-like characteristics.

In recent years, social scientists have learned a lot about what people are really like—how we respond to information, what makes us change, what scares us, what makes us happy or sad. At this point, it is not exactly news that people do not behave like the "rational actors" of economics textbooks. We are *Homo sapiens*, not *Homo economicus*. But many of the new findings are surprising. They show that subtle aspects of choice architecture have large effects on outcomes. One of the key findings is that complexity can be a really serious problem.

Did you know, for example, that thousands of students have not received financial aid, and hence have not been able to go to college, simply because financial aid forms have been too long and complicated? Or that numerous seniors have ended up in the wrong prescription drug plan, and therefore lost a lot of money, just because the number of choices is large and selection of the right plan is simply too hard? Or that one of the best ways to lose weight is simply to decide not to stock your refrigerator with fattening foods that you love? Or that a small, five-cent charge for the use of grocery bags can have a large effect in reducing the use of such bags? Or that people are far more likely to choose to have an operation if they are told that 90 percent of those who have had that operation are alive after five years than if they are told that after five years 10 percent are dead?

These and other findings are helping families, nonprofits, businesses large and small, and governments all over the world to identify fresh solutions to old and seemingly intractable problems. The findings bear on a host of questions that are being asked by both the private and the public sector. Under the Affordable Care Act, sometimes known as Obamacare, states are going to be setting up health insurance exchanges. The method of presentation will matter a lot. Good (and simple) presentation can save both taxpayers and consumers billions of dollars,[2] and bad (and complex) presentation can ensure that people lose just as much.

We are now equipped with a host of useful insights for thinking about regulation and its likely consequences. Those insights show the potential value of approaches that produce change without forcing anyone to do anything. A general lesson is that small, inexpensive policy initiatives, informed by behavioral economics, can have big benefits.

"Why, Then, Are We Doing This?"

One purpose of this book is to explore some evidence on government regulation, to catalogue recent practices and reforms, and to discuss the implications for regulatory policy. But there is a still more general theme, which involves the importance of ensuring that policies have strong empirical foundations, both through careful analysis in advance and through retrospective review of what works and what does not.

I well remember a conversation in Washington in which it became clear that no influential interest group would speak out in favor of a certain initiative, and someone asked, "Why, then, are we doing this?" Someone (it might have been me) had to offer the reminder, which is that we were doing it not to get public approval but because it was actually good, in the sense that it would help people on balance.

To get a bit ahead of the story, we now have a large set of tools by which to answer the right questions. Careful analysis of costs and benefits, based on science and economics, can be seen as a form of Regulatory Moneyball. For understanding the effects of policies and rules, the gold standard is provided by randomized controlled trials, used of course in medicine and science and increasingly emphasized in government as well.

To return to an earlier example: How would we know whether people will cheat less if they are required to sign forms at the start rather than at the end? The best way to find out is to have a randomized controlled trial, which can show whether there really is a significant effect. Many people, including officials in the Obama administration, have been concerned about the risks associated with using cell phones while driving. How do we know what those risks are? Laboratory evidence, showing effects on reaction time, is useful, but we don't really know what that evidence says about increases in accidents and injuries. The best information would come from a randomized controlled trial.

Two Systems in the Mind

In social science it has become standard to suggest that the human mind contains not one but two "cognitive systems." An understanding of the two systems tells us a lot about the importance of simplicity.

In the social science literature, authoritatively discussed by Daniel Kahneman in his masterful *Thinking, Fast and Slow*,[3] the two are called System 1 and System 2. System 1 is the automatic system, while System 2 is more deliberative and reflective. System 1 works fast. It is emotional and intuitive. When it hears a loud noise, it is inclined to run. When it is offended, it wants to hit back. Much of the time, it is on automatic pilot. It is driven by habits. It certainly eats a delicious brownie. It can procrastinate; it can be impulsive. It can be excessively fearful and too complacent. It is a doer, not a planner. It wants what it wants when it wants it. It has a lot of trouble with complexity.

System 2 is a bit like a computer or Mr. Spock from *Star Trek*. It is deliberative. It calculates. It hears a loud noise, and it assesses whether the noise is a cause for concern. It thinks about probability, carefully and sometimes slowly. It does not get offended. If it sees reasons for offense, it makes a careful assessment of what, all things considered, ought to be done. (It believes in deterrence rather than retribution.) It sees a delicious brownie, and it makes a judgment about whether, all things considered, it should eat it. It insists on the importance of self-control. It is a planner more than a doer. It can handle complexity.

Figure 2.2 offers a visual example of System 1 and System 2 in action. If you look at the two boxes, your System 1 immediately observes that they are different colors; the top box is dark gray and the bottom box is silver. But this is a mistake. If you put a finger in the middle of the page, you can see that both boxes are dark gray. The illusion is produced by the different backgrounds: light for the top box and dark for the bottom box. After you put your finger in the middle of the page, your System 2 acknowledges that

Figure 2.2. The color of boxes.

Source: Brain Games: Watch This! Pictures, http://channel.nationalgeographic.com/channel/brain-games/galleries/brain-games-watch-this-pictures/at/optical-illusion-37418/.

the two boxes are indeed the same color. But once you remove your finger, your System 1 may well say, "You have got to be kidding!"

Illusions of this kind are both fun and illuminating, so let's try another one. In Figure 2.3, where is the white knight? You probably think that the white knight is the one in the middle of the board. Isn't that obvious? Yes, but it's wrong. The two knights are the same color. The illusion that their colors are different comes (again) from their contrast with the background. System 2 gets this, but System 1 cannot.

These are visual illusions, and, as we will see, many human errors, including those that bear directly on public policy, are closely analogous. Here's a striking (and I think profound) demonstration of the relationship between System 1 and System 2: Some of the most important cognitive errors, including several that I discuss here, *disappear when people are using a foreign language.*[4] Asked to resolve problems in a language that is not their own, people are less likely to blunder. In an unfamiliar language, you are more likely to get the right answer. How can this be?

The answer is straightforward. When you are using your own language, you think quickly and effortlessly, and so System 1 has the upper hand. When you are using a foreign language, System 1 is a bit overwhelmed,

Figure 2.3. The dark knight rises.

Source: Mig Greengard, based on original "checkershadow illusion" by Edward H. Adelson, 1995, http://www.chessbase.com/puzzle/puzz10b.htm.

and System 2 is given a serious boost. Your rapid, intuitive reactions are slowed down when you are using a language with which you are not entirely familiar, and you are more likely to do some calculating and to think deliberatively—and to give the right answers. In a foreign language, you have some distance from your intuitions, and that distance can stand you in good stead.

There is a lesson here about the importance of approaches to policy and regulation that emphasize careful consideration of costs and benefits. Such approaches do not (exactly) use a foreign language, but they do ensure a degree of distance from people's initial judgments and intuitions, thus constraining the mistakes associated with System 1. In fact one of the biggest lessons I learned in government is that cost-benefit analysis operates like a foreign language, and one that helps people to focus on the right things. A high-level official, seeking to protect safety, once asked me with some irritation, "How do you put a price on a human life?" I loved him for his commitment to saving lives. But if public officials are willing to require people in the private sector to spend infinite resources to protect a single life, they'll ruin the economy (and a lot of lives in the process). System 2 recognizes that we have to make trade-offs—and that we will, inevitably, be making decisions about how much we should spend to reduce risks, even if we are speaking of mortality risks.

In some cases, an emphasis on costs and benefits played a big role in convincing officials, otherwise unsure about certain rules, that these rules were worth issuing, because the costs were low and the benefits were extremely high. In other cases, an emphasis on costs and benefits helped to show that rules deserved careful scrutiny or that they should not go forward, because the costs were extremely high and the benefits were low.

It is often said that people should just "blink" or "trust their gut," and in some circumstances, blinking and your gut, or System 1, will work well. People tend to know whom or what they like quite quickly, often at a glance. For example, employers tend to learn little or nothing about prospective employees from interviews.[5] Unfortunately, they think that they learn a lot more than they do. What they do learn is *whether they will like the person they are interviewing*. In many important contexts, especially those that are complex, new, or unfamiliar, you shouldn't blink, and you really shouldn't trust your gut.

We are all aware of situations in which we have a strong intuitive feeling of fear, desire, attraction, or revulsion. Sometimes that feeling is right, and once we do a little careful thinking, we can confirm our intuition. But often a moment's thought shows that the intuitive feeling is wrong and that it makes sense to pause and reconsider. If you're deciding how to invest your savings, your gut may speak clearly and simply. Please ignore it.

System 1 is much moved by features of choice architecture that would seem irrelevant to System 2. Indeed, you may deny that you are influenced by those features, and you may sincerely believe your denial. But it's nonetheless true. We are often blind to what moves us. If it is a bright, sunny day, you are more likely to make a risky investment than you would be if the day were gray and rainy. If you are asked to check a box to give money to charity, you are more likely to check that box if it is green rather than red. If you are asked to enroll in a savings plan or a health care program, it may matter a lot if the enrollment takes one minute or ten. If you're not sure which candidate to vote for, you may be influenced by whether the candidate's name appears first or last on the ballot.

I have said that System 1 tends to be emotional, and its emotional character creates both risks and opportunities. People may be immediately fearful of some risk—say, the risk associated with terrorism or the risk of losses in the stock market—even though the statistics suggest that there is no cause for alarm. A great deal of work suggests that people evaluate products, activities, and other people through an "affect heuristic."[6] When the affect heuristic is at work, people assess benefits, costs, and probabilities not by running the numbers, but by consulting their feelings. They might hate nuclear power or love renewable fuels, and those feelings may influence their judgments about the benefits and costs of nuclear power and renewable fuels. System 1 is doing all the work here.

In fact some goods and activities come with an "affective tax" or an "affective subsidy," in the sense that people like them more, or less, because of the affect, or feeling, that accompanies them. Advertisers and public officials try to create affective taxes and subsidies; consider public educational campaigns designed to reduce smoking or texting while driving. Many political campaigns have the same goal, attempting to impose a kind of affective tax on the opponent and to enlist the affect heuristic in their favor. In fact some political campaigns tend to appeal directly to System 1, not System 2.

At this point, you might ask, What, exactly, are these systems? Are they agents? How do they operate in the brain? Are they actually separate systems? In the case of conflict, who adjudicates? The best answer is that the idea of two systems is a simplification that is designed to distinguish automatic, effortless processing and more complex, effortful processing. When people are asked to add 1 plus 1, or to walk from their bedroom to their bathroom, or to read the emotion on the face of their best friend, the mental operation is easy and rapid. When people are asked to multiply 98 times 99, or to navigate a new neighborhood by car, or to decide which retirement plan best fits their needs, the mental operation is difficult and slow.

Different and identifiable regions of the brain are active when we perform either effortless or effortful tasks, and hence it may well be right to suggest that the systems have physical referents. An influential discussion states that "[a]utomatic and controlled processes can be roughly distinguished by where they occur in the brain."[7] The prefrontal cortex, the most advanced part of the brain and the part that most separates human beings from other species, is associated with deliberation and hence with System 2. The brain's amygdala has been associated with a number of automatic processes, including fear. And why do so many people focus on the short term and ignore the future? A striking study suggests that the brain offers some clues. In particular, an identifiable region of the brain is most active when we are thinking about ourselves. When patient people think of themselves a year from now, that region of the brain is quite active, but when impatient people think of themselves in a year, that region is far less so.[8] Impatient people think about their future selves in the same way that they think about perfect strangers. This finding bears on a question with which regulators all over the world must struggle: What should we do when people engage in behavior—smoking, drinking, overeating—that can create big trouble for them in the future?

On the other hand, different parts of the brain interact, and it is not necessary to make technical or controversial claims about neuroscience in order to distinguish between effortless and effortful processing. The idea of System 1 and System 2 is designed to capture that distinction in a way that works for purposes of exposition (and that can be grasped fairly immediately by System 1).

An understanding of the two systems helps to explain why, in thinking about both public policy and daily life, it is crucial to focus on a single question: *What happens if people do nothing at all?* This question is important because much of the time, nothing at all is exactly what people will do. Human beings tend to stick with their habits. They might not want to bother to take action to change the status quo, even if they would eventually benefit from doing so. The simplest thing to do is nothing, and doing nothing may be very appealing.

True, System 2 might be activated if the long-term benefits of action greatly outweigh the long-term costs. But System 1 might say, "I'm having a ton of fun right now. What's the rush?" The potential triumph of System 1 is clear in St. Augustine's prayer, "Give me chastity and continence, but not yet." Substitute "a good retirement plan" or "healthy eating" or "a visit to the dentist" for "chastity and continence," and you capture the wishes of a large portion of the population. For many of us, a lot of our well-being depends on whether the social environment allows us to prosper even if we do not act at all.

"You Didn't Build That"

Let's go beyond individual decisions and have a quick glance at the problem of poverty. What, exactly, makes the situation of poor people different from that of those who aren't poor? Part of the answer lies in choice architecture. Esther Duflo, one of the world's leading experts on poverty, says the following, in a passage that deserves to be widely known:

> We tend to be patronizing about the poor in a very specific sense, which is that we tend to think, "Why don't they take more responsibility for their lives?" And what we are forgetting is that the richer you are the less responsibility you need to take for your own life because everything is taken care of for you. And the poorer you are the more you have to be responsible for everything about your life. . . . Stop berating people for not being responsible and start to think of ways instead of providing the poor with the luxury that we all have, which is that a lot of decisions are taken for us. If we do nothing, we are on the right track. For most of the poor, if they do nothing, they are on the wrong track.[9]

The most important sentences here are the last two. Duflo's central claim is that people who are well off do not have to be responsible for a wide range of things, because others are making the relevant decisions, and to their benefit. In key respects, life is simple. If such people do nothing, things will be just fine. For many of us, clean drinking water, air that is safe to breathe, an effective police force, decent streets, protection of property rights, enforcement of contracts, a well-functioning constitutional system—all of these can be taken as given. We don't have to worry or even think about them. And they can be taken for granted because of the decisions and work of numerous people.

Of course it is true that many people with money have made some terrific choices and are rich for that reason, and a lot of poor people have made catastrophic choices and are poor for that reason. Remember the 2012 election-year campaign squabble over President Obama's line "You didn't build that"? President Obama was not denying that people build their own businesses; he was referring to the infrastructure, including roads and bridges, that enable business people to thrive. Here is the full quotation:

There are a lot of wealthy, successful Americans who agree with me—because they want to give something back. They know they didn't—look, if you've been successful, you didn't get there on your own. You didn't get there on your own. I'm always struck by people who think, well, it must be because I was just so smart. There are a lot of smart people out there. It must be because I worked harder than everybody else. Let me tell you something—there are a whole bunch of hardworking people out there.

If you were successful, somebody along the line gave you some help. There was a great teacher somewhere in your life. Somebody helped to create this unbelievable American system that we have that allowed you to thrive. Somebody invested in roads and bridges. If you've got a business—you didn't build that. Somebody else made that happen. The Internet didn't get invented on its own. Government research created the Internet so that all the companies could make money off the Internet.

Like Duflo, President Obama is referring to the social background, which gives people a great deal of help and which often creates the foundations that enable them to thrive. Let's be clear: If you're a successful businessperson, you probably did build that. But Obama was nonetheless right, and Duflo's point nonetheless holds. In countless contexts, you are being helped or hurt, a lot, by what track you are on if you "do nothing."

Migration, and Larry Bird

I have been treating System 1 and System 2 as separate and independent, but over time, understandings can migrate from System 2 to System 1. When you start to learn how to drive, System 2 is active and working really hard. Driving is complicated. System 1 is baffled. But as you gain experience, driving becomes second nature, intuitive, automatic. The same is true of sports. A tennis novice has to think really hard about exactly what to do in order to hit a topspin forehand. For a professional tennis player, nothing could be simpler. System 1 is educated to recognize the patterns immediately, and conscious thought is not required. An accomplished chess player automatically recognizes patterns and, after a quick glance at a board, knows the best moves to make. The same is true for musicians. Once you know how to play the guitar, a great deal of the work is automatic, and you don't have to think terribly hard about it. There is no miracle here—only a lot of practice.

When I started in government, I was a complete novice, and things that were automatic for many of my colleagues required a lot of thinking, and endless naive questions, for me. Who gets invited to a meeting on a clean air rule? When and how do I consult the chief of staff's office? To whom do official documents get circulated? Where, exactly, is the Oval Office? How do I respond to a meeting request from a labor union? After a year, many such things became second nature and simple.

Movement from System 2 to System 1 captures what it means to learn a number of skills. Is the opposite movement possible? Unfortunately, it is. If you are a terrific tennis player but don't play for a long time, you might have to think hard when you start again, and you'll probably play badly. The reason is that what was automatic is now self-conscious and deliberate, which means that you will be slower and worse. Many athletes find it frustrating and puzzling that after a short time away, their reactions seem way off. Even worse is the phenomenon of "choking."[10] What accounts for it? One answer is that choking occurs when an athlete somehow loses the ability to perform quickly and unconsciously and starts to think everything through. In sports, too much thinking can be fatal. A baseball player who is asked to think a lot about how he holds the bat is suddenly more likely to strike out. System 1 turns off, and System 2 has to pick up the slack. Unfortunately System 2 is just too slow.

Consider the strategy of Larry Bird, the immortal (and shrewd) Boston Celtic, when encountering the three-point specialist Leon Wood right before the three-point competition preceding the 1986 All-Star Game.[11] Bird began by saying, "Hey, Leon, you changed your shot lately? It looks different." Of course, Wood had not changed his shot, but the question got him thinking, and he was rattled. Bird's next tactic was to talk about the new red-white-and-blue basketballs, in special use for the competition. Bird reported that the balls "felt slippery." Wood felt even more rattled. With two quick provocations, Bird disrupted his opponent's System 1, and Wood ended up near last in the competition.

Bird won, of course.

3 HUMAN ERROR

Monsters of the Midway

When I started my career at the University of Chicago in the early 1980s, giants roamed the Earth and called Hyde Park their home. They were Babe Ruth's New York Yankees and Michael Jordan's Chicago Bulls. They were the Monsters of the Midway. They were the Dream Team.

The giants included George Stigler (Nobel Prize, 1982), Ronald Coase (Nobel Prize 1991), Gary Becker (Nobel Prize, 1992), Richard Posner (the most important figure behind the economic analysis of law), and Frank Easterbrook (maybe the nation's leading law and economics scholar at the time). The giants had a lot of influence not just throughout the nation but all over the world. The Reagan administration was enthusiastic about their ideas (and was populated by some of their intellectual offspring). The prevailing orthodoxy at the University of Chicago, the starting point for each and every conversation, was that human beings are rational, in the particular sense that their decisions maximize their own satisfactions. In short, people are terrific choosers, given what they care about.

True, the giants were not of one mind on this question. But if you challenged the view that human beings are rational, in the economic sense, you would get a withering look from one or another giant. The look said, very simply, that anyone who dared to question the rationality assumption was, well, not rational.

As a young law professor, I reacted to the Chicago orthodoxy with both awe and skepticism. Stigler, Coase, Becker, Posner, and Easterbrook were quick, funny, witty, cutting, tough, confident, and occasionally brutal.

Whether the question involved the choices of consumers, the behavior of government, racial discrimination, disability, poverty, or even addiction, the giants, invoking human rationality, seemed to have all the answers. (People get addicted because they like what they get addicted to!) At the same time, many of their answers seemed to me to be wrong. Human beings, I thought, were not really like that.

Unfortunately my skepticism was clumsy and clueless. In one early paper, delivered in front of a large room filled with giants, I argued that not only do people have preferences; people also have preferences about their preferences, and maybe we should pay attention to those. Maybe people want to smoke, but maybe they want not to want to smoke—and we might listen to what they want to want. Stigler responded, with some combination of gusto and contempt, that what I was saying sounded a lot like John Stuart Mill's distinction between higher and lower pleasures, and my argument seemed even stupider than Mill's. That certainly shut me up.

In the mid-1980s the cavalry arrived. Its young commander was Richard Thaler, an economist at Cornell, who was writing some brilliant papers about what people are really like, and about how they depart from economic understandings of rationality.[1] For example, Thaler argued, and demonstrated, that human beings value goods that they own more than they value the same goods in the hands of others. If you are given a mug or a lottery ticket, you'll probably demand more to give it up than you would have been willing to pay to get it in the first place. This finding complicates free market thinking, and it strikes a big blow against the work for which one of the giants (Ronald Coase) won the Nobel Prize.

Thaler also argued that money is not fungible and that we put it in different "mental accounts": vacation money, mad money, retirement money, money for kids, Christmas money, bill-paying money. On the usual economic assumptions, a dollar is a dollar, and it doesn't seem rational to treat money as nonfungible. Thaler's eye-popping work directed me toward research on judgment and decision making by two Israeli psychologists, Daniel Kahneman and Amos Tversky. That research turned my world upside down—or, more accurately, right side up.

In 1995 Thaler joined the University of Chicago, and we soon became good friends and coauthors, exploring how a more accurate understanding of human behavior could inform law and public policy. About a year later

Daniel Kahneman called and asked me to collaborate with him on some projects. I immediately exclaimed, "You're my hero!" Despite that unpromising beginning, he continued the conversation, and we ended up writing a series of papers together.

For many years, behavioral economics was not exactly a big hit in economics department or law schools, certainly not at the University of Chicago, which continued to be the bastion of rational choice theory. In the late 1990s Thaler and I gave one of our early papers at a seminar at the University of Chicago Law School. We argued that behavioral economics should change how we think about law and public policy—and indeed that some existing legal principles showed an intuitive appreciation of what people are really like. The giants came out in force, and they were not amused. The discussion was heated, intense, and at times a bit ugly. Because of the intensity and the ugliness, it was also memorable; a White House colleague, at the time a law school student, told me that people who were there will never forget it. But social scientists care about data, and the sheer accumulation of evidence made it impossible to dismiss what Thaler and other behavioral economists were saying.

George Akerlof, a big influence on and an important practitioner of behavioral economics, won the Nobel Prize in 2001. Kahneman himself received the Nobel in 2002. A 2005 recipient was Thomas Schelling, who inspired a great deal of behavioral research (including work on how people have preferences about their preferences—even better than John Stuart Mill's). Peter Diamond, who edited a book titled *Behavioral Economics and Its Applications*, was a Nobel recipient in 2010. Behavioral economics is now mainstream. All of the leading economics journals regularly feature behaviorally informed research.

By the way, Stigler (the most withering of Chicago's giants) died in 1991, but as of 2013, the rest of the giants remained active. Coase, 101 years young, cowrote a book on China and is hoping to start a new academic journal on human behavior. Becker continues to be a central figure in economics. Posner and Easterbrook are distinguished federal judges as well as active scholars. These days, even Chicago's giants use behavioral economics.

The work of Thaler, Kahneman, and Tversky has spurred a truly extraordinary outpouring of work on human decision making. In my view, that work counts as the most important development in the social sciences in the past half-century. (I know, I know, I am hopelessly biased. I even know that behavioral economics can help identify the sources of my bias.)

A number of popular books, including Kahneman's *Thinking, Fast and Slow*, outline behavioral findings. There is even a *Behavioral Economics for Dummies*. (And it's good!) A lot of recent work outlines the key empirical findings in detail.[2] My focus here is more narrow, in the sense that it is designed to capture what matters most for thinking about policy, simplification, and the future of government.

Strangers to Ourselves? Inertia Is Powerful

The Problem of Procrastination

According to standard economic theory, people will consider both the short term and the long term. We take account of uncertainties; we know that the future is unpredictable and that big changes may occur over time. We appropriately discount the future. It may be better to have money or a happy event a week from now than a decade from now. You might prefer $100 today to $300 in a decade. At the same time, $1 today is not as good as $100 tomorrow. System 2 certainly considers all of these points.

In practice, however, System 1 is often in charge. For some of us, the future is a foreign country—Laterland—and we don't know if we will ever visit it. Indeed, we might not know if the people who live there are really us, even if they bear our names and have our bodies. Our later selves may be strangers to our current selves.

If this seems a bit excessive, recall here the striking finding that an identifiable region of the brain—the ventromedial prefrontal cortex (vmPFC)—is most actively engaged when people think about themselves, and that in impatient people, this region is less active when they are thinking about their future selves. Those of us who are willing to defer gratification and to delay a current reward for a bigger reward in the future show an active vmPFC when we are thinking about our future selves. But less patient people, who want rewards immediately, do not show an active vmPFC when thinking about their future selves. As stated by the authors of the underlying study, "shortsighted decision-making occurs in part because people fail to consider their future interests as belonging to the self."[3] Some of us envision our future selves in the same way that we envision other people.[4]

For many people, including those who work in government, what may matter most is today, tomorrow, and maybe next week. Some people procrastinate or neglect to take steps that impose small short-term costs but that promise big long-term gains.[5] People may, for example, delay enrolling in a retirement plan, starting to exercise, seeing a doctor, ceasing to smoke, or using some valuable, cost-saving technology.[6]

One reason is that the long term is not salient and we do not focus on it, especially when strong emotions are associated with short-term benefits or short-term costs. If the short-term benefits involve something that tastes great or is really fun, they may dominate all other considerations. So too with short-term costs that seem high, such as a visit to the doctor's office or starting a diet.

Here is some suggestive evidence about the underlying problem: When people see pictures designed to show what they will look like a few decades from now, they are far more likely to save for the future.[7] In the relevant studies, experimenters provided people with digital versions of themselves, or avatars, and then they aged the avatars to a seventy-year-old version. An example is shown in Figure 3.1.

The results were impressive. Participants who were exposed to their future selves ended up doubling the amount of money that they allocated to their retirement account. Both college students and a wide range of adults showed the same basic pattern.

The photos are a pretty simple intervention. Why did they make such a difference? The reason is that when you see your future self, Laterland becomes real. Your System 1 is activated, and your future needs and wants are suddenly salient. Procrastination is less likely when your future self is visible to you.

Most of the time, of course, we don't see our future selves. They may be strangers to us, inhabiting Laterland, and we may not much care about those strangers. One implication is that we may well make choices that have short-term net benefits but long-term net costs—as is the case, for many, with eating unhealthy foods and smoking cigarettes. Another implication is

Figure 3.1. Digital aging procedure.

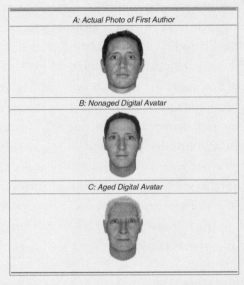

Source: Hal E. Hershfield et al., "Increasing Behavior Through Age-Progressed Renderings of the Future Self," *Journal of Marketing Research* 48 (November 2011): S23, S26 fig. 1.

that some of us fail to make choices that have short-term net costs but long-term net benefits—as is the case, for many, with choosing more energy-efficient products. (You might be able to save a lot of money if you do.)

Our failure to focus on the future helps to account for a lot of related problems. We may delay getting the car fixed, going to the doctor, or rebalancing our investments on the ground that not one of these is a lot of fun. Maybe tomorrow, or next month, will be better. There is a close connection between procrastination and myopia, understood as an excessive focus on the short term.[8] So too with inertia: Why change the status quo with respect to your investment portfolio when you can spend time with your spouse or watch television? Hyperbolic discounting,[9] which results in neglecting future costs, and associated problems of self-control are especially troublesome when the result is a small short-term gain (the joy of yet one more piece of chocolate) at the expense of large long-term losses (obesity or cavities or both).

Problems faced at the individual level can be problems for public officials too. Some policies would impose short-term costs but have major long-term benefits. Unfortunately, current voters, and hence current politicians, may have little incentive to adopt those policies. They may ask: Why deal with a budget deficit now, when any efforts to do so may not be much appreciated by today's citizens?

Many people hoped that in its first four years, the Obama administration would do a lot, both domestically and internationally, to address the problem of climate change. And some important regulations, including those increasing the fuel economy of cars and trucks, will reduce greenhouse gas emissions significantly. But many people were disappointed that Congress refused to enact greenhouse gas legislation and that international efforts produced only modest results. One reason involves time. The most serious harmful effects of climate change will be experienced by the citizens of Laterland. In the midst of a terrible economic period, some people thought, and still think, that Laterland can wait.

Help for Procrastinators

What can be done to get people to focus on the long term? Simple approaches are best.

When people are procrastinating or otherwise failing to protect their future selves, automatic enrollment in sensible programs is a really good idea. Without any action by government, you can make choices that will ensure that your own inertia works in your favor. If you sign up for automatic enrollment in a plan to rebalance your investments, you can save yourself a lot of time and trouble. Private institutions can help as well. If employers automatically enroll you in a good savings plan, you may be a lot better off than you would be if you have to sign up on your own.

Complex requirements, inconvenience, and lengthy forms are likely to make the situation worse, and maybe a lot worse. Consider how much Amazon and its customers have benefited from its "one click" purchasing program. (Let's put to one side impulse purchases, which are admittedly made easier by that one click.) One click is much easier than two or three, and so people buy a lot more books. For companies, one-click approaches can make a big difference. The same is true for governments. We can certainly imagine one-click government forms (and as we shall see, the Obama administration made some progress in that direction).

There is a lot of private and public interest in wellness programs, but if an employer makes it hard for you to sign up, you might take a pass. It is no accident that book clubs love to get people to commit to buying a book a month. The first books cost a penny, but after a while you may be paying a lot of pennies for a lot of books.

Default Rules

I have noted that both private and public institutions often establish "default rules"—rules that determine what happens if people make no affirmative choice at all. The importance of such rules is a tribute to the power of inertia. When people are asked whether they want to opt into a retirement plan, the level of participation is far lower than if they are asked whether they want to opt out. Automatic enrollment dramatically increases participation. Consider Figure 3.2, which captures the experience of several companies after they shifted to automatic enrollment.

As the figure suggests, automatic enrollment is an excellent way to increase savings. In fact, automatic enrollment can be far more effective than

Figure 3.2. 401(k) participation with and without auto-enrollment.

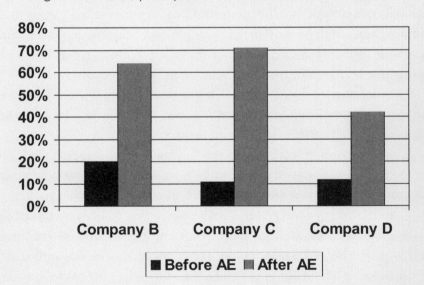

Source: Richard Woodbury, "How to Increase 401(k) Saving," *NBER Bulletin on Aging and Health* (Fall 2002), at 3, 3 fig. 1, http://www.nber.org/bah/fall02/401kSaving.html.

economic incentives, including significant tax subsidies.[10] Something similar can be said for organ donations.[11] If you want to increase the number of organs available for people who need them, an effective way to do so is to presume that people consent, at the time of death, to donate but allow them to allow opt out if they wish. I am not contending that this is the right policy; my only claim is that if we want to make more organs available for those who need them, we should be aware that the default rule really matters. The same holds true for clean energy. If it is the default, a lot of people will stick with it.[12]

Clear, Simple Paths

In my early months at the White House, we talked a lot about flu, not just because of the national risk posed by H1N1 (seen as a potentially serious problem at the time), but also because of the ordinary risks that each of us faced. To protect ourselves and our coworkers, we were advised to get a flu vaccine and were repeatedly informed that we could do so on the first floor of the Eisenhower Executive Office Building. The vaccine was free.

I was working on the H1N1 issue at the time, and I was focused especially on how to ensure that people got vaccinated. But of course when it came to getting my own vaccination, I delayed. Where, exactly, was that office that would give me the shot? How would I find it? Anyway, shots hurt, and most days I was busy. What would be the harm of waiting until tomorrow or next week? The delay got longer and longer.

One day I ran into my friend Dan Meltzer, the deputy White House counsel, on the first floor of the Eisenhower Building, and I asked him where he was going. He told me that he was going to get a flu shot. He knew exactly where to go, so I followed him and got vaccinated.

That is just an anecdote; here is some research. Suppose that you are informed of the benefits of a vaccine. If so, you are more likely to get vaccinated. (Fortunately, and no surprise there.) But if you are also given a map describing exactly where to go, you are a lot more likely to get vaccinated.[13] The map, specifying the path, makes a big difference.

Most of us agree that, other things being equal, healthy eating is better than unhealthy eating. But what is "healthy eating"? Many of us don't quite know, and so we might not be much influenced if we are encouraged to eat healthy. It is a lot more helpful to be specific—for example, by encouraging people to buy 1 percent milk as opposed to whole milk.[14] If you are concerned about reducing calories and fat, 1 percent is a lot better than whole. For eating healthy, such information is like a good map: clear and simple.

The word *actionable* is ugly and bureaucratic, but it is helpful insofar as it signals the immense importance of giving people a clear, concrete sense of what actions they might take if they want to get help or avoid hurt. Public health messages, from both the private and the public sector, should be actionable. (The same applies to leadership in organizations, to teaching, and of course to parenting.) The broader lesson is that when people are informed of the benefits or risks of engaging in certain actions, they are far more likely to respond to that information if *they are simultaneously provided with clear, explicit information about how to do so.*[15]

In many domains, the identification of a specific, clear, unambiguous path or plan has an important effect on our decisions. Vagueness can produce inaction, even when people are informed about risks and potential improvements.[16] What appears to be skepticism, intransigence, or recalcitrance may just be a response to ambiguity. People might not be thinking, *That's a bad idea.* Their real reaction might be, *I'm not sure what I'm being asked to do, so I'll just forget about it.*

Many commercial products do well because they are simple and intuitive. System 1 knows exactly how to handle them; it does not get baffled, and System 2 need not be invoked. Apple has succeeded in large part because of the simplicity of its products. Consider this statement from a review that is otherwise highly complimentary about a new Google product: "Nexus phone, Nexus tablet, Nexus sphere thing; what is Google thinking, anyway? If it truly wants to emulate Apple, it should minimize confusion, not foster it."[17]

Speaking of this problem, IKEA stores are hopelessly confusing, and some of us stay away from them because of it. After one baffling (okay, horrible and mildly traumatizing) visit, I certainly do. Note, however, that the confusion is almost certainly by design, entirely purposeful, a form of brilliant choice architecture, exploiting System 1. In the words of one observer, "By meandering through the confusing labyrinth of picture-perfect living spaces, the shopper is left feeling 'licensed to impulse purchase.' In short, the shopper becomes lost, cracks and buys the cheap wineglasses."[18]

At OIRA, one of my key goals was to do what we could to ensure that when people deal with government, they don't have to meander through confusing labyrinths, and they don't get lost (or have to crack and buy things). Having an understanding of behavioral findings, and working with many others in the Obama administration, I set out to reduce meanderings and frustration.

Framing

People are influenced by how information is presented or "framed."[19] System 2 cares about the content of information, not its presentation. What matters is what is said, not how it is said. But System 1 is much affected by "framing," and small differences matter a lot.

Suppose that you want to let people know that using energy-efficient products can save them money. Should you tell them that they will *gain* $300 if they buy efficient refrigerators and washer-dryers, or that they will *lose* the same amount of money if they don't?[20] The latter is much more effective. Patients considering surgery behave similarly. When told that 90 percent of those who have undergone the operation are still alive five years later, they are more likely to consent to the procedure than when told that after five years 10 percent are dead.[21] The basic finding holds not only for patients but also for doctors, who are more likely to recommend an operation when the frame is "90 percent are alive."

It follows that a product that is labeled "90 percent fat-free" will be more appealing than one that is labeled "10 percent fat." System 1 focuses on the "90 percent fat-free" and thinks the product sounds pretty healthy. But System 1 will also focus on the "10 percent fat" and get scared off. Even the proximity of certain words—"No cockroaches were recently in this glass"— alarms System 1.

These results matter for public policy. When making decisions about retirement, for example, an important question is, How long do you expect to live? If you are healthy and are asked what is the probability that you will *live to age eighty-five*, you will be likely to give a pretty high number. Maybe over 50 percent! But if you are asked what is the probability that you will *die by age eighty-five*, the number you give is likely to be under 50 percent.

Empirical studies find that the "live to" frame produces very different results from the "die by" frame.[22]

Why is this? One reason is that the question "Will I live to the age of eighty-five?" triggers a set of positive and negative thoughts in a certain sequence. The "live to" frame might well lead you to think of family members who have lived past eighty-five (maybe two of your grandparents did so) and about your current good health. But those thoughts and that sequence are different from what is triggered by the question "Will I die by eighty-five?" The "die by" frame might well lead you to think of family members who have died young (maybe two of your grandparents did so) and about any serious health risks that you have faced. System 1 is highly susceptible to framing effects, and the words *live* and *die* get it pretty worked up.

Here's an example that bears even more directly on the topic of this book. If people are asked whether they favor regulation and whether they think there should be more of it, most will answer no. But if people are asked whether they want to maintain or strengthen regulations protecting safe workplaces, safe food, and clean air, most will answer yes.

Is this inexplicable? Is there a paradox here? Should antiregulation conservatives celebrate people's negative reactions to regulation in general? I don't think so. Should pro-regulation progressives celebrate people's positive reactions to safety and clean air? I don't think so. System 1 doesn't much like "regulation," certainly not in the abstract, and so there is an immediate negative response, reflected in people's answers. (It would take a lot of work from System 2 to get people to have a positive reaction to "regulation" in the abstract, even supposing that they should.) But System 1 is upbeat about safety, and that too is reflected in people's answers. We can learn a lot about framing and psychology by seeing how differently people respond to questions about "regulation" or "regulation to protect food safety." But we can't learn much about people's considered judgments from their answers to such questions. The most general point is that our choices, including our choices about products and policies, are often not made solely on the basis of their consequences; choices are affected by the relevant frame.

In addition, *information that is vivid and salient is likely to have a much larger impact on people's behavior than information that is statistical and abstract.*[23] Attention is a scarce resource. Vivid, salient, and novel presentations trigger attention in ways that abstract or familiar ones cannot.

While System 2 loves statistics, they leave System 1 cold, and when most of us are deciding whether and how to respond to risks, numbers may not get our attention. All the statistics in the world about the risks of texting while driving can be less persuasive than a single anecdote about someone who died as a result.

Here are a few messages texted by drivers right before killing someone or dying in a crash: "LOL," "sweet," "where r u," "tell brad," and "hurry." An advertising campaign from AT&T, called "The Last Text," presented these actual text messages, accompanied by brief, vivid narratives of how the people died. There is every reason to think that it was more effective in changing behavior than would be any recitation of the statistical evidence.

Consider two questions:

1. How much would you be willing to pay for flight insurance that will pay your family $100,000 in the event of death from any cause?
2. How much would you be willing to pay for flight insurance that will pay your family $100,000 in the event of a terrorism-related death?

Remarkably, most people give a higher number in response to option 2 than option 1, even though that is palpably absurd.[24] By definition, the first flight insurance policy is worth more than the second, because it covers all deaths, including terrorism-related deaths! Why, then, are people willing to pay more for option 2? Because the idea of a "terrorism-related death" produces general fear and vivid images, and thus activates System 1. People's willingness to pay jumps accordingly.

Making something vivid is a way of making it salient, and salience matters greatly. Here is a point, and potentially a problem, for the operation of free markets. When we decide what to buy—whether it is a car, a refrigerator, a house, or a television—we should consider a wide range of features. But which features do you actually consider? Surely you think about the purchase price, which is highly salient. But other features are "shrouded attributes," important but far less salient. An example: The costs of energy may well be "shrouded" for some consumers. Do you really have a sense of the energy costs of your refrigerator? Many people do not. This point has potential implications for regulatory policy, including provision of information.

Why do people pay late fees? One factor is a combination of forget-fulness and lack of salience. Because late fees can be lucrative, companies don't have a big incentive to provide reminders. Mere reminders—that loan payments are coming due—significantly decrease late payments.[25] A behav-ioral lesson is that a simple reminder can be even more effective than an economic penalty.

A closely related question: Why do people pay bank overdraft fees? One answer is that such fees are not sufficiently salient to people. A careful study suggests that limited attention is indeed a source of the problem.[26] When people are asked to take general surveys about such fees, they are less likely to incur a fee in the following month. And when they take a number of surveys, the issue becomes so salient that overdraft fees can be reduced for as long as two years.

How inclined would you be to purchase a good with a price of $19.99 as opposed to $20.01? System 2 should think, "The difference is trivial. I won't notice it." But to System 1, the difference is salient, and $19.99 sounds like a lot less than $20.01. Does this matter in real markets? A study of more than 22 million used-car sales found that in assessing odometer readings, people focus on the digit on the far left—so much so that there is a big discontinuous drop in the sale price once the odometer goes over 10,000.[27]

An additional finding, of great importance in many domains, is that people dislike losses far more than they like equivalent gains. Suppose that I offer you the following gamble. You have a 50 percent chance of los-ing $200 and a 50 percent chance of winning $250. Would you take the gamble?

In terms of outcomes and probabilities, the gamble is a pretty good one. But most people won't take it. Weighing losses more heavily than gains, they won't accept a gamble even though it has a positive expected value: This is the behavioral phenomenon of "loss aversion." System 1 is playing a big role here. System 2 runs the numbers and calculates expected value. System 1 doesn't do that, and losses trigger intense concern. Careful re-search shows that even professional golfers display loss aversion. They do significantly better when putting to save par than when putting to make birdie. Indeed, neuroscientists have found that loss aversion is wired into the human brain.[28] And not just the human brain—monkeys are averse to losses as well.[29]

Many people have been interested in giving teachers economic incentives to improve their students' achievements. Unfortunately, many of these efforts just don't work. Is it possible to tweak them to make them more effective? An ingenious study enlists loss aversion.[30] Teachers were given money in advance and told that if their students did not show real improvements, they would have to give it back. The result? A big improvement in teachers' quality, as measured by a significant increase in students' math scores.

An appreciation of loss aversion offers important lessons for public policy. Consider recent efforts, by the District of Columbia, to decrease people's use of grocery bags. One approach was to offer a five-cent bonus to customers who brought reusable bags. The district tried that approach, and it had essentially no effect. People didn't much care about the five-cent bonus, so they ignored it. Recently the district tried another approach, which is to impose a five-cent tax on those who ask for a grocery bag. Five cents is not a lot of money, but many people do not want to pay it. The new approach, enlisting loss aversion, has had a major effect in reducing use of grocery bags.[31]

The general point is that if a company or a government wants to discourage behavior, a fee is likely to have a much bigger effect than a reward. Even small or nominal fees can have a big impact. It follows that a subsidy, including a tax credit, is likely to be far less effective than a tax—and indeed, that a pretty large economic subsidy may well have a weaker impact than a relatively small tax.

Social Influences

If you want to eat less, consider inviting someone thinner than you over for dinner. The reason is that our behavior is much influenced by what we think other people do (even though we may well be blind to that fact).[32] Human beings don't quite travel in herds, but most of us are affected by the beliefs and actions of others. With respect to obesity, proper exercise, alcohol consumption, smoking, being vaccinated, and much more, the perceived decisions of others can have a big influence on individual behavior and choice.[33]

If you are with people who eat a lot, you will probably eat a lot too.

Indeed, the body type of others in a dinner group has been found to affect people's food choices. Interestingly, those who are thin have a larger effect than those who are heavy.[34]

There has been a lot of recent interest in the "wisdom of crowds," captured in the idea that if you put a question to a lot of people and aggregate their answers or obtain some kind of statistical average, you'll often find the right answer.[35] If you ask a group of one hundred people what is the weight of one of their members, the average answer may well be stunningly accurate. For similar reasons, prediction markets, in which large numbers of people bet on likely outcomes, are often accurate. But the crowd turns out to be a lot less wise when people listen to one another. The reason is that people aren't making independent judgments anymore, and for crowds to be wise, their members need to be independent. Even in simple estimation tasks, the wisdom of groups starts to disappear when their members know each other's guesses. What is more, the guessers get a lot more confident.[36] In these ways, social influences can cause big problems, at least if people are listening to other people's mistakes.

How do people form political beliefs? Social influences matter greatly. Conservatives and liberals, when unaware of the views of others, have relatively predictable views about policies that usually divide them, such as welfare reform. That is not exactly surprising. But consider a striking finding from Stanford psychologist Geoffrey Cohen: While Republicans tend to favor a relatively stricter policy toward welfare recipients, they shift dramatically, and disapprove of it, when they are told that the Republican Party in fact disapproves of that stricter policy.[37] Democrats show the same willingness to abandon their private opinions in favor of the views of the Democratic Party. Perhaps most noteworthy, people firmly and sincerely deny that they are influenced by the position of their political party, even though they believe that other people (especially their political adversaries) are so influenced. Here, as in many other contexts, people are blind to what really influences them.

Consider the "social norm approach" to alcohol and drug abuse on college campuses.[38] The basic idea here is that students have an exaggerated sense of how much their fellow students are drinking and using drugs. They tend to think that the percentage is higher than it is. When they are alerted to the actual percentage—which is fairly low—the percentage goes down further.

Here is an illustration of the power of social norms from the United Kingdom, coming from the work of the Behavioural Insights Team, also known as the Nudge Unit. There, as in the United States, prompt tax payment is the general rule, in part because of the system of automatic payroll withholding. (A point for simplicity.) But small-business owners and people with significant nonpayroll income are required to send off a check to the government—and here there is a problem of significant noncompliance. In response, the British government writes standard warning letters. In 2011, equipped with the knowledge that people are more likely to comply with a social norm if they know that most other people comply, the government added a new statement to the letter, a kind of nudge, noting that the vast majority of taxpayers pay their taxes on time.

Letters with messages of this kind were sent to 140,000 taxpayers in a randomized trial. As the theory predicted, referring to the social norm ("9 out of 10 people in Exeter pay their taxes on time") produced big improvements: a 15-percentage-point increase in the number of people who paid before the six-week deadline, compared with results from the old-style letter. According to the tax authorities, this initiative, if used generally, could produce £30 million in extra revenue each year.

Social influences help to account for large-scale social movements, potentially even revolutions. Consider a stylized example. Imagine that Alan concludes that smoking is dangerous and so never smokes. Betty, otherwise a potential smoker, may be convinced by Alan and so refrain from smoking. Carl, mildly inclined to smoke, may think that if Alan and Betty think that smoking is dangerous, that belief must be true. It will take a confident Deborah to resist the shared judgments of Alan, Betty, and Carl. The result of this set of influences can be an *informational cascade*.[39] When a political cause or candidate for public office starts to take off, as Barack Obama did in 2008, an informational cascade may well be a key factor. (The same is true, by the way, of popular songs, movies, and TV shows.)

People also care about their reputation, and for that reason, they may be influenced by a desire to avoid the disapproval of others.[40] You may engage in certain behavior—support a cause, smoke a cigarette—only to avoid the opprobrium of others. A possible result is a *reputational cascade*. Sometimes people take to speaking and acting as if they share, or at least do not reject, what they view as the dominant belief.

For purposes of regulation, an understanding of social influences has an important implication: compliance without a need for enforcement. Often rules are placed on the books, but it is expensive to enforce them, especially when budgets are tight. Does this mean that the rules are pointless? Not necessarily. Both enacted law and regulations can provide important signals; they have *expressive functions*.

When a state requires people to buckle their seat belts or not to text while driving or not to leave children unattended in a car, it gives us a sense of what the authorities, and perhaps the public in general, expect us to do. Rules convey information about what actions make sense. When people comply with laws forbidding indoor smoking or requiring the buckling of seat belts, they are responding to social norms or the expressive function of those laws.[41]

Mistakes About Risks

Not long ago, I bought a new cell phone. It was expensive, but there was also a $100 mail-in rebate. All I had to do was cut out a portion of the cell phone box and mail it to the company. Annoying, maybe a bit stupid, but easy enough to do. When purchasing the phone, I was sure I would do what I needed to do to get my money back. But I delayed for weeks and eventually lost the box.

Some of us are pessimists, and some of us are realists, but most of us are optimists. With respect to risks, most of us believe that we are above average, meaning that we think that we are less vulnerable than most people.[42] Odds are that you believe that you are less likely than others to suffer from life's misfortunes, including automobile accidents, heart attacks, and divorce. Though most people are aware that about 50 percent of marriages end in divorce, brides and grooms typically believe that the chance that they will get divorced is far lower than that.[43] (Even divorce lawyers, who really should know better, greatly underestimate their chances of getting divorced.) Perhaps more surprisingly, one study found that smokers do not underestimate the statistical risks faced by the population of smokers, but they nonetheless believe that their personal risk is less than that of the average nonsmoker.[44]

What can be done to counteract unrealistic optimism? The best answer is not a whole lot. The tale of my unmailed, unredeemed $100 rebate is pretty typical. In a revealing study with the happy title *Everyone Believes in Redemption*,[45] people were asked to predict the likelihood that they would redeem a mail-in form; their actual redemption rates were far lower than their predicted rates. Moreover, and sadly, the very consumers who were most likely to choose a product requiring future action were the ones who were most likely to guess wrongly about what they would actually do!

The authors tried to counteract excessive optimism with three nudges: (1) simply informing people about the (low) actual redemption rates of a previous group, (2) reminding people about the deadline for redemption, and (3) making it a lot simpler for people to redeem. In a finding with important implications, the first two nudges utterly failed; only the third worked. It did so not by reducing optimism, which seemed intractable, but by simplifying life and thus making optimism more realistic.

Some of the most well-known work in behavioral economics stresses people's use of heuristics, or mental shortcuts, in making judgments about risks. You may not know whether a particular event is likely, and in the absence of personal knowledge, you may rely on a heuristic. We have already encountered one example, known as *social proof*: What do other people think? Not knowing for sure, and not wanting to make the effort to investigate a complex issue on the merits, you ask about the views of trusted others. Heuristics typically work in the following way. You face a hard question to which you don't really know the answer. System 2 would have to do a lot of work to figure it out. Instead of trying, you think of an easier question, one that is relevant to the hard one, and you answer the easier question instead. System 1 can do that just fine.

An example is the *availability heuristic*. Our judgments about probability are often affected by whether a recent event comes readily to mind.[46] If an event is cognitively "available," we might well overestimate the risk. If an event is not cognitively available, we might well underestimate the risk.[47] When people are deciding whether it is dangerous to walk in a city at night, to text while driving, or to smoke, it matters a lot whether they know anyone who experienced a bad outcome. System 1 is obviously important here. While System 2 might be willing to do some calculation, System 1 works quickly and automatically.

In short, *availability bias* can lead to big mistakes about the probability of bad outcomes.[48] The bias can take the form of either hysteria or complacency. A finding: On hot days, people are more likely to believe that climate change is real, and they are more likely to support efforts to reduce greenhouse gas emissions.[49]

My goal has been to isolate behavioral findings that have particular importance for regulatory policy. As we will see, many of those findings point in valuable directions; they show real opportunities for saving money and saving lives. Nations all over the world are already taking advantage of those opportunities. Smart businesses are doing the same thing.

Nothing here means that incentives don't matter. Of course they do. Human beings care a lot about costs and benefits. Increases in gas prices decrease driving, and such increases make people more inclined to purchase fuel-efficient cars. Incentives include far more than money. If you believe that carrots make you healthy, or that red meat is bad for you, you may well change your eating habits. When the price of a product rises, or when it becomes clear that use of a product can make you sick, the demand for the product is likely to fall (at least, and this is a significant qualification, if these effects are salient).

Let us agree that if we want to do something about the largest problems, the best approach may well be to change incentives. In the Obama administration, we took strong steps to increase the fuel economy of cars, not by nudges but by mandating big increases in the fleet-wide MPG average. True, those mandates were informed by behavioral economics. And true, we added some nudges as well (see chapter 4). But to limit air pollution, reduce dependence on foreign oil, and save consumers a lot of money, we relied mostly on commands, not nudges.

But apart from material incentives, two other things have independent importance. The first is the social environment; the second is the set of prevailing social norms. It is often said of real estate that only three things matter: location, location, and location. The adage can be applied to choice architecture as well. Recall the effects of the big bowl of chocolates in my office suite. Consistently with this little tale, studies show that if healthy foods are prominent and easily accessible, people are a lot more likely to choose them.[50] One study finds that people will eat 8 to 16 percent less if food is made only slightly more difficult to reach—for example, by decreasing its proximity by ten inches.[51]

The broader point is that when some aspect of the social environment is altered, significant changes may occur—as, for example, when a new default rule is provided for savings plans, or when healthier choices become simpler and easier to make. And when some people, cities, and states do well and others poorly, the reason will often have a lot to do with whether the social environment is harmful or helpful. I have already referred to the work of Esther Duflo on poverty. Consider the words of Duflo and her co-author Abhijit Banerjee: "The poor bear responsibility for too many aspects of their lives. The richer you are, the more the 'right' decisions are made for you. The poor have no piped water, and therefore do not benefit from the chlorine that the city government puts into the water supply. If they want clean drinking water, they have to purify it themselves."[52]

Markets or Government?

Some people think that behavioral economics and an appreciation of the role of System 1 justify a greater role for government. If we know that people are likely to err, shouldn't government do a lot more to correct their mistakes?

This is a good question, but it would a mistake to say that once we understand behavioral economics, we will necessarily be inclined to expand government's power. Among other things, public officials are human and they can err as well. True, we might expect System 2 to exert a lot of authority in government, and in my own experience, most officials in the executive branch do not rely on their intuitions but carefully investigate evidence and facts. Nonetheless, public officials often respond to what citizens want, and what citizens want is likely to show the influence of System 1.

Availability bias, for example, can play a significant role, leading people to emphasize recent events suggesting that a problem is serious, while neglecting other problems because no recent event comes to mind. Self-interested private groups aggravate the problem, enlisting availability bias by drawing official attention to bad outcomes, or promoting complacency by repeatedly drawing official attention to the absence of bad outcomes.

It is true, however, that some of the key behavioral findings help to identify a series of *behavioral market failures*, providing new grounds for government action. Indeed, an understanding of this point helped inform several regulatory decisions in the Obama administration, including mandated increases in fuel economy; energy efficiency requirements for refrigerators, clothes washers, and other appliances; and disclosure requirements of many kinds. An increase in fuel economy will (other things being equal) result in less pollution, and thus fewer deaths and illnesses. Fuel economy standards also increase energy security by reducing the nation's dependence on foreign oil. But most of the monetary benefits of fuel economy standards come from savings to consumers, who will spend far less money at the pump. Other consumer benefits—and they are not trivial—come from saving time. I have a hybrid, and when I bought my fuel-efficient car, I did not focus on these savings at all. But they are really important. It is not a lot of fun to have to stop at the gas station or to see the meter showing that you're going to have to go there soon. If you have a car with good gas mileage, you don't have to look at the meter very often.

Here is the problem. From the standpoint of conventional economic theory, maybe the private savings—the money and time saved—shouldn't count. The free market provides consumers with a lot of options. If they want to buy fuel-efficient cars, they can do that. If they aren't choosing those cars even though they're available, why should government get involved? But if we are alert to the behavioral problems, we will see a possible set of answers.

In 2012 the Department of Transportation referred to

phenomena observed in the field of behavioral economics, including loss aversion, inadequate consumer attention to long-term savings, or a lack of salience of relevant benefits (such as fuel savings, or time savings associated with refueling) to consumers at the time they make purchasing decisions. Both theoretical and empirical research suggests that many consumers are unwilling to make energy-efficient investments even when those investments appear to pay off in the relatively short-term. This research is in line with related findings that consumers may undervalue benefits or costs that are less salient, or that they will realize only in the future.[53]

Here, then, is an explicit recognition of the possibility that behavioral market failures might justify regulation.

But it remains true that even if we have to supplement the standard accounts of market failures, it does not necessarily follow that more regulation is justified. Maybe reliance on the private sector is best. The regulatory cure might be worse than the disease. It might be poorly designed and ineffective; it might be too expensive; it might reflect the power of self-interested private groups who hope to benefit from it.

It would be absurd to say that behaviorally informed regulation is more aggressive than regulation that is not so informed. The argument is instead that such an understanding can help to inform the design of regulatory programs—and make them more likely to succeed. And in some contexts, we will be able to come up with new nudges, taking the form of creative solutions to seemingly intractable problems.

We Need to Learn

The empirical literature is large and, thank goodness, it is growing. For those who want to improve regulation, it would be especially valuable to have a better understanding of how the relevant findings apply within diverse groups.[54] With respect to unrealistic optimism, procrastination, and loss aversion, are men and women the same? Old people and young people? Rich people and poor people? Are college graduates different from those who have not finished high school? How do people differ across nations and across cultures?

We do know that there is a plenty of diversity out there. Some people are more optimistic than others; some people procrastinate more than others; and some people are not so averse to losses. For purposes of policy, this kind of diversity may matter.[55] If a policy would benefit men and hurt women or confer benefits on the rich but not the poor, maybe we should reconsider it and see whether a different or more fine-tuned approach would be better. Perhaps we could devise a policy that would help those who need help without hurting those who do not.

The conceptual and empirical issues are complex, and they have not yet been fully sorted out. A lot more work remains to be done. But even at this stage, we can identify helpful lessons for regulatory policy. Let's begin with disclosure.

4 PLATE, NOT PYRAMID

For decades. the United States relied on the Food Pyramid to promote healthy eating (Figure 4.1). Created by the Department of Agriculture, MyPyramid.gov, displaying the iconic Pyramid, was one of the most visited websites in the entire federal government. Generations of children have been subjected to it. Imagine briefly that you are one of them. Your teacher asks you to study the Pyramid and come back with a plan for a nutritious meal.

Figure 4.1. USDA Food Pyramid.

Source: "Bye-Bye, Pyramid—Hello, Plate: Timeline of Food Guidelines," CBS News (March 8, 2012), http://www.cbsnews.com/2300–204_162–10008001–9.html.

Now ask yourself what you should be eating if you care about nutrition. Maybe the shoeless person climbing (away from the food? toward the top?) holds a clue. But wait. What is so good about the top? What is that white apex supposed to represent? Is it heaven? Is it thinness? At the bottom, why are so many foods crowded into each other? Are you supposed to eat all of those things? At once? What's that large stripe between "fruits" and "meat and beans"? And what is that brown thing at the lower right? Is it a shoe? Did it belong to that climbing person? Are you supposed to eat it?

The Pyramid has long been criticized as hopelessly uninformative. In the words of Chip Heath and Dan Heath, authors of the wonderful bestseller *Switch*, "[I]ts meaning is almost completely opaque." They point out that nothing about the Pyramid or its markings reflects "people's actual experience with food." The consequence is a message that "confuses and demoralizes."[1]

People won't change their behavior if they can't identify any kind of path. A lot of people are interested in healthy eating, but they don't know how to go about it. The goal is exceedingly important. If Americans ate more nutritious meals, they would themselves benefit, and the nation as a whole would benefit too, through greatly reduced medical costs and greater productivity. In fact obesity is one of the nation's most serious public health challenges, and we would save many lives and a lot of money if we met that challenge. The government has strong reasons to help Americans who are inclined to eat more nutritiously. The Food Pyramid was supposed to promote that goal. But it didn't really work.

Having found the Food Pyramid impossibly confusing, I was greatly impressed by these objections. So were several others in the Obama administration, including those in the White House. It mattered that Michelle Obama's "Let's Move" campaign was squarely focused on the problem of childhood obesity, which has been growing at an alarmingly rapid rate. With that problem in mind, a number of us were interested in exploring how best to give parents relevant information. Revising the Food Pyramid was an obvious place to start. The Executive Office of the President contains a number of offices and policy councils, and several of us set up a meeting with officials from the U.S. Department of Agriculture (USDA), which is responsible for the Food Pyramid. They had some loyalty to the old Pyramid, but they agreed that it made sense to rethink the whole approach.

In consultation with officials in the Executive Office of the President, the USDA discussed its options with a wide range of experts with backgrounds in both nutrition and communication. In the end, the USDA replaced the Pyramid with a new icon, consisting of a plate with clear markings for fruit, vegetable, grains, and protein (Figure 4.2).

Figure 4.2. USDA Food Plate.

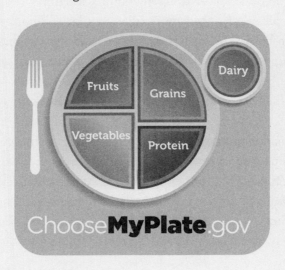

Source: ChooseMyPlate.gov, US Department of Agriculture, http://www.choosemyplate.gov.

The plate gives clear, simple guidance, working not unlike a map. Of course, it doesn't require anyone to do anything. But it makes clear that if half your plate is fruits and vegetables, and if the remaining half is divided between rice (or some other grain) and meat (or some other protein), you're likely to be having a healthy meal.

At ChooseMyPlate.gov, the USDA made sure that the plate is accompanied by straightforward verbal tips, giving people information about what they might do if they want to make good nutritional choices. Imagine that you are a parent interested in serving up nutritious meals to your children. (Maybe you actually are, or will be before long.) Stop reading for a moment and explore ChooseMyPlate.gov and then come back. You might have encountered these:

- Make half your plate fruits and vegetables.
- Drink water instead of sugary drinks.
- Switch to fat-free or low-fat (1%) milk.
- Choose unsalted nuts and seeds to keep sodium intake low.[2]

These statements have the key advantage of avoiding ambiguity. The tips are clear and actionable. For the future, "Plate, Not Pyramid" is a terrific organizing principle. True, we can't exactly build a social movement around it, but the principle needs to be kept in mind in a lot of domains. A friend of mine in government, having experienced an unexpected series of successes in an important international negotiation, once exclaimed to me over the phone, "Plate, not Pyramid!"—meaning that the successes were possible because she had been able to be clear about exactly what she sought. The principle holds for employers, parents, public interest organizations, corporate lobbyists, advertisers, negotiators of all kinds, human rights advocates, and government. Simply put, the principle is this: Avoid ambiguity and be specific about the favored path. This is a good principle for orienting disclosure policies, which can be a powerful, exceedingly useful nudge, and which must be a central part of simpler government.

Three Goals of Disclosure

Disclosure of information is a low-cost, high-impact regulatory tool, replacing or complementing other approaches.[3] To see why, it is important to distinguish between *summary disclosure*, often provided at the point of purchase, and *full disclosure*, typically provided on the Internet. Summary disclosure helps consumers directly through clear, simple information, typically provided on products themselves; consider the "nutrition facts" label on many food packages. Full disclosure, as I use it here, involves the provision of a lot of information on the Internet, giving opportunities to those in the private sector, most especially technological innovators, to use, package, and repurpose it in helpful ways.

For full disclosure in action, have a look at data.gov, the website created by the Obama administration in an effort to "democratize data." One example is the government's release of information about airline on-time performance and causes of flight delays—a release that has helped give rise to valuable apps. Whether summary or full, properly designed disclosure requirements can help people to make more informed decisions and much improve the operation of markets.

As a simple nudge, disclosure can promote three quite different goals. The first is nicely captured by Supreme Court Justice Louis Brandeis's suggestion that sunlight operates as "the best of disinfectants." What Brandeis meant was that sunlight—allowing people to see what is being done or not being done—can help improve performance. The reason is that public knowledge and scrutiny encourage both individuals and institutions to perform better. A dramatic example is Harvard economist Amartya Sen's finding that in the history of the world, no society with democratic elections and a free press has ever experienced a famine.[4] In such societies, sunlight tends to be omnipresent, and it operates to deter official choices that would lead to mass starvation. Because of the power of disclosure, open societies are more likely to attend to emerging problems, relieve suffering, and generally make people's lives better. We should use sunlight far more often than we do. The worldwide Open Government Partnership, spearheaded by the Obama administration, is motivated in large part by this idea (see www .opengovernmentpartnership.org).

In terms of domestic policy, an important example is Congress's decision in 1986 to require companies to disclose toxic releases. Designed largely as an information-gathering tool, it has actually worked to reduce such releases, because no company wants to be known as one of the Dirty Dozen in its state. With this precedent in mind, the Obama administration decided not only to require companies to disclosure their greenhouse gas emissions but also to produce a clear, usable website allowing people to track greenhouse gas emissions in the United States.[5] Thus Gina McCarthy, the EPA's assistant administrator for air, stated, "We have great hopes that the information itself will be a strong driver for greenhouse gas reductions."[6] Of course, it is possible that the hope will not be realized; a great deal depends on the incentives of those who emit greenhouse gases. But in many contexts, disclosure helps to promote accountability for both private and public institutions, altering behavior for the better. A current example is medical errors, which are the fifth leading cause of death in the United States. Greater transparency, allowing the public to see the magnitude of errors and to make comparisons across doctors and hospitals, could save a lot of lives.[7]

A second goal of disclosure is to provide people with information they can readily find and use. This is not a point about accountability and improved performance; it is about giving people knowledge that enables them to make better choices about nutrition, child care, motor vehicles, energy, health, investments, and much more. When government releases data with respect to motor vehicle safety or the performance of infant safety seats, it provides consumers with indispensable information and, in the process, can provide a helpful nudge toward better decisions. Consider here President Clinton's 2000 decision to unscramble Global Positioning Service (GPS) signals, which enabled millions of people to make countless informed decisions about what route to take while driving on the streets and sailing on the seas. (This is a terrific illustration of the potential of disclosure, and I will return to it.) Many of the nations participating in the Open Government Partnership are making a lot of data available to their people.

A third goal of disclosure is to improve decisions made by the government itself, by ensuring that its officials will have access to the dispersed information of the nation's citizens. While in government, I was acutely aware of how much I did not know. Even if government officials are specialists, they need to learn from the public. When judging the potential effects of rules designed to promote food safety or to protect air quality, public officials cannot possibly have complete knowledge. They have to find out what is known by other people, especially those in the private sector. Every day, policies and rules are improved in this way.

In his most important contribution, Friedrich Hayek, Nobel Prize winner and powerful critic of socialism, urged that no government planners, however expert and well-motivated, can know as much as society knows, simply because human knowledge is widely dispersed.[8] The public as a whole knows far more than any expert or board of experts. Hayek was defending the free market's price system, which he described as a "marvel" simply because it aggregates diverse information. The price system remains a marvel, and it is an indispensable part of a free society. But it is not the only mechanism by which we can obtain dispersed information. Modern technologies create other mechanisms that Hayek could not possibly have imagined.

With such technologies, there are growing opportunities for government to learn from members of the public—to identify the likely consequences of decisions in advance, to reduce the risk of error, and to correct mistakes after they are made. Before implementing regulations, the government usually puts them before the public for comment; it cannot, and does not, finalize rules before it learns what the public has to say. This process is an important check on mistakes. It is also extraordinarily informative. Public officials often learn a great deal from the concerns and objections of citizens. (I certainly did.)

Modern technologies also make it increasingly possible to inform people about the nature and effects of their past decisions, to assemble and apply statistical data, and to expose false or deceptive claims. Consider "comparison friction," or the difficulty that most of us have in making easy comparisons among complex products.[9] (Or not so complex: Have you tried to buy a vacuum cleaner lately?) We will soon be in a position to reduce that friction, collecting a lot of relevant data and presenting them in a way that allows easy comparisons. Some of the most exciting possibilities involve disclosure of information held by the government. The Open Government Initiative of the Obama administration was designed with the knowledge that private developers would mine and adapt data in ways that could dramatically improve people's lives. The possibilities of disclosure are in their infancy, and we can only glimpse what is to come—but the promise is extraordinary. Consider a few examples.

Beyond the MPG Illusion

Under the law, automobile manufacturers have long been required to disclose the fuel economy of new vehicles, as measured by miles per gallon (MPG).[10] The idea behind the law is straightforward: Providing consumers with information about fuel economy could have significant economic (and environmental) benefits.

Figure 4.3 illustrates an old label. The label is useful, as far as it goes, and the information that it conveys does help to promote informed choice. The label is better than the Food Pyramid (I think). At the same time, it is far from ideal. If you are considering a car bearing this label, how will you

Figure 4.3. Old fuel economy label.

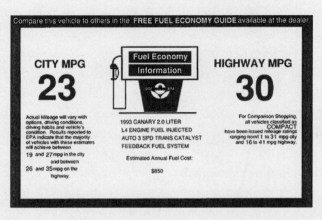

Source: Fuel Economy Label, US Environmental Protection Agency, http://www.epa.gov/ fueleconomy/images_label/label_pre2008_650.gif.

compare it with one that costs a bit more but has higher MPG numbers, or with one that costs a bit less and has lower MPG numbers? And what exactly does MPG mean, for you and for what you care about?

Suppose that your big question is how to save money, and you want to know whether a car with a high sticker price and high MPG numbers will cost you more or less than other cars over the next five years. You may ask: Is this high-MPG car really worth it to me, simply in terms of money? To many consumers, what matters most is cost, and on this label the annual fuel cost is buried in tiny print. But suppose what you care about is the environment, and what you really want to know is something about the relationship between air pollution and MPG. This label doesn't help very much.

There is also a fundamental problem with the MPG measure, which is that it can be highly misleading. Contrary to most people's intuitions, MPG is a nonlinear measure of fuel consumption, thus giving rise to the "MPG illusion."[11] For a given distance, a change from twenty to twenty-five MPG produces a larger reduction in fuel costs than does a change from thirty to thirty-five MPG, or even from thirty to thirty-eight MPG. To see the point more dramatically, consider the fact that an increase from ten to twenty MPG produces more savings than does an increase from twenty to forty MPG—and an increase from ten to eleven MPG produces savings

almost as great as an increase from thirty-four to fifty MPG![12] Figure 4.4
displays the nonlinearity of the MPG measure.

Figure 4.4. Gallons of gas used per 10,000 miles driven as a
function of fuel efficiency of cars (expressed in MPG).

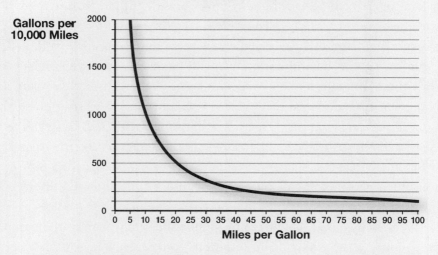

Source: Richard P. Larrick and Jack B. Soll, "The MPG Illusion," *Science* 20 (June 20, 2008):
1593–94.

From this figure, unlike the MPG label, you can readily see that there
are huge gains in going from a low-MPG car to a mildly higher-MPG car—
but when you get to the high numbers, the gains level off. The problem
can be put in terms of System 1 and System 2. While your System 2 can
figure all this out (though it has to do some work), your System 1 is likely
to find the whole issue baffling. From a series of studies, we know that many
consumers do not understand the nonlinear nature of the MPG measure;
they tend to interpret MPG as linear with fuel costs.[13] If that is the consumers' assumption, the MPG measure can lead to poorly informed decisions;
people's intuitive comparative judgments across cars are based on a fundamental mistake.

Because of the MPG illusion, consumers tend to *underestimate* the fuel
cost differences among low-MPG vehicles and to *overestimate* the fuel cost
differences among high-MPG vehicles.[14] As a result, car buyers may well
underestimate the benefits of trading a low-MPG car for one that is even

slightly more fuel efficient. At the same time, they may overestimate the benefits of trading a high-MPG car for one that has even higher MPG.

The MPG measure hardly eliminates comparison friction. Because of the MPG illusion, it may well increase it. Other measures would be far less confusing. Consider, as one example, a metric that turns MPG on its head: gallons of gas used per one hundred miles driven. Such a measure *is* linear with fuel costs and can help consumers make more informed choices.[15] A measure of this kind is in general use in Europe, and it appears to work well.

In the Obama administration, many of us were aware of the problems with the MPG measure, and we were keenly interested in developing a better label. We discussed the problem with officials at the Environmental Protection Agency and the Department of Transportation; the agencies responded enthusiastically. In 2010, DOT and EPA put two alternative labels before the public (see Figures 4.5 and 4.6). Both were designed to provide consumers with clearer and more accurate information about the effects of fuel economy on fuel expenses and on the environment.[16]

We presented both options to the public and received many thousands of comments—some of them empirical, some highly insightful, some

Figure 4.5. EPA and DOT proposed alternative fuel economy label, Option 1.

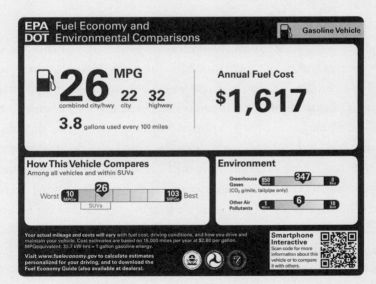

Source: Proposed Fuel Economy Labels, Environmental Protection Agency (August 2010), http://www.epa.gov/fueleconomy/label/label-designs.pdf.

Figure 4.6. EPA and DOT proposed alternative fuel economy label, Option 2.

Source: Proposed Fuel Economy Labels, Environmental Protection Agency (August 2010), http://www.epa.gov/fueleconomy/label/label-designs.pdf.

highly technical, some based on intuitions, some a form of cheerleading, others a form of booing and hissing. I will outline some of the comments shortly, but having just discussed the dispersed nature of human knowledge, I should note that many of the comments were exceptionally helpful and that receiving helpful comments is the norm, not the exception. In my time in government, I read thousands of public comments, and my staff read far more. (You can find public comments on pending rules by visiting regulations.gov, a website that we worked hard to improve and redesign. The website's words, "Your Voice in Federal Decision-Making," are not puffery. They reflect reality.) Indeed, the importance of receiving such comments may have been the chief lesson I received during my time at OIRA.

The dispersed information of the public—usually citizens of the United States, but sometimes noncitizens as well—is an essential part of the rule-making process. Time and again, proposed rules were subject in advance to intense thinking and scrutiny, but public comments revealed that we had missed something—sometimes something crucial. By listening to what people had to say, we avoided serious errors. By the way, we weren't affected by public applause or by public booing and hissing, which were predictable. Some segments of the public seem to think that what matters is the volume of the positive and negative comments, whereas what really matters is their substance and content.

Back to our subject. Which of the two labels would you choose? The first label emerged from a careful process in which we used focus groups to test a variety of options. Members of our focus groups—ordinary people, recruited to produce their own evaluations—generally liked the clean, simple, prominent statement of annual fuel cost. Several variations on this label were given to the focus groups, which supported the label that we proposed. We also did some testing of whether people could understand the label, and here too the first label did quite well.

The second label emerged from a more unusual and more creative process. The EPA convened a group of experts in a number of fields, including communications and marketing. To my great surprise, the experts were not just modestly critical of the first label. They hated it! They thought that it was too dry, too complicated, too bland, too number-focused, and too statistical. In their view, it would not have much of an impact on consumers. They argued for a clear, simple letter grade—A for excellent, B for good, C for average, and so forth—on the ground that it would convey an immediate, understandable message. While the experts did not speak in terms of System 1 and System 2, it was clear that they sought a label that System 1 could get automatically and that would not force System 2 to work much, if at all. They wanted simplicity.

The experts also argued that the new label should give people a clear sense of a car's five-year fuel expenditure (or savings) as compared with the average. The logic here is straightforward. Many people keep cars for five years or more. If they buy a fuel-efficient car, a key question is the effects of ownership on their bank account. At the time of purchase, it would be extremely helpful for people to have a sense of how much they would be spending or saving over the full five years. We agreed that the experts made some strong points, and when we proposed the two labels, we really did not know which was best. We wanted the public to help us find out.

I have referred to the problem of comparison friction. For some products, comparison is easy, and price alone suffices. If a candy bar costs $10, it had better be a pretty special candy bar, and a $75 laptop is an amazing deal. But suppose you spend $1,200 annually on electricity bills. In your community and in light of your options, is that a lot or a little? If you are spending $900 annually on your cell phone, do you have a good deal or a terrible one?

To be able to answer, you would want, first, to be able to make a comparison between the service or product you have and alternative services or products. Second, you would want information about what you might do to drive your cost down. To make such comparisons people (and System 2 in particular) have to do some work. How many of us do that work? Is there a way to make it easy for us?

Consider an important study by the economist Jeffrey Kling and his colleagues.[17] They conducted a randomized field experiment in which some people received a letter containing personalized cost information about their options under the Medicare Part D prescription drug plan. People in a control group did not. Even without the letter, that information was easily available to the control group; it was both free and widely advertised. Nonetheless, there was a big effect from the small, simple nudge of providing the information rather than requiring consumers to have to work to get it. The people who received the letter were a lot more likely to switch plans and save real money—about $100 per year. Kling and his coauthors conclude that even when the cost of acquiring information is small, comparison friction can be a major problem.

With respect to the fuel economy labels, many public comments picked up on this theme, emphasizing the importance of enabling people to make easy comparisons. This was why many people, especially in the environmental community, loved the letter grade. They found it simple and compelling, and they predicted that it would have a significant and beneficial effect on choices. By itself, a letter grade helps to overcome comparison friction. Everyone knows that "A" is better than "C."

But many other people, including those in the automobile industry, strongly preferred a "just the facts" approach. In particular, they contended that the letter grades were too evaluative and prescriptive, putting the government's thumb far too heavily on the scales. Undoubtedly their self-interest was at work. They feared that a low letter grade could reduce sales.

Who wants to buy a car with a big C on it? But they also had a more interesting argument, which was that consumers might take the grade to suggest
the government's evaluation of the overall merits of cars. A car might get a
C on fuel economy but nonetheless be a terrific car. A grade of C might suggest, wrongly, that the government believes that the car is lousy on balance.

Whether intentionally or not, the industry critics were showing an
awareness of the importance of the affect heuristic discussed in chapter 3:
People often form a quick, affective reaction to products, and that reaction
influences their judgments. (Ever been affected by the number of stars that
a critic gave a movie?) A C could produce a quite negative affect even if the
car has plenty of wonderful features.

We had a lot of internal discussion of the merits of the competing labels.
Some of us liked the letter grades a lot, but we were ultimately convinced
that the industry critics had some good points. The grades could indeed
suggest that government was grading cars, not just fuel economy. After considering the comments, DOT and EPA chose a label that borrows from
both proposed labels (see Figure 4.7).[18]

As with the first proposed label, the chosen approach discloses a lot of
factual information, including annual fuel costs. But in keeping with the

Figure 4.7. New fuel economy label.

Source: A New Fuel Economy Label for a New Generation of Cars, Environmental Protection
Agency, http://www.fueleconomy.gov/feg/label/docs/EPA_FE_Label-052311.pdf.

second label, the chosen approach adds a clear statement about anticipated fuel costs (compared with the average) over a five-year period. This information should help to counteract the MPG illusion and inform consumers about the economic effects of fuel economy over the period of ownership. The new label also includes information about gallons used per one hundred miles.

There is a broader lesson from this tale. With respect to energy conservation, helping consumers know, very concretely, what energy-efficient choices save them (or what energy-inefficient choices cost them) might help overcome undue focus on the costs and benefits that are obvious only at the time of purchase. See, as one example, Figure 4.8, which is the Federal Trade Commission's energy-efficiency label for refrigerators, clearly identifying annual costs.

Figure 4.8. FTC EnergyGuide label.

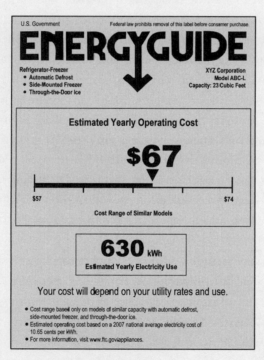

Source: Press release, Federal Trade Commission, "Concluding Two-Year Rulemaking, FTC Announces New EnergyGuide Label" (August 7, 2007), http://www.ftc.gov/opa/2007/08/energy.shtm.

Unhiding Costs

The Food Pyramid, the fuel economy label, and energy-efficiency labels are simple nudges, designed to make markets work better by informing consumers. There are many other examples.

A long-standing complaint about airline fees is that they are hopelessly opaque. Because of hidden fees, an astonishingly low $9 ticket might entail a much less welcome $100 fee. That's an extreme case (though real; one airline has charged a $100 *carry-on* luggage fee), but starting in 2008 unexpected costs became more common. One consequence is that many fees have not been easily taken into account by consumers. Another consequence is that the process of competition works far less well than it should. Airlines have had an incentive to hide some of their fees, and because government taxes and fees were not included in the up-front fare quote, people did not have a complete sense of their out-of-pocket costs.

In 2011, the Department of Transportation took significant steps to reduce the problem. By regulation, the Department required airlines to disclose prominently all potential fees on their websites. These include fees for baggage, meals, canceling or changing reservations, and advanced or upgraded seating. Even better, airlines have to include all government taxes and fees in every advertised price. Notably, some airlines sued to invalidate the regulation, complaining especially about the requirement to include taxes and fees and invoking the First Amendment, no less, to say that the requirement was unconstitutional. (The airlines lost.)

People have also long complained that credit card contracts come with confusing terms, including hidden costs. System 2 has to do a lot of work to understand these terms, and it might well give up in frustration. The problem is compounded, as the law professor Oren Bar-Gill has explained, by other behavioral market failures.[19] Some people, for example, are unrealistically optimistic about their own behavior—most obviously, they believe that they will stay within spending limits and avoid running up balances—and their optimism can lead them to lose a lot of money.

A key goal of the Credit Card Accountability, Responsibility, and Disclosure Act of 2009 (Credit CARD Act)[20] is to ensure that credit card users are adequately informed and that they receive advance notice of changes in terms. The act shows a good understanding of the importance of simplification, and it includes a lot of nudges. Among other things, the act

- Requires clear and conspicuous disclosure of annual percentage rates (APR) and finance charges
- Prohibits an increase in APR without forty-five days' notice
- Prohibits the retroactive application of rate increases to existing balances
- Requires clear notice of the consumer's right to cancel the credit card when the APR is raised

The act also requires a number of electronic disclosures of the terms of credit card agreements, ensuring that both the Federal Reserve Board and the public can easily find and retrieve the information.[21]

Perhaps the most familiar example of summary disclosure is the "Nutrition Facts" panel on most food packages. Notwithstanding the intense controversy that preceded its original adoption in 1983, it is now a central part of America's choice architecture. For many years, however, no such panel could be found on meat and poultry products. In the Obama administration, we filled that gap. In 2011 the Department of Agriculture required ground meat and ground poultry to have a nutrition label. The panels must contain information about calories and both total and saturated fats.[22]

Notably, the rule explicitly recognizes the importance of framing. If a product lists a percentage statement, such as "80 percent lean," it must also list its fat percentage.[23] This requirement should help to avoid the confusion that can result from selective framing. A statement that a product is 80 percent lean, standing by itself, makes leanness salient, and may therefore mislead people. By the way, this part of the rule is historic: it is the most explicit acknowledgment of the power of framing in American regulatory law.

It is widely understood that the Affordable Care Act, otherwise known as Obamacare, is designed to promote accountability and informed choice with respect to health care.[24] What is not sufficiently appreciated is that the Affordable Care Act is in part a series of disclosure requirements. For example, the act calls for disclosure of "information that allows consumers to identify affordable coverage options."[25] To this end, it requires the establishment of an Internet portal to enable people to find health insurance plans, including information about eligibility, availability, premium rates, cost sharing, and the percentage of total premium revenues the insurer spends on health care rather than on administrative expenses.[26]

The Affordable Care Act also enlists disclosure to constrain increases in health insurance premiums. The act requires the secretary of the Department of Health and Human Services (HHS) and the states to establish a process for the annual review of "unreasonable increases" in premiums. That process in turn requires health insurance issuers to justify any apparently unreasonable increase before it can be implemented. Moreover, insurers are required to post information about premium increases and their justifications prominently on their websites.

Under the act, HHS also requires insurance companies to provide clear summaries of relevant information to prospective customers,[27] including the annual deductible, a statement of services that are not covered, and a statement of costs for going to an out-of-network provider. The HHS template offers other information as well, some of which is presented in Figure 4.9.

Figure 4.9. Sample insurance coverage template.

_______________ : _______________ Policy Period: ______ – ______

Summary of Coverage: What this Plan Covers & What it Costs **Coverage for:** __________ | **Plan Type:** ____

This is not a policy. You can get the policy at www.insurancecompany.com/PLAN1500 or by calling 1-800-XXX-XXXX. A policy has more detail about how to use the plan and what you and your insurer must do. It also has more detail about your coverage and costs.

Important Questions	Answers	Why this Matters:
What is the premium?	$	The premium is the amount paid for health insurance. This is only an estimate based on information you've provided. After the insurer reviews your application, your actual premium may be higher or your application may be denied.
What is the overall deductible?	$	
Are there other deductibles for specific services?	$	
Is there an out–of–pocket limit on my expenses?	$	
What is not included in the out–of–pocket limit?		
Is there an overall annual limit on what the insurer pays?		
Does this plan use a network of providers?		
Do I need a referral to see a specialist?		
Are there services this plan doesn't cover?		

Source: Department of Health and Human Services, Proposed Template: Summary of Coverage and Benefits, HealthCare.gov, http://www.healthcare.gov/news/factsheets/labels08172011b.pdf.

Under another provision of the act, chain restaurants are required to disclose calorie information on their menus. They are also required to make available to customers nutritional information about their food, including amounts of fat, saturated fat, cholesterol, sodium, total carbohydrates, complex carbohydrates, sugars, dietary fiber, and protein.[28] In 2011, we proposed rules to implement these requirements.

How, Not Only Whether

As the requirement to include lean and fat percentages suggests, disclosure as such may not be enough. It is important to consider *how, not only whether, disclosure occurs.*[29] Even accurate disclosure of information may be ineffective if the information is too ambiguous, abstract, vague, detailed, complex, or overwhelming to be useful.[30] Clarity and simplicity are critical. Summary disclosure should be designed for System 1, not System 2.

A good rule of thumb is that disclosure should be concrete, straightforward, simple, meaningful, timely, and salient. In other words, Plate, not Pyramid. Recall as well that people's tendency toward unrealistic optimism can affect their judgments about serious risks, including those associated with smoking and distracted driving. In such circumstances, disclosure might be designed to make these risks more vivid, even graphic, as required by the Family Smoking Prevention and Tobacco Control Act of 2009 (see chapter 6).

Simplicity, Competition, Markets

Consumer protection cannot possibly be understood without an appreciation of behavioral economics and of the importance of simplicity. I was privileged to participate in the lengthy discussions over the design of the Consumer Financial Protection Bureau, and behavioral findings, accompanied by an appreciation of the risks of complexity, played a role in those discussions.

Congress ultimately charged the Consumer Financial Protection Bureau with ensuring that people "know before they owe" with respect to mortgages, school loans, credit cards, and much more. In language that draws directly on behavioral research, Congress authorized the bureau to issue rules ensuring that information is "fully, accurately, and effectively disclosed to consumers in a manner that permits consumers to understand the costs, benefits, and risks associated with the product or service, in light of the facts and circumstances."[31]

To accomplish this, the bureau is authorized to issue model forms with "a clear and conspicuous disclosure that, at a minimum—(A) uses plain language comprehensible to consumers; (B) contains a clear format and design, such as an easily readable type font; and (C) succinctly explains the information that must be communicated to the consumer."[32] In addition, and importantly, the director of the bureau is required to "establish a unit whose functions shall include researching, analyzing, and reporting on . . . consumer awareness, understanding, and use of disclosures and communications regarding consumer financial products or services" and "consumer behavior with respect to consumer financial products or services, including performance on mortgage loans."[33]

During my years in the Obama administration, simple disclosure was a major theme, and there are a lot more examples in this vein. In order to promote competition and to avoid deception, the Department of Labor issued a rule requiring employers to provide workers with key information about pension plans. The rule requires clear, simple disclosure of information about fees and expenses in such a way as to allow meaningful comparisons, in part through the use of standard methodologies in the calculation and disclosure of expense and return information.[34]

A rule from the Department of Education, designed to promote transparency and consumer choice with respect to for-profit education, was among the most controversial issued by the Obama administration, and it faced intense opposition by the for-profit sector. Nonetheless, we went forward with it. Key provisions require institutions to disclose costs, debt levels, graduation rates, and job placement rates.[35] Under the rule, institutions must disclose, among other things:

- Occupations that the program prepares students to enter
- On-time graduation rate for students completing the program

- Tuition and fees charged to students for completing the program within a normal time
- Job placement rate for students completing the program
- Median loan debt incurred by students who completed the program

These disclosures must be included "in promotional materials [the institution] makes available to prospective students" and be "[p]rominently provide[d] . . . in a simple and meaningful manner on the home page of its program Web site."[36]

President Obama built on this example in proposing a more general College Scorecard, shown in Figure 4.10. Notice that the scorecard contains both absolute and relative information; it is designed to allow for comparisons. One of its purposes is to promote informed choice. Another is to

Figure 4.10. College Scorecard.

Source: College Scorecard, WhiteHouse.gov, http://www.whitehouse.gov/sites/default/files/image/college-value-profile.pdf.

promote better performance on the part of colleges. If a university's students have a lot of debt and don't get jobs, the scorecard provides it with strong incentive to do better. The White House developed the initial proposal into a clear, easy-to-use College Scorecard (http://www.whitehouse.gov/issues/education/higher-education/college-score-card), providing simple information about costs, graduation rates, loan repayments, borrowing, and much more. Here as elsewhere, sunlight can have a big effect.

Full Disclosure

The disclosure requirements discussed thus far are designed to inform consumers at the point of purchase or decision, usually with brief summaries of key information. Such summary disclosures are often complemented with far more detailed information, typically found on public or private websites. I have noted that disclosure of this sort has a special virtue: If it is done properly, it can be adapted by the private sector, which can repackage the data in multiple ways, making them as useful as possible.

Recall President Clinton's 2000 decision to make the GPS widely available by unscrambling the signals. That decision, unlocking data of immense social value, produced huge economic and social benefits, in large part because it provided information that the private sector has been able to use and to adapt in countless ways. Government is doing and can do a lot more in this vein. HealthData.gov, the one-stop resource for high-value government health data, is constantly being improved. (It's worth a look.) The "Nutrition Facts" label is supplemented by a great deal of nutritional information on government websites.[37] Humanrights.gov, created as part of the Open Government Initiative, offers an extraordinary amount of material about human rights. I have emphasized the importance of the website data.gov, which offers over 350,000 data sets, many of them adaptable for private sector use; there is immense potential here to replicate the GPS experience in ways large and small. Private developers are paying close attention.

Many disclosure requirements are designed to promote public understanding of social problems and help produce solutions by informing people about current practices. I have mentioned disclosure of toxic releases, which was required by the Emergency Planning and Community Right-to-Know

Act of 1986.[38] At first this law seemed to be largely a bookkeeping measure, calling for a Toxic Release Inventory.[39] It turned out to be an unanticipated public health success story, spurring significant reductions in toxic releases throughout the United States.[40] Knowing that public attention can help promote public goals, the Occupational Safety and Health Administration (OSHA) placed a significant subset of its fatality, illness, and injury data online, in a step designed to promote safer workplaces.[41] The Department of Justice has published dozens of data sets involving crime, enforcement, and prison.[42] The Department of Labor's "Searchable Enforcement Database" provides the public with one-stop access to an astonishing wealth of data collected by Department agencies in areas including safe and healthful work conditions, minimum wages and overtime pay, and employment discrimination.[43] The EPA has taken a similar approach.[44] Generalizing from these practices, President Obama issued a memorandum in 2011 requiring agencies with broad regulatory compliance and enforcement responsibilities to make their activities accessible, downloadable, and searchable online. A central goal is to promote accountability. With the same ends in mind, the Office of Management and Budget's Open Government Directive requires high-value data sets to be placed online.[45]

In addition to making data more accessible, agencies are making data more usable. An example is eXtensible Business Reporting Language. XBRL is an open standard for creating electronic reports and exchanging data via the Internet. It allows anyone to download and analyze large amounts of data using a simple spreadsheet. The Securities and Exchange Commission has required large companies (those with a market capitalization over $5 billion) to submit all filings in the XBRL format. The rule, titled "Interactive Data to Improve Financial Reporting,"[46] is intended not only to make financial information easier for investors to analyze but also to assist in automating regulatory filings and business information processing. Interactive data have the potential to increase the speed, accuracy, and usability of financial disclosure and eventually to reduce costs.[47]

Smart Disclosure

The idea of Smart Disclosure is sparking enthusiasm not only in the United States but all over the world. In brief, Smart Disclosure refers to *the timely release of complex information and data in standardized, machine-readable formats in ways that enable consumers to make more informed decisions.* It typically takes the form of providing the public with direct access to key information and data sets. The information that is disclosed might be used by ordinary people; but it is more likely to be adapted by private intermediaries who make it simple, clear, and intelligible. Such information might involve, for example, the range of costs associated with various products and services, including costs that might not otherwise be transparent.

The interest in Smart Disclosure is motivated by two independent concerns. The first is that people often have too little information about the nature and the consequences of their own past decisions. By contrast, companies may well have exactly that information. They may know (and increasingly do know) a tremendous amount about the nature and effects of your choices with respect to health care, finance, cell phones, rental cars, energy, books, and much more. Knowledge of those choices, and their effects, can improve people's decisions in the future; consumers should have access to that knowledge.

The second concern is that even when the private or public sector discloses information, it may not do so in a way that can be readily used. For example, the information may not be machine-readable. It may not be easily adapted by the countless people in the private sector who stand ready to work on information to make it usable by ordinary people. Smart Disclosure is meant to fix this problem.

Consider the Blue Button, used by the Veterans Administration (VA) to provide veterans with access to their health care information. In the words of the VA: "VA's Blue Button allows you to access and download your information from your My HealtheVet personal health record into a very simple text file or PDF that can be read, printed, or saved on any computer. It gives you complete control of this information—without any special software—and enables you to share this data with your health care providers, caregivers, or people you trust." Veterans who log onto My HealtheVet at www.myhealth.va.gov and click the Blue Button can save or print information from their own health records.

The My HealtheVet personal health record includes emergency contact information, test results, family health history, military health history, and other health-related information. It has generated an exceedingly enthusiastic response; tens of thousands of veterans have used it to download their records. A wide range of people, not merely veterans, stand to benefit from this sort of disclosure.

Can something similar be done for energy use? In 2012, utilities and electricity suppliers across the country committed to provide more than 15 million households with an online "Green Button," giving them access to data about their energy use with a simple click. Armed with their own data, homeowners and building owners are able to use online services to manage their energy use and cut their bills. The promise here is extraordinary. In a randomized controlled trial, residential customers who were given detailed information about prices and usage, essentially in real time, ended up saving a lot of money.[48] They were able to reduce their usage from between 8 and 22 percent—far more than the control group. This finding suggests the possibility of future savings involving cell phones, water, heating oil, natural gas, and more.

Here too we are at the tip of an iceberg. With Smart Disclosure, it should eventually be easy for consumers to get secure access to their own health care, energy, financial, and education data. Smart Disclosure also promises to provide new market opportunities for the many entrepreneurs and start-ups now creating new apps and services. What has been complex and hard to find can be made simple and accessible in an instant. It may be too much to expect one-click government, but let's be optimistic; we can get a lot closer. And if government can move in that direction, there is no question that private institutions will get there too.

5

AUTOMATIC FOR THE PEOPLE

Suppose that you are watching your favorite television show on channel 52, and after it ends, a show comes on that you don't much like. Will you change the channel? If you are like a lot of other viewers, the answer is no. As shows get more popular, the shows that follow them get more popular too. Why? Because the channel that you are watching is the default—it is what you will continue to see if you do nothing at all.[1] In Italy, a 10 percent increase in the popularity of a program has been found to lead to a 2 to 4 percent increase in the audience for the program that follows it. Unsurprisingly, television stations exploit this behavior; if they did not, they could lose up to 40 percent of their profits!

I propose the following aspiration for governments and the private sector alike, suitable for many domains: *Make it automatic*. For governments, the goal should be to ensure that if people do nothing at all, things will go well for them. And if people are required to take action, government should make the process is as simple and automatic as possible. Put differently, government should try to ensure, when it can, that what has to be done can be handled quickly and easily by System 1.

Many companies prosper because they excel at making things automatic. Part of the genius of Apple products is that their amazingly complex technologies build on simple patterns that people find intuitive and familiar. iPad and iPhone users never encounter complex instruction manuals filled with technical jargon and impenetrable diagrams. Why shouldn't interactions with government be as simple as interactions with the iPad?

Both public and private institutions often require people to fill out complex forms before they can receive benefits, licenses, permits, grants, em-

ployment, entry, or security clearance. Are all of these really necessary? The
Obama administration eliminated tens of millions of hours in paperwork
requirements, and there is much more to get rid of. The federal government could eliminate many millions more—probably hundreds of millions.
Time is money, and at a reasonable hourly rate, we are talking about billions
of dollars in savings.

As one of my final acts in government, I directed all agencies to test
their new forms to get a sense of the burdens they would impose in the real
world, and then to figure out how to make them simpler. I also directed
agencies to test their existing forms before renewing them, and to refine or
simplify them on the basis of what they learn. (I confess that when requiring
these steps, I had not forgotten my own frustration in filling out innumer-
able forms to qualify for federal employment.) If filling out forms cannot
be automatic, at least it can be easy rather than hard and at least we can
reduce the burden on those who must comply. If System 1 is unable to fill
out a form, we should take steps to make sure that System 2 does not have
to struggle.

Deciding by Default

We have seen that starting points, or default rules, greatly affect outcomes.
Here is a little example. Credit card machines have been installed in taxis
in New York City. But what's the tip? The machine gives you three options:
30 percent, 25 percent, or 20 percent. If you want to give less, you can,
but it takes a little work. Customers are effectively defaulted into one of
the three options. There is every reason to think that tips are increasing as a
result. Calculations are highly speculative, but according to one admittedly
very rough assessment, the result has been to increase the average tip from
10 percent to 22 percent, which would mean that cabdrivers are taking in
an additional $144 million each year.[2]

In 2011, several of us organized a conference at the White House on
information disclosure. Along with others, Dick Thaler, my friend and
coauthor, sent out materials in advance to the 300 registrants, who came
from more than sixty federal agencies. In those materials, people were told
that unless they specifically requested otherwise, they would get the healthy

lunch option. The materials explained: "Healthy options for lunch may include, but are not limited to, a bean sprout and soy-cheese sandwich on gluten-free soda bread." The materials also offered a "special reward" to anyone who sent in an e-mail with the subject line: Full Disclosure.

The bean spout and soy-cheese sandwich sounds pretty awful, and I doubt that many people actually wanted it. How many people do you think would opt out? As it happens, 80 percent of attendees failed to do so, and just 1 percent got that reward. On the morning of the event, the participants groaned when told that most of them had people had "selected" the soy-cheese sandwich for lunch. Now, Thaler is a nice guy, and he was joking, and people ended up with pretty good sandwiches. Still, it is noteworthy that the well-educated participants ended up signing on for a really unappealing sandwich (and missing out on a promised reward).

Default rules can be found in your health insurance plan, your savings plan, your credit card and cell phone agreements, and your mortgage. As we have also seen, the default rule tends to stick. Where people end up may well depend on where they start. Because System 1 often says, "Yeah, whatever," and because System 2 has other things to do, the default has a big effect. (A noteworthy exception, on which more below: Upon marriage, the default rule is that people keep their surname. But the vast majority of women switch.)[3]

An excellent way to make things automatic is to establish default rules that serve people's interests even if they do nothing at all. In many contexts, important goals can be achieved through sensible default rules that preserve freedom of choice and that help to avoid the rigidity, cost, and unintended bad consequences of mandates and bans.

How much privacy do any of us have online? The answer may well be a function of the default rule. Suppose that a public or private institution— the Social Security Administration, your employer, your preferred search engine, Facebook, Twitter, your favorite website—says that your personal information will not be shared with anyone *unless you click on a button to allow it.* Now suppose instead that the same institution says that your personal information will be shared with the entire world *unless you click on a button to forbid it.* Will the results be the same?

Far from it.[4] If people are asked whether they want to opt in to information sharing, a lot of them will either ignore the question ("Yeah, whatever") or respond with some version of "No, you've got to be kidding." In either case, the result is the same, and their information will not be shared. If people are asked whether they want to opt out of information sharing, a lot of them will again say "Yeah, whatever," especially if they have to think a little bit and read something complicated in order to switch. In that case, their information will be shared.

Consider the current settings on Chrome, the Google browser. If you want to use the web anonymously, you can, by clicking on "New Incognito Window." But there is no option for selecting "Incognito" as your default setting. You have to click on it every time you open your browser. I predict, with a lot of confidence, that if people could opt into Incognito, making it their default setting, they would do exactly that. I also predict that if the default setting were Incognito, a lot of people would not opt out. Clearly Google believes that it is important to manipulate the default so as to permit, but discourage, the use of Incognito. Google may be right; maybe going to Incognito is not in people's interest. The only point is that Google is acting as a choice architect, and its decisions have an impact.

During my painful confirmation process, I was accused of being in favor of stealing human organs. The accusation was (and remains) false (I am pleased to report). But return to a question to which I have briefly alluded: What is an easy way to increase the number of kidneys available for people who need them? The answer is automatic enrollment in a national organ donation program.[5] Nations that "presume consent," in the sense that they require people to opt out of a presumption that they are willing to donate their organs after death, end up with far higher donation rates than nations that ask people to opt in.

In Austria, for example, the organ donation consent rate is over 99 percent, while in Germany the rate is just 12 percent. Is this because of some deep cultural difference between the two nations? Not at all. It is because of the different default rules.

Of course, it is possible to doubt whether presumed consent is a good idea. In view of the sensitivity of the issue, it may be best, at least in some nations, to dispense with any default rule and to require people to make an active choice. What is clear is that if there is a default rule it will matter a lot—and automatic enrollment saves lives. To see the power of default rules in the domain of public health, consider the fact that in sub-Saharan

Africa, many people with tuberculosis are also infected with HIV, and TB is often the first clinical presentation of an HIV infection. An experiment found that when TB patients were tested under voluntary procedures, by which they must explicitly opt in to receive HIV/AIDS testing and counseling, only 7.7 percent did so. Under opt-out guidelines, nearly 21 percent did.[6] In the future, default rules will be an important way of protecting public health and safety.

Many people have been interested in increasing consumers' use of "green energy"—energy sources that do not significantly contribute to air pollution, climate change, and other environmental problems. While such energy sources are available in many places, few people choose them (notwithstanding the fact that in response to questions, many people say they would do so). Nonetheless, two communities in Germany do show strikingly high levels of green energy use—well over 90 percent. This is a dramatic contrast to the level of participation in green energy programs in other German towns, which is around 1 percent. The reason for the difference is that in the two relevant communities, people are automatically enrolled in green energy programs, and they have to opt out.[7]

Opt In, Opt Out in the United States: A Brief Guided Tour

Savings

In the United States, employers have long asked workers whether they want to enroll in 401(k) plans; under a standard approach, the default rule is nonenrollment. Even when enrollment is easy, the number of employees who enroll, or opt in, has been relatively low, certainly in the initial years.[8] A consequence is that a lot of workers end up with insufficient savings for retirement.

Recently a number of employers have changed the default to automatic enrollment. As I noted in chapter 3, the results are clear. Recall that automatic enrollment can be far more effective in encouraging savings than economic incentives in the form of tax subsidies. When employees must opt out of automatic enrollment, many more of them end up enrolled and are thus put in a position to retire with far greater savings.[9] This is so even when opting out is easy. Notably, automatic enrollment benefits all groups, with increased savings for Hispanics, African Americans, and women in particular.[10]

Congress noticed. In 2006 Congress passed, and President Bush signed, the Pension Protection Act,[11] which draws directly on behavioral findings by encouraging employers to adopt automatic enrollment plans. The act provides a number of incentives to make it easy for employers to adopt such plans.[12] Building on those efforts, President Obama directed the Internal Revenue Service and the Treasury Department to undertake new initiatives to promote automatic enrollment.[13] The result? Countless Americans will have more money in retirement, when they are most likely to need it. The reason does not lie in anything fancy, like financial education or messy regulatory interventions. It is the default rule.

Health Insurance

What works for savings plans can work for health insurance too. Consider the "individual mandate" in the Affordable Care Act, which requires people to obtain health insurance (with generous financial assistance for those who need it). To say the least, the mandate generated a heated national debate—a debate that may not have been put to rest when, in 2012, the Supreme Court upheld it by a narrow 5–4 vote. What I want to emphasize here is that some people who hate the individual mandate nonetheless favor automatic enrollment, and that automatic enrollment is helpful even when an individual mandate is in place.

For example, Republican Senator Tom Coburn, a strong conservative, has argued vigorously in favor of automatic enrollment.[14] In the long congressional dispute over health care reform, he contended that automatic enrollment would significantly increase coverage while ultimately leaving people free to opt out. Senator Coburn was right to say that automatic enrollment would produce a big increase in coverage. Some projections suggest that, as compared with requiring people to opt in, automatic enrollment would ensure that millions of additional people would end up with health care, even without a mandate.[15]

In the Obama administration, we devoted a lot of discussion to automatic enrollment, with careful consideration of what the evidence actually shows. One result of that discussion is an important provision of the Afford-able Care Act: Alongside the individual mandate, the act requires automatic enrollment. The basic idea is that with automatic enrollment, the govern-ment can facilitate people's compliance with the individual mandate—and make things a lot easier and simpler for people to boot. More specifically, the act provides that employers with over two hundred employees must automatically enroll them in health care plans, while also allowing employ-ees to opt out.[16]

The requirement demonstrates a general point, which is that automatic enrollment can supplement a mandate, or for that matter a ban. Automatic enrollment makes it easier for people to do what they are required to do. If they do nothing, they are in compliance (and covered).

It might, of course, be asked: Why are people allowed to opt out if they are also facing an individual mandate? The answer is straightforward: There may be good reasons to opt out! For example, a husband might have health insurance through his wife's policy, and so he might want to opt out. Automatic enrollment eases the process for employers and employees alike, but for those who have another policy, it preserves the ability to opt out if they like.

What about health insurance for children? For some states, and some parents, enrollment in health plans is time-consuming and confusing, and because of the power of inertia, many children do not end up in plans for which they are perfectly qualified. In 2010 the Center of Medicare and Medicaid Services took a major step toward addressing this problem.[17] New guidelines permit states to enroll and renew eligible children automatically in Medicaid or the Children's Health Insurance Program. The result is that a lot of kids are insured who otherwise would not be.

School Meals

Since 1946, the federal government has done a great deal to provide free meals, both lunch and breakfast, to schoolchildren. Under the National School Lunch Program, more than 31 million children, in more than 101,000 public and private nonprofit schools, receive low-cost or free lunches. Those at or near the poverty line do not have to pay a penny.

A long-standing problem has been that numerous eligible children are not enrolled in the program. One reason is that enrollment is not easy. Many parents don't know about the program, and even if they do, they don't take the necessary steps to enroll their kids. The National School Lunch Act takes ambitious steps to introduce what should be seen as a form of automatic enrollment.[18] Under the "direct certification" program, children who are eligible for benefits under other programs are "directly eligible" for free lunches, without the bother of filling out additional applications.[19] As a result of direct certification and implementing rules, the number of children who are receiving free meals is in the hundreds of millions.

Payroll Statements and More

As more and more people have access to the Internet, paper notification seems increasingly obsolete, a quaint relic of the past, a lot like vinyl records and rotary phones. For many of us, paper notifications—about, say, wages and health insurance payments—are a distraction and a waste. It might be best to presume that people would prefer to receive information electronically, while allowing those who lack an Internet connection, or who otherwise prefer paper, to opt out. This is precisely what the Department of Homeland Security has done, setting the default for DHS payroll statements to electronic, thus reducing costs while allowing people to stick with paper if that is what they want.[20]

Changes of this kind promise to save a lot of money for both the private and the public sector. In 2012, we took major steps to ensure that investors would receive clear and timely information about their savings plans, including information about fees and potential conflicts of interest.[21] Here is a good, simple nudge. But it's important to keep regulatory costs low, and if this information has to be provided on paper and delivered by mail, the expense is a lot higher. An opt-out system, with an electronic default, would save private companies a great deal of money. And that, in turn, could save you money. Electronic defaults, it needs to be remembered, also ensure that the costs of paper notification will not be passed on to employees and consumers.

Childhood Obesity

The "Let's Move" campaign, First Lady Michelle Obama's signature effort to fight the epidemic of childhood obesity, is encouraging better eating habits and increased physical activity. Real progress is being made. In 2012, obesity rates finally started to go down in major American cities, including New York, Los Angeles, and Philadelphia. But progress is not rapid, because this is an unusually tough problem. One way to move toward solving it is through the functional equivalent of default rules.

Here's how. As I have noted, a lot of empirical work identifies *easy accessibility* as a contributor to the problem of obesity. What is most accessible may not literally be a default rule, but the social environment produces something a lot like defaults for food choices. If healthy foods are easily accessible, people are far more likely to choose them, and the same is true for unhealthy foods. Convenience and accessibility can significantly increase caloric intake.[22] Some studies have found that when fast-food restaurants are located near schools or residences, both children and pregnant women gain a lot of weight.[23] And when unhealthy foods are made even slightly less accessible, their consumption is reduced.[24]

Even small differences, such as the sizes of plates and portions, can have large effects. These small differences operate as nudges and even default rules. How much people eat is a function of how much food is at hand. As the psychologist Brian Wansink has demonstrated in a series of important (and hilarious) studies, a lot of eating is "mindless," in the sense that System 1 is in charge and System 2 is dormant, and people tend to eat whatever is put in front of them.[25] Often we overeat what we do not much like, simply because of the context in which we find ourselves. All this happens rapidly and unconsciously, even automatically.

Wansink calculates that people make more than two hundred food-related decisions every day. Most of those decisions are made quickly and intuitively, by System 1, without any kind of deliberate assessment. A few years ago, moviegoers in Chicago found themselves with a free bucket of popcorn. Unfortunately the popcorn was stale; it had been popped five days earlier and stored so that it would actually squeak when eaten. People weren't told that the popcorn was stale, but they didn't love it. One moviegoer said, "It was like eating Styrofoam packing peanuts."

Wansink designed the experiment so that about half of the moviegoers received a big bucket of stale popcorn and half received a medium-size bucket. After the movie, he asked the recipients of the big bucket whether they might have eaten more because of the size of their bucket. Most denied the possibility, saying, "Things like that don't trick me." They were unaware of what really influenced them. On average, recipients of the big bucket ate about 53 percent more popcorn—even though they didn't really like it.

Another experiment required some special equipment. People sat down to a large bowl of Campbell's tomato soup and were told to eat as much as they wanted. What they did not know was that the soup bowls were designed to refill themselves (with empty bottoms connected to machinery beneath the table). The bowl never emptied, no matter how much people ate. Many people just kept eating until the experiment ended.

The general rule seems to be "Give them a lot, and they eat a lot." Those who receive big bowls of ice cream eat much more than those who get small bowls. If you are given a half-pound bag of M&Ms, chances are that you will eat about half as much as you would had you been given a one-pound bag. The reason is simple: Packages suggest the appropriate amount to eat. In fact most people do not stop eating when they are no longer hungry. They look to whether their glasses or plates are empty. Few of us leave our ice cream bowls half-finished.

Americans are far more likely to be obese than the French; in recent years, the American obesity rate has been between two and three times as high as the French. Why? The reason is not that French diets are free of high-calorie food (far from it). A contributing factor appears to be portion size. In cookbook recipes, supermarkets, and restaurants, portion sizes are a lot smaller in France.[26] In the United States both plates and portions have increased dramatically over time. A really good nudge would be to make them smaller. Consider the graph in Figure 5.1.[27]

Surprisingly simple approaches can get people to eat a lot less. Many restaurants ask consumers if they would like to "supersize" their order. What about asking people if they would like to "downsize"? One study found that when people were prompted to downsize their meals, they ate significantly less at fast-food restaurants.[28] Indeed the effect of this prompt was found to be greater than that of calorie labeling!

The central finding is that many people think that portions are too big.

Figure 5.1. Portion sizes expanding.

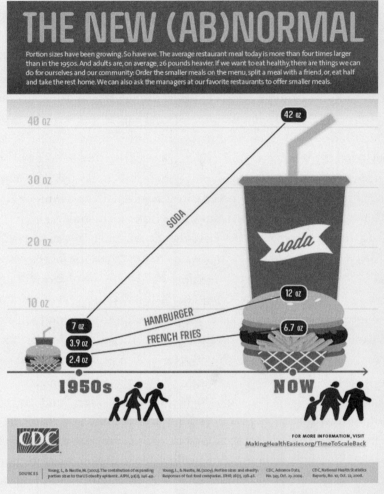

Source: Centers for Disease Control, "The New (Ab)Normal," http://makinghealtheasier.org/
newabnormal.

When asked, "Would you like to cut more than two hundred calories from
your meal by taking a half-portion of your side dish?" they answer yes about
35 percent of the time. Not only did the "downsize" question result in reduced calorie consumption; it also cut the participating restaurants' costs.
Another central finding of the study is that verbal prompts can serve some
of the functions of default rules.

Indeed, companies that are interested in helping people to lose weight are increasingly relying on default rules and nudges.[29] For example, Weight Watchers is attempting to ensure that healthy choices are effectively the default. Members can use the company's app to follow healthy routines, receiving automatic messages emphasizing fruits and vegetables. Weight Watchers is encouraging the use of choice architecture as well, by advising participants to put fatty foods on a higher shelf. In the future, we should expect a lot more private creativity in this vein.

Why Defaults Work

A great deal of research explores exactly why default rules have such a big effect on outcomes.[30] There appear to be three contributing factors.

The first involves inertia and procrastination, which I discussed in chapter 3. To change the default, people must make an active choice to reject it. In view of the power of inertia and the tendency to procrastinate, people may simply continue with the status quo.

The second factor involves what people might see as an implicit endorsement of the default rule. If your employer automatically enrolls you in a savings plan, or if your state automatically presumes that people consent to organ donation, you might think that most people, or most informed people, believe that these are the right courses of action, and you might trust them well enough to follow their lead. Many people think that the default was chosen by someone sensible and for a good reason. They believe that they should not depart from it unless they have information that would justify a change.[31]

The third factor is that the default rule establishes the reference point for decisions. Recall the phenomenon of loss aversion. People dislike losses from a reference point.[32] Suppose you are getting paid $5,000 per month and are asked if you'd like to receive instead $4,800 a month, with $200 going into your savings account. You might not be happy about that. But what if $4,800 is your reference point? Suppose that that is yours, along with $200 per month going into savings. Asked if you want less money going into your savings account, you might not be happy about that. Where you start sets your reference point.

There are many areas in which the reference point and hence loss aversion matter. Suppose the default rule favors energy-efficient lightbulbs. You are then asked whether you want less efficient bulbs instead. The loss, in terms of efficiency (and eventually money), may loom large, and you will continue to purchase energy-efficient lightbulbs. But if the default rule favors less efficient lightbulbs with lower up-front costs, you might well favor less efficient lightbulbs, because you like those lower up-front costs enough to stick with the default.[33]

Which Default Rule?

Private and public institutions can achieve important goals, and do so while maintaining freedom of choice and at low cost, by selecting good default rules and avoiding harmful ones. But which default rule should we select? How do we know which is helpful and which is harmful?

A reasonable approach is to *select the default rule that reflects what most people would choose if they were adequately informed.*[34] If we know that a particular default rule would place people in the situation that informed people would select anyway, we have good reason to adopt it (with the understanding that those who differ from the majority may opt out). Suppose that we know that 80 percent of people, given a lot of information, would choose to enroll in a savings plan. That's a pretty good reason to favor automatic enrollment.

Of course, it is possible that this approach is too crude. Suppose that of two default rules, A and B, 55 percent of informed people slightly prefer A. Suppose too that 45 percent of people strongly prefer B; maybe their circumstances make B hugely better, whereas for the 55 percent, the choice is a matter of relative indifference. We should probably select B. The example shows that it is important to ask not only which approach would be preferred by informed people, but also about the intensity of their informed preferences.

The most natural way to think of the choice is in terms of costs and benefits. If a default rule turned out to stick, what would be the costs and what would be the benefits? In the example just given, default rule B would almost certainly be better. We could also imagine cases in which the choice between default rules is hard, and in such cases active choosing might be better (more on this below).

Risks: Self-Interest, Mischief, and More

It may have occurred to you that default rules can be badly chosen or mis-used, and that some can be extremely harmful. Imagine, for example, a voting system in which your vote is automatically registered as favoring the incumbent—but you can opt out if you like. Or imagine a nation that defaults you into a certain religion—but that allows you to opt out. Or a rental car company that defaults you into all sorts of costly insurance poli-cies and expensive payment plans, while allowing you to opt out.

Fortunately, market forces constrain some of the most harmful default rules. Before long, customers are not likely to go to companies that impose a series of terrible defaults. For this reason, many default rules are good ones; consider the default settings for your computer and your cell phone, which are probably pretty helpful. In some cases, however, companies have an incentive to exploit System 1, especially when the relevant attributes of the product are shrouded and not salient.

As a potentially fiendish example, consider the practice of "negative op-tion marketing." This practice occurs when people who accept a "free" prod-uct are automatically enrolled in a plan or program that carries a monthly fee (unless they explicitly opt out).[35] You might, for example, get a free hotel room, but as a result, you are enrolled in a program that charges you $15 per month. The monthly charge might be mentioned quietly and obscurely, if at all, and if it is mentioned, people might be given (quietly) the option to opt out.

I am hardly immune to negative option marketing; few of us are. When my credit card company graciously offered to provide me with a free three-month subscription to several magazines of my choice, I happily accepted the offer. Decades later I found myself subscribing to those same magazines, even though I had no interest in them and even though I was subscribing at full price. It was not until I faced the prospect of government employ-ment, and the resulting salary cut, that I took the trouble to cancel my subscriptions.

Negative option marketing has an unfortunate effect, which is that it exploits the tendency toward inertia in a way that can cost people a lot of money. You might not see the monthly bill, or if you see it you might assume that all is well, and you might not cancel the plan until you have (automatically) paid a great deal. Unsurprisingly, the Federal Trade Commission has expressed serious concerns about negative option marketing.[36]

It is easy to imagine both private and public analogues. Consider, for example, an automatic enrollment policy that puts an unreasonably large amount of your salary into savings, or that defaults you into a health insurance plan that is a bad deal for your circumstances, or that signs you up for an exercise plan that you don't need and maybe hate. Automatic enrollment can be a waste or even a disaster. The risks are real and important, but they do not argue against default rules in general. We cannot do without them. The question is which ones are best. (True, there is a qualification— involving active choosing—which, again, I promise to discuss shortly.)

In evaluating the use of automatic enrollment, the particular circumstances certainly matter. If automatic enrollment is not made clear and transparent to those who are enrolled, it can be considered a form of manipulation. The problem is worse if it is not in people's long-term interest.

Making It Personal: The Wave of the Future?

Most default rules apply to everyone within the relevant population. If you work for the Sensible Sneaker Company, its default rules (say, for health insurance and retirement plans) may well apply to everyone who works there. If you are a public employee in Australia, the default rules of the government of Australia might well apply to all employees. Other default rules are *personalized*. In principle, there can be default rules especially designed for each of us: for Joe Smith, Mary Jones, Lady Gaga, Kobe Bryant, Sarah Palin, Barack Obama, Brad Pitt, you, and everyone else. In the fullness of time, we are likely to be headed in the direction of personalized default rules. And in principle, the design of such personalized rules would be a great boon.

A personalized default might be based on your own past choices or those of people like you. For example, Amazon.com provides recommendations to its customers on the basis of past choices; it knows that if you like science fiction by David Ambrose (and you really should), you'll probably like science fiction by Neil Gaiman as well. In a loose sense, Amazon.com creates personalized default rules in the form of visible, salient choices.

Similar approaches might be used to design default rules in many areas. Once enough information is available about Joe Smith, we could design for Joe Smith default rules with respect to health insurance, privacy, rental card agreements, computer settings, and everything else. Personalized default rules can also be dynamic, in the sense that they can change over time. The best default rules for Joe this year might be very different from the best rules for Joe next year. In principle, the default rules could change on a moment-by-moment basis. As private and public institutions receive increasing amounts of information about each of us, this prospect is becoming less like science fiction and increasingly the stuff of daily life. Many websites (again consider Amazon) are already moving in this direction, providing defaults or at least suggestions for you based on your own past choices.

True, this possibility raises serious questions about privacy. You might be pretty embarrassed to find that you are being defaulted to certain choices with respect to books (stories about time travel?), magazines (focused on the private lives of movie stars?), and music (actually Taylor Swift is pretty good!), and you might not want anyone to know about those defaults. Note, however, that privacy issues might themselves be handled by personalized default rules. If you tend to prize privacy, and if your past choices reflect that preference, your personalized default rules will be chosen to promote privacy. With personalization, you'll be defaulted into what you've chosen before, and that can be true for privacy as for everything else.

Less ambitiously, personalized default rules might be based on group characteristics, such as geographic or demographic variables. For example, age and income might be used in determining appropriate default rules for retirement plans. When I rejoined the Harvard faculty, the university defaulted me into such a plan, a Vanguard Target Retirement Fund. (The default stuck. I hope it's good.) If you are sixty, your default allocation should be different from what it would be if you are thirty, and if you are making a lot of money, your default might be different from what it would be if you are making a little. The general idea is that your default rules would track what would be best for "people like you."

Evidence suggests that for retirement plans, default rules that respect diversity (especially with respect to age) are possible, and that they can increase the probability of enrollment in the default plan by 60 percent! They can also create very large gains for participants.[37] We could easily imagine similar approaches to health insurance, privacy, credit cards, cell phone plans, and much more.

The key advantage of personalized default rules is that they are likely to be more accurate and fine-grained than "mass" default rules. As technology evolves and information accumulates, it should be increasingly possible to produce personalized defaults (privacy included) on the basis of people's own choices and situations. Of course the rise of personalization will create risks, but there will also be promising opportunities to use default rules to promote people's welfare.

What's in a Name? Nonsticky Default Rules

We have seen that default rules are sticky, but let's not overstate the point. If you have a really strong preference, and if you hate the default, you'll probably opt out, even if doing so is a big bother. It follows that default rules will not stick when those who are subject to them think they are a bad idea.

Return to the question of changing names upon getting married.[38] All states in the United States have the same default rule: Both men and women retain their premarital names when they get married. Note that we could easily imagine a large number of default rules:

- The husband's name stays the same, but the wife's name changes to that of her husband. Indeed, that approach, however discriminatory, would mimic people's behavior, at least in the United States.
- The husband's name changes to that of his wife, and the wife's name stays the same.
- The spouses' names are hyphenated.
- Unless you opt out, your marital name is Smith (or Dylan, or Kennedy, or Pie, or Simpler, or Australia; you get the idea).

So there is nothing inevitable about the current default rule. What are its effects? In the overwhelming majority of cases, men stick with the default. A very small percentage of men change their names. By contrast, the overwhelming majority of women do so (probably more than 80 percent). In that respect, the default rule does not seem to have a large effect on women (though admittedly, the percentage of women with their husband's names would probably be even higher if that were the default).

Why doesn't the default rule stick for women? Three factors seem to be important. First, many women (often affected by social norms and perhaps pressures) affirmatively want to change their names, all things considered, and their desire is not unclear.[39] This is not a complex or unfamiliar area in which people are unsure about their preferences, or in which their preferences are, in a sense, constructed by the default rule. Second, the issue is salient to them, and because marriage is a defining event, the timing of the required action is relatively clear. Procrastination and inertia are therefore less important. Third, for some or many of those who do it, changing their name is a kind of celebration. It is not the sort of activity that people seek to defer. When the relevant conditions are met—clear preferences, clear timing, and positive feelings about opting in—the default rule is unlikely to matter much.

Indeed, clear preferences are likely to be sufficient. Suppose that you are automatically enrolled in a plan that puts 80 percent of your income into savings, or 60 percent of your income into your nation's treasury (after taxes!), or 40 percent of your income into your worst enemy's savings account, or 40 percent of your income into the toilet. You'll probably opt out. A study in the United Kingdom found that most people opted out of a savings plan, admittedly less awful than those just described, but with an unusually high default contribution rate (12 percent of before-tax income).[40] Only about 25 percent of employees remained at that rate after a year, whereas about 60 percent of employees remained at a lower default contribution rate.

A clear implication is that "extreme" defaults are less likely to stick. A more puzzling implication, based on the lower incomes of those who stayed with the default in the study just described, is that default rules may be stickier for low-income workers than for their higher-earning counterparts. One reason may be that low-income workers have a lot to worry about,[41] and so are less likely to take the trouble to think through and alter the default rule. Another may be that low-income workers have less confidence in their own judgments, and so they allow the default allocation to stick.

There are other situations in which the default rule does not have a big impact. Workers are not much affected if a significant fraction of their tax refund is defaulted into US savings bonds. In significant numbers they opt out, apparently because they have definite plans to spend their refund, and little interest in putting it into savings.[42] The general lesson is that default rules will have a weaker effect, and potentially no effect, when people have a strong preference for a certain outcome.

This finding is both bad news and good news. The bad news is that choice architects may not be able to use default rules to achieve their goals. The good news is that the ability to opt out is an important safeguard against stupid or malicious defaults. In some situations, however, defaults may not stick even though they *are* important safeguards.

Consider the Federal Reserve Board's 2010 effort to protect people from bank overdraft fees. The Board's regulation forbids banks to charge a fee for overdrafts from checking accounts unless the account holder has explicitly enrolled in the bank's overdraft program.[43] One of the goals is to protect customers, and especially low-income customers, from ending up taking the equivalent of punitively high-interest loans—indeed, interest of up to 7,000 percent. In principle, the regulation should have had a big effect, and an understanding of the power of default rules helped to motivate it. But the available evidence suggests that the effect may well be modest, because people are rejecting the default in large numbers.

Why? As the law professor Lauren Willis has shown in an important article,[44] a big reason is that banks greatly dislike the regulation, want to be able to charge overdraft fees, and have used a number of tools to facilitate opt-in. Appreciating the power of simplification, they have taken steps to make opt-out as easy as possible—for example, just by pushing a button on an ATM. They have also engaged in active marketing and created economic incentives to get people to opt out. Showing an impressive understanding of behavioral economics, they are exploiting loss aversion and consumer confusion to encourage account holders to think that they will lose money if they do not opt in. Consider the following excerpt from one bank's marketing materials:

YES: KEEP MY ACCOUNT WORKING THE SAME WITH SHARE-PLUS ATM AND DEBIT CARD OVERDRAFT COVERAGE.
NO: CHANGE MY ACCOUNT TO REMOVE SHAREPLUS ATM AND DEBIT CARD OVERDRAFT COVERAGE.

As Willis quotes a bank employee, "People are scared of change so they'll opt-in [to overdraft] to avoid change." The general lesson is that if regulated institutions are strongly opposed to a default rule and have easy access to their customers, they may well be able to use a variety of strategies, including behavioral ones, to encourage people to move in the direction the institutions prefer. They can enlist simplification, loss aversion, and other ideas to achieve their goals. If public officials want to make the default rule sticky, they may have to take further steps to discourage opt-out.

Active Choices

I have suggested that default rules are inevitable, but I have also noted an important qualification. Choice architects may instead avoid any default rule and *require active choices*. Those who really distrust choice architects, including public officials (or, for that matter, private corporations), and who want to avoid being influenced by them, will have a lot of interest in active choices. They will want to avoid default rules of any kind and put the questions directly to individuals.

Under this approach, people are required to make an actual choice among various options; they are not defaulted into any particular alternative. With respect to health care, privacy, and savings, for example, regulators and corporations could reject both opt-out and opt-in and simply require people to indicate their preferences. To be sure, the word "require" is ambiguous. What is the sanction if people fail or refuse to choose? One possibility would for employers, public or private, to say that employees could not start work unless they choose their health insurance or savings plan. Another possibility would for the government to say that in order to get certain licenses or benefits—perhaps a driver's license—people have to indicate their preferences about (for example) organ donation.

Consider three points in favor of active choosing:

1. *Active choosing overcomes inertia.* A key virtue of active choosing is that it increases the likelihood that people will end up with their preferred outcomes. Think again about savings plans, health insurance, and privacy settings. The problem with opt-in is that it may

mean that some people will end up with outcomes that they would not prefer if they were asked to make a choice. You might be a lot better off if you are asked, "Which health insurance plan do you like best?" than if you are automatically enrolled in a plan chosen by your employer.

2. *Active choosing is a safeguard against uninformed, confused, or evil choice architects.* Suppose that a private institution is producing the default rule, and it really doesn't know a lot about what informed people would choose. If so, active choosing might be a lot better. Or suppose that the government is producing the default rule. If public officials are biased or inadequately informed, and if the default rule is no better than a guess, that rule might lead people in the wrong direction. Or perhaps those setting out a default rule are highly informed, but are calling for it precisely because it will help some preferred interest group and will *not* benefit those on whom it will be imposed. If you don't trust public officials, private institutions, or influential interest groups, you might like active choosing best.

3. *Active choosing handles diversity.* As compared with either opt-in or opt-out, active choosing can have major advantages when a single approach is unlikely to fit diverse circumstances. If one size does not fit all for health insurance or savings, then we might want to ensure that people make choices on their own. (Recall, however, that personalized defaults, fitting individual circumstances, can help to overcome this problem.)

On the other hand, active choosing can have significant disadvantages:

1. *Active choosing imposes burdens on choosers.* Suppose the situation is unfamiliar and complicated. Suppose that people lack information or experience. If so, active choosing may be unhelpful, and it may impose unjustified, unwelcome, or excessive burdens. You probably would not like it if, at the time of purchase, you had to choose every default feature of your cell phone or your computer. You might not want to spend the time required to obtain the necessary informa-

tion and decide what choice to make. The existence of default settings saves you a lot of time, and most of those settings are probably fine. In fact life is full of a lot of default settings, and if you had to choose each of them on your own, you would quickly run out of time. (I will have a lot more to say about this point when discussing the nanny state in chapter 9.)

2. *Active choosing imposes burdens on providers.* Default rules can be good, even great, for those who provide products or services, including government. The reason is that such rules avoid costs, and possibly high costs, which might result in increased prices. Without a series of default rules, private and public providers might have to devote a lot of time and resources to providing patient, tedious explanations spelling out all the various options and the relevant pros and cons to consumers or users. As providers know, those consumers and users may well have far better things to do.

3. *Active choosing can increase errors.* A central goal of active choosing is to make people better off. But if the area is unfamiliar and confusing, active choosing might have the opposite effect. If you have to answer a set of technical questions, and if the choice architects really know what they are doing, then people will probably do better with defaults.

With these points, we can identify the circumstances in which active choosing does or does not make sense.[45] When the group is diverse, when choice architects are unsure which approach is best, when choosers prefer to choose, and when the topic is not unduly technical or complex, active choosing is a good idea. But when a particular default rule fits well with the informed preferences of the relevant group, when the area is highly technical, and when choosing would be an unwelcome burden, a default rule should probably be preferred over active choosing. Personalized default rules, reducing the errors associated with one-size-fits-all approaches, can provide some of the advantages of active choosing without the costs. For this reason, personalized default rules are clearly going to play a big role in the future.[46]

Just Simplification

I have emphasized that complexity can have serious unintended effects, including indifference, delay, and confusion. These bad effects can, in turn, undermine important social goals by reducing compliance or by making it less likely that people will benefit from various policies and programs. There is a close relationship between this point and the idea of Plate, not Pyramid. Unfortunately, we can find pyramids everywhere. With respect to forms in particular, undue complexity can severely discourage applications, thus undermining public programs. Simplification can have surprisingly large benefits.

As a prime example, consider the Free Application for Federal Student Aid (FAFSA), which is filled out every year by about 14 million households seeking federal aid for college. FAFSA has long contained well over 100 questions. The length and complexity of the application have discouraged a lot of people from completing it. This is a big problem. By reducing the likelihood that people will get the help they need to go to college, complex forms can seriously harm their prospects, and in the very period when the economy most needs more educated job applicants. In 2005, a congressionally authorized committee called the Advisory Committee on Student Financial Assistance nicely sketched the problem: "Millions of students and adult learners who aspire to college are overwhelmed by the complexity of student aid. Uncertainty and confusion robs them of its significant benefits. Rather than promote access, student aid often creates a series of barriers— a gauntlet that the poorest students must run to get to college."[47] Careful studies show that the complexity of the form has reduced access to college and that, all by itself, simplification can make it more likely that people will submit the application, get financial help, and enroll.[48]

In recent years the Department of Education has taken these findings and concerns extremely seriously. In my time in government, reforming the FAFSA form was a high priority for the Obama administration, including the Department of Education and OIRA. Because OIRA oversees the Paperwork Reduction Act, it is in an excellent position to help eliminate redundancy and excessive complexity. The Department made major changes to the FAFSA form, removing unnecessary questions and reducing the number of questions through "skip logic" (a survey method that skips over some questions on the basis of answers given to earlier questions). Especially important, it is allowing key information to be retrieved electronically.[49] A new initiative, described as a "major administrative breakthrough," allows online users automatically to transfer tax data, held by the IRS, directly into their FAFSA applications.[50] To be sure, problems remain, and additional simplification can and should be achieved.[51] But the recent initiatives are enabling many additional students to receive aid to which they are entitled.

Similar progress might be made in a lot of other domains. Consider, again, the simple switch from paper to electronic reporting systems. In 2010 the Treasury Department undertook a major initiative to do exactly that. The department finalized a rule to provide electronic payments to essentially everyone who is receiving Social Security, Supplemental Security Income, Veterans, Railroad Retirement, and Office of Personnel Management benefits.[52] These steps are saving over $400 million in the first five years—and increasing accuracy and convenience in the process.[53]

These steps are in line with a directive I issued in 2010, asking all government agencies for new initiatives that would substitute electronic for paper signatures, increase administrative simplification, allow for "fillable fileable forms," and reduce burdens on small businesses.[54] Strongly supported by others in the Obama administration, my directive produced no fewer than seventy-two initiatives from various agencies, all designed to reduce burdens and increase simplification.[55] In total, those initiatives are expected to eliminate millions of hours of paperwork and reporting burdens each year.

In 2011 I followed the 2010 directive with a new one, also emphasizing simplification and focusing on small businesses and benefit programs.[56] The request drew particular attention to the potential harms of complexity, specifically noting that "the process of renewing or applying for benefits can be time-consuming, confusing, and unnecessarily complex, thus discouraging participation and undermining program goals. Sometimes agencies collect data that are unchanged from prior applications; in such circumstances, they might be able to use, or to give people the option to use, pre-populated electronic forms."[57]

The multiple benefits of increased simplicity are evident in an important initiative from the Department of Treasury involving Social Security and Supplemental Security Income: the "Direct Express" card program.[58] As a result of the program, many people are now automatically receiving their money via a prepaid debit card. This initiative increases, at the same time, both convenience and accuracy, thus reducing paperwork and costs. It provides particular help for those who lack bank accounts, and indeed 95 percent of users say that they are satisfied with it, an extremely high number for a government program.[59] (It is worth visiting godirect.org, part of the Go Direct educational campaign, which is also part of the Department's transition to all-electronic payments. In the spirit of the "Plate, Not Pyramid" principle, the site reflects the Department of Treasury's efforts to keep everything simple.)

Here too there is real promise for the future. Other programs might build on this approach, specifically helping those without bank accounts, by giving them such accounts or the functional equivalent.[60]

Structuring Choices

In the traditional view, more choices are always better than fewer. If you now have five options, you would probably like to have ten, and if you have ten options, you'd probably like to have twenty, and if you have twenty, you would probably be better off with fifty. On this view, having more choices helps and never harms people. If another option is no better than the existing ones, people can simply decline to choose it. From the standpoint of System 2, more choices really are better. And while System 1 may not know exactly how to choose among a large menu of options, it may not much object to a lot of choices with respect to ice cream, cell phones, CDs, tablets, and shoes.

In general, more choices are indeed desirable. Markets respond to what people want, and for countless goods, markets are producing a dizzying array of options, fitting the diversity of human tastes and preferences. But an increasing body of research offers some important qualifications, especially in unusually complex situations.[61] The underlying concern is straightforward: *choice overload*. As choices proliferate, the burdens of choosing increase, and as the number of options mounts, the situation gets harder to handle. Even for System 2.

If you are looking for a small refrigerator, and you have 250 apparently reasonable options, you might have no idea how to choose. You might hate the idea of studying hundreds of refrigerators to discover which is best. You might wish that the market, or someone, would narrow your list to (say) fifteen. And under less than ideal circumstances, the proliferations of options may lead to bad outcomes. Maybe people will get frustrated and not choose at all. System 1 might think, "This isn't a lot of fun; I'll do something else." Maybe people will get confused and make less than optimal (or even awful) choices.

It is true and important that the market itself can provide assistance. If there is a demand for them, advisers of various kinds should turn up, helping to inform and structure people's choices. And companies can compete along the dimension of complexity. If people are frustrated by multiple options, "keep it simple" companies may arise instead. Nonetheless, the problem of choice overload is real, and it can have unfortunate effects on government programs.

The concern is not hypothetical. For example, there is evidence that as the menu of investment options in a 401(k) plan expands, enrollment may decline[62] and asset allocations may worsen.[63] The reasons are not mysterious. If you have a ton of options, you might get baffled, and you might not enroll at all. And if you have a large menu of options, you might not be careful or sufficiently informed, and your choice might not be the best one.

Consider an important and much-studied example. Under Medicare Part D, seniors are given access to prescription drug plans that promise to save them a lot of money. But from how many plans should seniors be asked to choose? Ten? Twenty-five? Fifty? A hundred? At first glance the right answer seems clear: the more, the better. But Nobel Prize winner Daniel McFadden and his colleagues have shown that if seniors are given a lot of choices and little guidance, they may make big mistakes and waste a lot of money.[64] In fact we now have a lot of evidence that as a result of the so-called Medicare Part D maze, people are making many bad choices.

What can be done? Responding to the problem, the Department of Health and Human Services, working with OIRA and others in the Obama administration, took two significant steps designed to maintain freedom of choice while also reducing unhelpful and unnecessary complexity.[65] First, the rules now say that if plan sponsors provide several offerings, they must ensure that those offerings have meaningful differences. This step is designed to reduce redundancy and confusion. Second, the new rules eliminate plans with persistently low enrollments. The theory here involves the "wisdom of crowds." By definition, those plans have failed the test of the market. They increase the complexity of choices without adding value.[66] By eliminating such plans, the new rules increase simplification while nonetheless allowing a large number of plans.

The broadest point is that both private and public institutions often fail because they make things difficult. Sometimes they make things difficult because they do not select simple, sensible default rules. Sometimes they create inadvertent problems because they list, and do not structure, a wide range of options. Often the best approach is to make things automatic, so that if people do nothing at all, they'll be just fine.

6

INVISIBLE GORILLAS AND HUMAN HERDS

Imagine that you are without a GPS and trying desperately to find a tucked-away restaurant in a rural area of Vermont. As it is, you are fifteen minutes late for your reservation. You stop and ask for directions. The gas station attendant nods knowledgeably and assures you, "Don't worry. You can't miss it." He then describes the unmarked road you must turn left on, just a couple of miles farther on. And then he adds, "Just turn left after the tall pine tree." That's a bit of a problem, maybe a disaster. There are a lot of pine trees in the area, and many of them are tall. So let's change the story a bit. Imagine instead that he says, "Just turn left after the big billboard with the naked basketball player on it." Odds are that you will head off with a little more confidence that you'll arrive soon.

Every minute of every day, an extraordinary amount of information comes before us. We are influenced by what we notice. There is a lot that we do not notice, so there is a lot that does not influence us. For businesses, individuals, and government, a simple step toward promoting important goals is to make certain features of a product or a situation more *salient* to people.

Here is an example.[1] Experimenters have tested what people notice by asking them to watch a ninety-second movie in which six ordinary people pass a basketball to one another on a basketball court. The task? To count the number of passes.

After the movie is shown, the experimenter asks people how many passes they were able to count. Then the experimenter asks, "And did you see the gorilla?" Most people laugh at the question. *What gorilla?* Then the movie is replayed. If you aren't counting passes, you see a gorilla enter the scene, plain as day. The gorilla isn't at all hard to see. In fact you can't miss him. He even pounds his chest briefly before leaving the scene. But when counting passes, most people don't see him. Even though you now know the trick, it's worth Googling *The Invisible Gorilla* to find a link to the video; you might spring it on an unwary friend and see what happens. Figure 6.1 is a screenshot, showing the gorilla clearly.

Figure 6.1. The invisible gorilla.

Source: Daniel J. Simons and Christopher F. Chabris, "Gorillas in Our Midst: Sustained Inattentional Blindness for Dynamic Events." *Perception* 28 (1999): 1059, 1070 fig. 3.

Why do most people miss the gorilla? (I confess that I did the first time I watched the video.) The answer is that viewers are watching players passing the basketball, and they are counting passes, which is pretty hard work for System 2. They are not monitoring the screen to see who, or what, enters and pounds his chest. The gorilla is not salient for those who are counting passes, and so it fades into the background and is therefore invisible.

The lesson for businesses, individuals, and government is that we are all at risk of missing a lot that is happening in the background (and possibly even the foreground) of our lives. What's more, some of what we're not seeing is really important. We might miss it even if our life depends on our seeing it. The psychologist Daniel Kahneman puts it nicely: "The gorilla study illustrates two important facts about our minds: we can be blind to the obvious, and we are also blind to our blindness."[2] Magicians are, of course, acutely aware of this point, and they exploit both our blindness and our blindness to our blindness. The famous illusionist David Copperfield writes, "If I can gather your attention and fix it on something specific, there's a good chance that you won't notice things that are happening right in front of you."[3]

In free markets, many sellers try to act like magicians. They focus your attention on "something specific" and try to ensure that you won't notice things that are in some sense right in front of you. If a credit card issuer wants you to overlook a 29 percent APR, its advertisements will go to great lengths to focus your attention on something else, perhaps a free introductory offer. Those who offer mortgages and cell phone agreements use similar strategies. One goal of the Dodd-Frank financial reform law, and in particular of the Consumer Financial Protection Bureau that it creates, is to make sure that consumers don't ignore invisible gorillas. In designing the law and the bureau, we were acutely alert to the risk that when companies provide information, they might do so in a way that is too complex and confusing for consumers to understand.

A general challenge, for the private sector as well as government, is to make what is really important visible. Public-spirited and otherwise sensible efforts to provide information or to create certain incentives may not be enough. They may fail simply because they lack salience. Like the gorilla, they fade into the background. If a car's fuel economy label is not salient, it won't matter much even if it is perfectly accurate. Insurance companies may provide a lot of information about benefits and coverage, but if people do not pay attention to that information when picking one plan over another, it will not be helpful.

Informed by a sense of human psychology and the importance of simplicity, the government needs to take special steps to help people see invisible gorillas.

"Smoking Can Kill You"

Smoking is the leading killer in the United States. It causes over 430,000 deaths per year. The Centers for Disease Control find annual smoking-related medical costs of $96 billion, alongside $97 billion in lost productivity.[4] Notwithstanding the risks, over 46 million Americans smoke. We know that increasing the price of cigarettes can have a big effect in reducing those costs. In 2009, the federal cigarette tax was increased dramatically, from 39 cents to $1.01. There is every reason to think that this tax increase is helping to cut smoking and hence saving lives and costs, and that a bigger increase would have a bigger effect. Incentives really matter, and the best way to reduce consumption of something is usually to increase its price. But disclosure of health-related information can matter too, at least if that information is salient.

The United States has long had warnings on cigarette packs, stating simply that smoking "can be hazardous to your health." This is a pretty mild warning. For most people, including most smokers, it is an invisible gorilla. It is just part of the background. There is an important lesson here, which is that when something is familiar, it starts to become invisible. When you go to a new city, you tend to notice everything: colors, buildings, people, landscapes. System 1 is on the alert and soaking in the details. The sense of acute vividness that people get when visiting new places comes from the fact that a lot is unfamiliar and thus stands out from the background. When you return home, not so much stands out (even if home is pretty amazing).

It was in part to make the gorilla visible, so to speak, that the Smoking Prevention Act was enacted in 2009. The act responds to the importance of salience in requiring new and more graphic warnings. Under the law, cigarettes must have one of the following labels:

WARNING: Cigarettes are addictive.
WARNING: Tobacco smoke can harm your children.
WARNING: Cigarettes cause fatal lung disease.
WARNING: Cigarettes cause cancer.
WARNING: Cigarettes cause strokes and heart disease.
WARNING: Smoking during pregnancy can harm your baby.
WARNING: Smoking can kill you.

>   **WARNING:** Tobacco smoke causes fatal lung disease in nonsmokers.
>   **WARNING:** Quitting smoking now greatly reduces serious risks to
>   your health.

The law also directs the Food and Drug Administration to issue regulations requiring packages to contain color graphics describing the health consequences of smoking, thus grabbing the attention of System 1.

After a long period of deliberation, including assessment of practices in other nations and a lot of public input, the FDA, working closely with OIRA and many other parts of the federal government, selected nine images. They are vivid, even disturbing, and for that reason likely to be highly salient. See Figure 6.2.

In addition, the FDA required the phone number 1-800-QUIT-NOW to appear as part of the graphic health warnings. The FDA's goal was not only to get people's attention but also to make current smokers aware of this resource and thus increase the likelihood that smokers who want to quit will be successful. Here the required phone number functions like a map. I have emphasized that if we want to encourage desirable behavior, it can be exceedingly helpful to provide people with a clear path that they can easily follow.

A crucial question, of course, is the likely effect of such warnings. Inevitably we are reduced to a degree of guesswork. This is not the fault of Congress or the FDA; it is in the nature of the problem. We don't have randomized controlled experiments, and so we don't (yet) have a precise sense of the effect of graphic warnings on smoking in the United States. Of course, government must often proceed in the face of considerable uncertainty with respect to both benefits and costs. (I will have a great deal more to say on this point in chapter 7.)

With close reference to the experience in Canada, which imposed graphic warnings of its own, the FDA projected that the new warnings would reduce the number of smokers by 213,000 in 2013, with smaller but still significant reductions through 2031. In addition, the FDA estimated that the warnings would deter between 16,544 and 19,687 people from starting to smoke, and in the process prevent numerous deaths and illnesses. The FDA acknowledged the uncertainties but unambiguously concluded, on the basis of evidence, that graphic warnings were likely to have significant health benefits.

Figure 6.2. Graphic cigarette warning labels.

Source: Overview: Cigarette Health Warnings, US Food and Drug Admininistration, http://
www.fda.gov/TobaccoProducts/Labeling/Labeling/CigaretteWarningLabels/ucm259214.htm.

The graphic warnings are a distinctive kind of nudge. However graphic,
the warnings maintain freedom of choice; they do not prevent anyone from
buying a pack of cigarettes. They directly target System 1, trying to make
the health consequences of smoking salient and to enlist the affect heuristic
in the direction of reduced smoking. For many decades, cigarette companies went to great lengths to connect smoking with fun, youth, energy,
relaxation, coolness, hotness, and sex. The health consequences of living in

Marlboro Country were anything but salient. With the graphic warnings, the FDA sought to meet fire with fire, associating smoking with illness, distress, pain, and death. It sought to do this not just with a behaviorally informed public education campaign (though it is doing that as well, and the campaign is plenty graphic, even gruesome[5]), but also by requiring cigarette packages to display warnings to consumers.

Is there a problem with this particular kind of nudge? Some people think so. They insist on a distinction between government efforts to require sellers to provide truthful information ("just the facts") about their products, which are viewed as perfectly legitimate, and government efforts to require sellers to produce visceral negative reactions to their products, which are objectionable. On this view, there is nothing wrong with the Food Plate and the current fuel economy label. It is also fine to require disclosure of the fees that investors must pay and of the basic requirements and features of health insurance plans. But it is not fine to direct sellers to produce strong, hostile emotional reactions to their own products. One way to understand this objection is to say that while government can compel speech so as to educate System 2, it cannot compel speech so as to alarm System 1.

A federal judge made this distinction in invalidating the FDA regulation that required the graphic health warnings.[6] In his view, government has no business requiring the producers of a product to include warnings that are meant not to inform but to frighten and disgust.

This distinction is certainly intelligible. Even if we agree with it, we can accept some government efforts to promote salience, so long as what is salient is purely factual rather than emotional. But should the distinction matter? Is System 1 off-limits? In the private sector, of course, efforts to produce strong visceral reactions are standard; advertisers do this all the time. Automobile companies, the cell phone industry, soft drink companies, cigarette companies—indeed, it is hard to think of a line of products for which someone *isn't* trying to do exactly that. And there is general agreement that it is fine for government to produce strong emotions through its own pronouncements. Campaigns that are designed to reduce drunk driving, drug use, and texting while driving commonly appeal to people's feelings. The only disputed question is whether government can require producers of a product not merely to disclose facts but also to include warnings that trigger emotional reactions.

It is certainly possible to interpret the First Amendment to mean that this is not the legitimate role of government. On this view, requiring companies to produce revulsion about their own products is an unacceptable intrusion on their freedom. But why should we accept this view? Cigarettes pose serious health risks, and they are addictive. The resulting costs to individuals and to society are very high. To be sure, the government does not seek to ban cigarettes. But for products that pose such risks, and that cost a lot of lives, there does not seem to be anything objectionable about nudges in the form of emotionally evocative warnings.

As of this writing, the legal status of the graphic health warnings remains unsettled. One court of appeals has upheld them; another has struck them down, largely because of its judgment that the FDA produced insufficient evidence that the warnings would work.[7] We should pause, just briefly, to wonder how the First Amendment to the Constitution, originally designed to promote democratic self-government, has been transformed into a weapon against reasonable efforts, by the elected representatives of the people, to regulate the marketing of a product that causes over 430,000 deaths each year. But that is a tale for another day. Whatever the legal fate of the graphic health warnings on cigarette packages, they suggest the possibility of triggering public attention by making certain gorillas far more visible.

Increased Salience as a Nudge

Salience is especially important in the context of health risks of many kinds. Recent efforts to respond to the problem of childhood obesity are designed to make that problem more salient and to draw people's attention to numerous small choices that, in the aggregate, contribute to the problem of obesity. Consider, as one example, the simple suggestion that pediatricians calculate the body mass index (BMI) of young children and inform parents of the results. This suggestion is an effort to increase the salience of important health-related information. It responds to the fact that attention is a scarce commodity, and if attention is triggered, people's behavior is likely to be affected.

Here is a good way to lose weight: Weigh yourself every morning. Here's a good way not to lose weight: Get rid of your scale. Whether you like them or not, the efforts of New York City's Mayor Michael Bloomberg to regulate the size of soft drink containers is partly an effort to increase salience by drawing people's attention to the seriousness of the obesity epidemic.

Research suggests that efforts to make the costs of energy use more salient can alter decisions and significantly reduce those costs.[8] For example, people can be informed of how much energy they use, how their use compares with that of their neighbors, and how much they spend compared with what their neighbors spend. Opower, a company that makes impressive use of behavioral economics, specializes in providing people with social comparisons of this kind, above all through its innovative Home Energy Report. An example is in Figure 6.3.

Opower's nudges have had a major effect.[9] Over four million households now receive Home Energy Reports, and they are saving people hundreds of millions of dollars as a result. (See opower.com for details.) These and related interventions can save consumers a lot of money and also reduce pollution.[10] Consider, for example, the fact that energy costs are generally salient only once a month, when people are presented with the bill. Efforts to increase the salience of such costs by displaying them in real time can produce gains for consumers. In fact behaviorally informed interventions,

Figure 6.3. Home energy report.

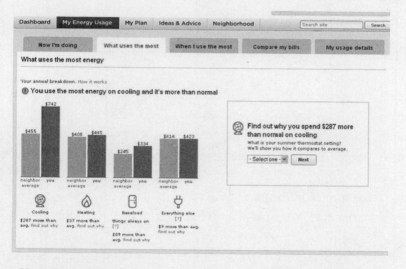

Source: Home Energy Reports, Opower, http://opower.com/what-is-opower/reports.

exploiting salience, could have a bigger effect than significant economic incentives.

Incentives as Invisible Gorillas: Shrouded and Unshrouded Attributes

Everyone agrees that incentives matter, but in order for them to matter, they have to be salient. Usually this isn't a big problem. If you have to pay $8 for a gallon of gas, you'll notice. If one tablet costs $200 and another $900, the numbers will be salient to you at the time of purchase. Purchase prices are almost always salient.

Even here, however, there is room for creativity. I have mentioned the fact that in 2010, the District of Columbia changed the law to require grocery and convenience stores to impose a small charge for grocery bags (just five cents per bag). When you pay by credit card at the checkout machine, you are specifically asked how many bags you want, and you are asked if you are willing to pay the small charge. You might think that people would always say yes because the amount of the charge is so small, but a lot of people decline. Because of loss aversion, and the salience of the charge, many fewer bags are given out.[11] A nickel isn't a lot, but many people treat it like a visible gorilla.

Consider a few other examples.

Checks or Withholding?

In the context of fiscal policy, a big goal might be to stimulate spending. Government may want to get money into people's hands so that they will spend it and thus promote economic growth. If that's the goal, what is the best way to get money to people? Consider two possible approaches:

1. Put money in people's hands by sending tax refunds as checks.
2. Put people in people's hands by reducing tax withholding.

There are obvious advantages to Option 2: it is simpler and less expensive to administer. It can cost a lot of money to send out checks. Moreover, standard economic theory suggests that the delivery method shouldn't make any difference. Extra spending money is extra spending money, and it ought not to matter how people get it.

But evidence suggests that the standard theory is quite wrong. If you want to increase spending, a check is far better than an economically equivalent reduction in withholding.[12] A good explanation involves salience. A check pulled from an envelope and held in your hand is much more visible than a reduction in withholding. Indeed, one study found that a majority of households did not even notice the withholding changes. Households that did not get a mailed check, but simply found a small increase in their paychecks, were far less likely to use the money for significant purchases.[13]

Framing Alcohol Taxes

States impose alcohol taxes in order to raise money and to discourage excessive consumption of alcohol. Is the only question the amount of the tax, or does choice architecture matter too? What would you expect the outcomes to be for two apparently equivalent approaches?

1. Alcohol taxes are specifically called out in the posted price.
2. Alcohol taxes are applied at the cash register.

The answer is that identifying the tax in the posted prices really matters and has a much larger impact on consumption.[14] The reason is that with Option 1, the taxes are salient when people are deciding whether to purchase. With Option 2, the tax is not so salient, and it does not get noticed until people have already decided what they want to buy.

Messaging Taxes

Government sometimes imposes taxes in order to discourage certain behavior, such as smoking. Does it matter if government makes it clear that it is imposing the tax for exactly that reason—or is the tax enough? If we are focusing on incentives, the tax would seem to be all that matters. But it is quite possible that the message matters too.[15] If people are clear that the tax is imposed in order to protect health, it might have a larger deterrent effect.

This is an important possibility, and it remains to be thoroughly tested; if the speculation is correct, it would represent a noteworthy wrinkle in the findings described thus far. With respect to regulation, we need to know what people *see* and also what they *hear*. Some incentives are more visible than others, and if the goal is to change behavior, it is important, and sometimes crucial, to increase visibility. But some incentives come with messages, which people may or may not hear. It is one thing to see what a product costs, or even to see that a product costs a certain amount because of a tax. It is another thing to know the government's *reasons* for applying that tax—and whether the tax reflects the government's view that a product is potentially dangerous or harmful.

Human Herds

Odds are that you'll be more certain there was no gorilla in that video if you are sitting in an auditorium filled with other people who insist that there was no gorilla in that video. In fact your brain may itself show that you are actually convinced, and not merely saying that you are.[16] As we have seen, social practices and norms have a big influence on our decisions. Often we do what others do.

For example, a really terrible way to discourage bad behavior is to tell people that everyone else is acting badly. If a political candidate laments that members of his party aren't voting, or if a university emphasizes that most of its undergraduates are getting drunk every weekend, or if a national park emphasizes that theft is everywhere, they may well end up increasing the very behavior that they are trying to change.[17] Whether good or bad, behavior is contagious, which creates both a challenge and an opportunity for nudging.

We often think that success or failure is inevitable and that intrinsic quality is what counts. But this is a big mistake. Intrinsic quality usually matters, but contingency and accident can make all the difference. As the sociologist Duncan Watts has shown, it was hardly inevitable that the *Mona Lisa* would be the most famous painting in the world.[18] For most of its life, it was hardly that. Its fame owes a great deal to dramatic and hardly inevitable events, including a theft in 1911 that greatly increased its prominence.

Without those events, many fewer people would have heard of it. Hard to believe, but it's true.

Choose your favorite movie, musician, and novel. If one or more of them is successful, there is a good chance that luck, in the form of early attention or the noticeable enthusiasm of a few people, played an indispensable role. For those of us who love *Chariots of Fire*, Steve Earle, *Gone Girl*, and A. S. Byatt's *Possession*, these are especially painful thoughts. We might even say that people are prone to the *inevitability illusion*. They tend to think that whatever happened was inevitable, even if it happened because of chance—even if serendipitous social factors (who is talking to whom, and how much, and when) were indispensable.

If you are doubtful, consider a study of music downloads by Watts and his coauthors.[19] In the study's control group, people could hear and download one or more of seventy-two songs by new bands. They were not told anything about what anyone else had downloaded or liked; they were left to make their own independent judgments. To test the effect of social influences, Watts and his coauthors also created eight other subgroups. In each of these subgroups, members would see how many people had previously downloaded individual songs in that subgroup.

Watts and his colleagues were testing the relationship between social influences and consumer choices. What do you think happened? Would it make a small or a big difference, in terms of ultimate numbers of downloads, if people could see the behavior of others?

The answer is that it made a huge difference. While the worst songs (as established by the control group) were never at the very top, and while the best songs were never at the very bottom, essentially anything else could happen. If a song benefited from a large number of early downloads, it could do really well. If it did not get that benefit, almost any song could be a failure. As Watts and his coauthors later showed, manipulation is pretty easy, because popularity is a self-fulfilling prophecy.[20] If a site shows (falsely) that a song is getting downloaded a lot, that song can get a tremendous boost and eventually become a relative hit.

Because of social influences, the success of cultural products is highly unpredictable. We usually don't know which books, songs, movies, and artists will get the kinds of early attention that can make all the difference between big success and dismal failure. Maybe William Shakespeare, John Lennon,

Franklin Delano Roosevelt, and Martin Luther King Jr. were all bound for iconic status. It's hard not to think so. But maybe not. Even for such figures, social influences were hugely important and may well have been indispensable. In an imaginable world, one or all of them never made it.

Learning from Sugar Man

Consider in this light *Searching for Sugar Man*, a stunning documentary about an unsuccessful Detroit singer-songwriter named Sixto Rodriguez, who released two long-forgotten albums in the early 1970s. Almost no one bought them, and his label dropped him. Rodriguez stopped making records and worked in construction and as a demolition man.

What Rodriguez did not know was that he had become a spectacular success in South Africa—a giant, a legend, comparable to Elvis Presley and bigger than the Beatles and the Rolling Stones. Describing him as "the soundtrack to our lives," South Africans bought hundreds of thousands of copies of his albums. *Searching for Sugar Man* is about the contrast between the failed career of Detroit's obscure demolition man and the renown of South Africa's mysterious rock icon.

The film is easily taken as a real-world fairy tale, barely believable, the kind of story that gives new meaning to the phrase "You couldn't make this up." But it is a bit less extraordinary than it seems, and it offers a profound lesson not only for music but for business, politics, and government as well.

Here's the lesson, in a nutshell: Social dynamics—who is conveying enthusiasm to whom, and how loudly, and where, and exactly when—can separate the rock icon from the demolition man, and mark the line between stunning success and crashing failure. Social dynamics made Rodriguez in South Africa and broke him in the United States. Plenty of hit movies, chart-topping songs, and bestsellers, made possible by bandwagon or cascade effects, could easily have switched places with flops that you've never heard of.

Actually the implications are far broader than that. Simple and apparently small nudges, growing out of an appreciation of the power of social influences, can make a big difference. During the 2010 congressional races, certain Facebook users received a social message, a clickable "I voted," including six pictures of randomly selected Facebook friends who had previously clicked that "I voted" button.[21] Presented with those pictures, people were more likely to vote—and as a result of the experiment, hundreds of thousands of Americans ended up voting who would not otherwise have done so. We could easily imagine a parallel experiment with the message "I didn't vote," and it would almost certainly depress voting. In fact, we could easily imagine many influential clickable messages on social media ("I bought a fuel-efficient vehicle," or "I stopped smoking," or "I love the Chicago Bears," or "I bought a Sixto Rodriguez CD").

Successful entrepreneurs, social movements, and politicians benefit from the same dynamics that produce best-selling albums. Franklin Delano Roosevelt and Ronald Reagan were immensely talented and appealing, but countless people voted and worked for them only because they saw that other people were doing so. Other immensely talented and appealing politicians go nowhere, only because they fail to catch an early wave. Science fiction's "parallel worlds," exploring how differently history might have turned out, are not as far-fetched as they seem.

True, we can always try to reclaim inevitability by generating after-the-fact explanations of both success and failure. It's tempting to think that Rodriguez did well in South Africa because his songs spoke especially well to that nation's citizens. Maybe Rodriguez did poorly in the United States because of anti-Hispanic prejudice. Maybe, but beware of the inevitability illusion. With a few twists of fate and the right social nudge at the right time, Rodriguez could have become a big star in the United States. And without some serendipitous word of mouth in the early stages, he wouldn't have become an icon in South Africa.

Sparks

One implication is that the choices of early deciders, with respect to goods, policies, and products of many kinds, can have a major effect. A more general implication is that in deciding what choices to make, each of us gets a lot of information from consulting the choices of others. Both a problem and an opportunity arise here. The problem is that if a few people start to move in a certain direction—toward violence, toward discrimination, toward self-destructive behavior—the ultimate consequences can be horrible, even tragic, for a large number of people. Revolution, hatred, and suicide can be contagious; a small spark can light a big fire.

Why is large-scale political change, as in the fall of communism and the Arab Spring, so hard to predict? The political scientist Susanne Lohmann and the economist Timur Kuran have shown that the answer is closely connected to the music download study and the tale of Sixto Rodriguez, and it lies in social influences.[22] Information is an important factor: People learn from others, and once a few people begin to rebel, a cascade may develop, reaching a tipping point where once-compliant citizens enter a full-scale rebellion. Reputation is also a factor: People care about what others think of them, and once rebellion starts, rebellious acts are no longer punished, socially speaking, but instead rewarded. As social pressures switch from favoring quiescence to promoting rebellion, large-scale change can become inevitable. Political entrepreneurs of various sorts, including rebels, show an awareness of this insight. If private and public institutions seek to produce desirable behavior, an understanding of the underlying dynamics can help.

Click It or Ticket and Beyond

These points have implications for regulatory policy. In the early 1980s, an overwhelming majority of drivers—over 80 percent—failed to use seat belts, and this failure led to thousands of preventable deaths. Since that time there has been a dramatic change in lifesaving behavior, with an increase in just a few decades from usage rates under 15 percent to well over 70 percent.[23] Social norms have shifted in concert with regulatory changes. Seat belt buckling was once inconsistent with such norms, in part because it signaled either a kind of cowardice ("I am a fearful person") or an accusation against the driver ("I don't trust you to drive safely"). It has now become standard practice. Far from resisting seat belt buckling, the vast majority of us buckle quite happily.

In the Obama administration, we made serious efforts to deal with distracted driving, one of the key emerging issues with respect to highway safety. System 1 is a big problem here. Many of us find the little red light flashing on our phone highly seductive. Who is contacting us? Maybe the message is fun? A friend? A potential romantic partner? Is there an invitation of some kind? To a party? Maybe the message is work-related and we need to get to it immediately. Even if the red light isn't flashing, maybe we are bored, or could benefit from sending a message right now, or would just enjoy making a little human contact?

Department of Transportation Secretary Ray LaHood made it a high priority to address the problem. An early step occurred on October 1, 2009, when President Obama issued a somewhat unusual and highly publicized executive order that bans federal employees from texting while driving.[24] All by itself, and despite its limited scope, this executive order had a major effect. It drew national attention to the issue and helped to energize action at the state level and in the private sector. Numerous states began to impose similar bans. The United Nations itself banned texting while driving by its employees, emphasizing traffic safety and the worldwide problem of distracted driving in a public event, featuring the UN secretary-general and Ambassador Susan Rice, that I was privileged to attend.

Shortly after President Obama signed the executive order, the Department of Transportation held a public summit on distracted driving, with a range of speakers, including public officials and people who had done empirical work on the topic. I walked into the summit one afternoon expecting to see a few dozen people around a conference table. Instead I entered a huge room filled with hundreds of people, all staring at the speakers with rapt attention. The summit attracted a lot of news. In 2009 Webster's Dictionary declared *distracted driving* to be the "word of the year." Because of federal action, mostly in the form of a few simple nudges, people were devoting unprecedented attention to reducing the relevant risks.

Congress did not, of course, enact a law to forbid texting while driving. The Department of Transportation took several regulatory actions to reduce texting while driving, but they were hardly radical. The Department banned texting by those who transport hazardous materials and who drive large commercial trucks. In addition, the Department strongly encouraged action at the state and local level, and also worked with employers to get them to discourage their workers from texting while driving, perhaps through advice, perhaps through prohibitions. Distraction.gov has a lot of details. The problem of distracted driving remains extremely serious, but in some parts of the country, a norm is developing in favor of keeping people's hands on the wheel and eyes on the road.

We need to do much more on this problem. We need to learn more about the risks of texting while driving and also about the risks of using a cell phone while driving. The empirical questions here have yet to be sorted out.[25] We also need to understand the effects of new automobile technologies, including those that involve interactive dashboards, and we need to ensure that those technologies are not creating undue risks. If the technologies move in a certain direction, they will create obvious dangers, as the Department of Transportation has recognized.[26] System 1 may miss invisible gorillas, but it is drawn to all sorts of distractions, not least while people are driving. We need to make sure that the results do not include more injuries and deaths. Social norms will be central to that endeavor.

Childhood Obesity

With respect to childhood obesity, a social norm in favor of healthy eating and proper exercise could produce huge health benefits. In 1998, a study found that the social costs of obesity exceeded $99 billion in 1995,[27] nearly 6 percent of the total national health expenditure, and the cost is undoubtedly far higher today. Here, as elsewhere, public-private partnerships can play a key role, with those in the private sector helping to spur emerging norms that promote better choices by and for children.

In particular, the "Let's Move" initiative has emphasized such partnerships. Of course there have been regulatory efforts, including evidence-based nutrition policies for school meals. But most of the initiative has involved working cooperatively with those outside the federal government, not to regulate but to educate and to nudge. And the effort seems to be having an effect. Here's a little evidence.[28] On Halloween in 2012, researchers randomly assigned children to one of two sides of a large porch. On one side of the porch, there was a big photo of Michelle Obama. On the other side, there was a big photo of Ann Romney. Here, then, were two kinds of nudges, in the form of pictures of prominent women. The question: Would kids' choices, as between fruit and candy, be affected by the photos?

The answer was clear. The photo of Michelle Obama was an effective nudge. It made children far more likely to select fruit. About 38 percent of children nine and older choose fruit when they saw her picture; of those who saw the picture of Ann Romney, just 19 percent did so. Interestingly (but not amazingly) there was no such effect on children under nine, probably because they were not aware of the "Let's Move" campaign.

Without imposing regulatory requirements, that campaign has had a real impact in the United States, above all because of work with state and local governments and with the private sector, which have been taking meaningful steps to combat obesity. I have noted that in major cities, there have been recent reductions in childhood obesity rates, with real decreases from 2007 to 2011, including a 5.5 percent decrease in New York City. Both nudges and school nutrition policies, implemented in the Obama administration, appear to be contributing factors. As in the case of distracted driving, far more remains to be done, above all to understand which approaches have the biggest impact in informing decisions and promoting health. But consider just a few examples:

- Michelle Obama collaborated with Walmart to promote healthier choices.[29] As part of that collaboration, Walmart committed to reformulating thousands of everyday packaged food items by 2015, reducing sodium 25 percent and added sugars 10 percent and removing all remaining industrially produced trans fats. Walmart is also reducing the costs of healthier options, thus making those costs comparable to the costs of less healthy choices, and at the same time reducing the costs of fruits and vegetables.[30] Finally, Walmart has developed a "healthy seal" to help consumers to identify healthy choices.[31]

- A number of companies, including Kraft Foods, General Mills, Coca-Cola, Pepsi, and Kellogg, will remove a total of 1.5 trillion calories from their products by 2015 in an effort to combat childhood obesity.[32] Their initiatives include reduction of product sizes and introduction of lower calorie foods.

- A coalition of the Fruit and Vegetable Alliance, the Food, Family and Farming Foundation, and the United Fresh Produce Association is putting six thousand salad bars in schools across the country, making fresh vegetables a more accessible choice for children.

- The Food Marketing Institute and the Grocery Manufacturers Association are promoting informed choices through a "Nutrition Keys" label, designed in part to combat childhood obesity.[33]

- McDonald's is providing calorie information on its menus (both at restaurants and at drive-throughs). McDonald's also introduced a "Favorites under 400" menu, containing lower-calorie options, and is taking steps to move meals in the directions suggested by official federal recommendations and the Food Plate.[34]

These examples have many analogues. Consider the problem of "bill shock," which occurs when people are unexpectedly faced with high cell phone charges as a result of exceeding their monthly limits. The Federal Communications Commission (FCC) proposed a rule that would require cell phone companies to give people advance notice of overcharges. In response to the proposed rule, companies decided to take action to give such notice voluntarily, in a highly public announcement with the FCC.

It is important, and true, that the voluntary action might not have been undertaken without the prospect of a rule. But it is noteworthy that the companies chose not to fight the rule, publicly or in court, but instead to take action to inform consumers.

There is a larger lesson here. Some of the most important reforms come when someone in the private sector begins with a simple idea or initiative, which in turns attracts the attention of public officials, who in turn promote greater private-sector interest (perhaps by considering official action), thus creating a kind of virtuous circle, or even a cascade, with highly beneficial consequences. Of course, the same processes can lead in bad directions as well. But if the goal is to save money and lives, private-public partnerships, focusing on norms and minimizing or even avoiding regulation, may be the best option.

7

REGULATORY MONEYBALL

How do we know if a new regulation is a good idea? Suppose that a rule would make the air a bit cleaner or reduce the risk of death on the highways. Is it good for that reason?

Facts and Values

Here is a possible response. Debates about regulation are really debates about values, not about facts. When people disagree about a rule that would protect clean air or increase highway safety, it is because of what they most value, not because of disagreements about the evidence. Facts are not irrelevant, but they are hardly the main event.

A lot of evidence shows that with respect to regulation, values can have priority.[1] If you have certain predispositions, you will be inclined to believe that climate change is real, that nanotechnology is dangerous, that nuclear power is a bad idea, and that gun control saves lives. If you have different predispositions, you will be inclined to the opposite beliefs. Predispositions with respect to values help to account for people's factual judgments on these and many other questions. If we are asking what, in fact, explains people's disagreements about facts, one answer would be their disagreements about values.

On some of the largest issues, values and predispositions do play a critical role. I saw this in Washington every day. At the same time, we shouldn't overstate the point. Most people's values do not lead to a clear judgment about whether to require rearview cameras in cars. (Do they reduce accidents? By how much?) They do not tell us whether we should reduce levels of ozone in the ambient air from 75 parts per billion to 70 parts per billion or 65 parts per billion, or for that matter 20 parts per billion. (Would such reductions have big health benefits or not?) Taken by themselves, values don't answer the question whether we should increase the fuel economy of cars to 40 MPG or 50 MPG or 60 MPG or 70 MPG, and whether we should do so by 2020 or 2025.

To answer these questions, the facts are indispensable. Without facts, you might rely on heuristics of various sorts. With System 1 in charge, you might think: My first priority is safety, and so of course I want to do whatever can be done to make to air cleaner. Or you might have recently sat among a group of friends who think that the free market works pretty well and that regulators tend to be overzealous and to get pushed around by interest groups. Certainly, these sorts of general commitments can help to orient thinking, but they are too abstract to provide concrete answers. To do that, you need to explore the details.

This is an opportunity, not an obstacle. If regulators discover that a rule would do very little to increase highway safety but would add $600 to the cost of every new car, they have learned enough to know that the rule is hard to defend. After they learn such facts, those previously inclined to favor the rule might well change their minds. And if we know (hypothetically) that a rule requiring rearview cameras in cars would prevent many deaths (say, nine hundred per year) and cost very little (say, $1 per car), the argument for that rule would be hard to resist.

Of course, people's values differ. In some cases their values will lead in competing directions no matter what the evidence says. What I am emphasizing here is the opposite point, and the more interesting and neglected one: When the evidence is clear, it will often lead people to the same conclusion even if those very people differ intensely with respect to values. If a regulation would save many lives and cost very little, people are likely to support it regardless of their party identification; and if a regulation would produce little benefit but impose big costs, citizens are unlikely to favor it regardless of whether they like elephants or donkeys.

When laws and regulations are being written, officials ought to do a lot more than consult their predispositions and their intuitions. System 1 should not be the nation's regulatory czar. To be sure, people's deepest moral commitments matter, and on some issues those commitments may turn out to be decisive; consider civil rights. And certain values are inescapable. If you do not agree that preventing the death of a child is good, or that requiring an expenditure of $1 billion is bad, then it will be difficult to enlist facts in the service of reaching a resolution. But we often have sufficient agreement on what is good and what is bad, so that the key questions are: How many deaths would be prevented? How much would it cost to prevent them?

How Do You Know?

My own experience in government was that in tough cases, the real issues usually involved the facts, not values, and certainly not which interest groups to favor. When people in government are discussing a rule, a central task is to ascertain those facts. What would a rule accomplish? What would it cost? If people are able to get clear on the actual effects of a rule—whether it involved highway safety, energy efficiency, clean air, workplace safety, or education—they are far less likely to disagree.

I am not denying that prior commitments influence people's judgments about regulations. In fact some people in government (and elsewhere) appear to have a heuristic: *In the face of doubt, protect public safety*. Other people in government (and elsewhere) appear to have a different heuristic: *In the face of doubt, don't interfere with the private sector*. In addition, people in government, no less (or more) than anyone else, are influenced by the set of people with whom they speak. A brilliant essay by the political scientist Russell Hardin refers to the "crippled epistemology of extremism."[2] By this Hardin means to emphasize that many extremists have extreme views not because they are stupid or crazy but because of the narrow set of people from whom they learn. And it is not only extremists who suffer from a crippled epistemology; at least to some extent, most of us do. We cannot possibly know everything or talk with everyone. Government officials know a lot, and they talk with a lot of people, but their information is also limited. Inside and outside government, people learn from those with whom they interact, and limited interactions can ensure limited information.

I have emphasized that during my years in government, the desires of interest groups, taken simply as such, were not particularly important. (Recall that at OIRA, we tried to avoid sewer talk.) And people did not ever "cave in" to interest-group pressure; I saw literally no cases in which that happened. But if people in the private sector presented arguments, with evidence, about the importance of going in a particular direction, those arguments could matter, whether they came from people seeking or resisting regulation.

What I did see was important and, in its way, even inspiring: a significant and beneficial impact from a sustained analysis of the likely consequences of regulation and a careful assessment of its costs and benefits. That assessment could subject the claims of self-interested outsiders to critical scrutiny. It could broaden the viewscreen. It could, and did, narrow and clarify the stakes, often bringing people together regardless of what they had heard or what they thought they were most concerned about.

Let's come back to *Moneyball*. Many sports, including football and basketball, now have their own Billy Beanes and Paul DePodestas, asking not about anecdotes or about players' looks, height, and weight, but about what kinds of contributions players actually make to winning. In sports, careful statistical analysis is replacing intuitions, analogies, anecdotes, and the availability heuristic. System 2 is increasingly in the forefront. As players are to sports, regulations are to society. They also need rigorous evaluation. We need to learn as much as we can about what kinds of contributions rules are likely to make. Without an analysis of their consequences—of their costs and benefits—we will be in a poor position to obtain that knowledge. Indeed that analysis can help reduce complexity, if only because complexity can be costly. We need Regulatory Moneyball, not because it solves all our problems but because it solves a lot of them and because it helps to clarify why some questions are hard ones.

Cost-benefit analysis is not an algorithm, and it should not (and in my experience did not) put government in an arithmetic straitjacket. But it is an indispensable means of helping regulators to make sensible choices. Just as ordinary people can benefit from a nudge, so too can government. At a minimum, an analysis of costs and benefits is an important way to nudge regulators. Indeed requiring such analysis is a way of creating a good choice architecture for those who make the rules.

Cost-Benefit Analysis as Nudging Government

Why, exactly, is cost-benefit analysis good? My basic answer here is simple: Careful analysis can provide a kind of System 2 check on the operations of System 1.

That check is helpful, even indispensable, for each of us in ordinary life. It is helpful, even indispensable, for government as well. At OIRA I saw this repeatedly. Attention to benefits and costs helped to trigger concern with big problems and to deflect concern with small ones. It forced interest groups to ask the right questions and to provide more helpful information—not to threaten public disapproval or reprisal but to discuss consequences for real human beings. True, a lot of what they said was self-serving (they are interest groups, after all), but it was relevant nonetheless. By itself this point argues for engaging in cost-benefit analysis, simply as a means of generating relevant information.

If that information is helpful, why, exactly, might it inform people's judgments? Part of the answer is that an assessment of the likely consequences of a proposed regulation might move us in a direction very different from our initial inclinations. System 1 may assert a commitment to public safety, but after analysis, System 2 might question if a rule meaningfully promotes that goal. Or System 1 might think that nothing is amiss, and regulation is a silly idea, but after analysis. System 2 might conclude that we really need to take some precautions. In short, System 1 might be alarmed or complacent, and cost-benefit analysis can strengthen the hand of System 2. There are several points here.[3]

As we saw in chapter 3, people tend to think that potential events are more probable if they can recall actual incidents when such events occurred. In the face of a horrific shooting at a school, fear of a similar shooting can be very high, but it is reduced after memories of the horror start to fade. If floods have not occurred in the immediate past, people who live on floodplains are far less likely to purchase flood insurance; in the aftermath of an earthquake, sales of insurance for earthquakes rise sharply—but sales decline steadily from that point, as vivid memories recede.[4]

Public officials, no less than ordinary people, are susceptible to the availability heuristic. And in a democracy, officials, including lawmakers, may react to public alarm. Within the executive branch, there is a lot of analytic discipline. OIRA is filled with people who focus not on what events come to mind but on whether risks are serious and have the potential to cause harm. Under both Republican and Democratic administrations, OIRA, the Council of Economic Advisers, the National Economic Council, and others do not want to impose costly regulations unless there is good reason to believe that they will deliver significant benefits. After thirty years of experience, the culture of cost-benefit analysis is now well ingrained. In fact President Obama's embrace of such analysis played a big role in fortifying and even cementing that culture. When he endorsed cost-benefit analysis in an executive order signed in January 2011, he gave a clear signal of the importance of relying not on anecdotes but on a careful assessment of the likely consequences.

Nonetheless, the availability heuristic can create problems. If citizens are worried about abandoned hazardous waste dumps or are extremely concerned about the risk of airplane accidents, they will ask for aggressive regulation in response. The number of people actually at risk from hazardous waste dumps (sometimes not a lot) or the relative safety of air travel (exceedingly safe) might not be given enough attention.

Cost-benefit analysis is a natural corrective, above all because it focuses attention on the actual effects of regulation, sometimes including the surprisingly small benefits of regulatory controls. To this extent, cost-benefit analysis is unquestionably a way of forcing System 1 to pause for a moment and of fortifying the role of System 2—of ensuring that a full accounting, and not a recent event, is the basis for action.

Of course, the availability heuristic does not operate in a social vacuum. If something bad happens and is memorable, the fact of its occurrence may generate an informational cascade, with significant consequences for private and public behavior and possibly distorting effects on regulatory policy. Cascade effects help explain widespread public concern (entirely justified in some cases but excessive in others) about abandoned hazardous waste dumps. They spurred public fears of the pesticide Alar and of risks from plane crashes. Cascade effects helped produce massive dislocations in beef production in Europe in connection with "mad cow disease." They have given rise to Europeans' fears of genetic engineering of food and Americans' fears of "pink slime" in beef.

Self-interested private groups can exploit these forces, often by using the availability heuristic. Consider the fact that European companies have tried to play up fears of genetically engineered food as a way of fending off American competition. In these circumstances, the effect of cost-benefit analysis is clear. It subjects fears and concerns to a kind of technocratic scrutiny, to ensure that the demand for a regulatory response is rooted in reality rather than rumor and myth and to ensure as well that government is regulating risks even when the public demand (because insufficiently informed) is low.

Some people are subject to "alarmist bias."[5] Suppose that as your airplane is about to take off, your pilot tells you the following: "The risk that the plane will crash is really low. Air travel is safe, and the chance that we will all die is extremely small." Though you had been calmly reading the newspaper a moment before, you might now feel really frightened. One reason is salience. For many of us, the mere discussion of risks can increase our concern, even when the discussions take the form of apparently trustworthy assurances that the level of danger is relatively small.[6]

In chapter 3 I referred to evidence that people's feelings of worry are sometimes sensitive not to the *probability* of the bad outcome but to the *severity* of the bad outcome. Vivid mental pictures of widespread death or catastrophe can drive a demand for risk regulation. The role of cost-benefit analysis is straightforward here as well. Just as the Senate was designed to have a "cooling effect" on the passions of the House of Representatives, so cost-benefit analysis might ensure that policy is driven not by hysteria or alarm but by a full appreciation of the relevant risks. If the alarm survives an investigation of consequences, then it is fully rational, and an immediate and aggressive regulatory response is entirely appropriate.

Nor is cost-benefit analysis, in this setting, only a check on unwarranted regulation. It can and should serve as a spur to regulation as well. If risks do not produce visceral reactions, partly because the underlying activities or outcomes do not produce vivid mental images, cost-benefit analysis can show that regulatory controls are warranted. The cost-justified elimination of lead in gasoline, brought about by the Reagan administration, is a case in point, and it has had terrific public health benefits. In government I saw a large number of cases in which high benefits and low costs spurred enthusiasm for regulatory initiatives. Rules increasing energy efficiency for appliances made their way through the process in part because their benefits were far higher than their costs.

Let's look at one example a bit more closely. Under the Montreal Protocol, which is designed to protect the ozone layer, nations are required to phase out emissions of ozone-depleting substances. The Reagan administration aggressively supported the Montreal Protocol notwithstanding earlier conservative resistance to (and even ridicule of) efforts to protect the ozone layer. Indeed, the Reagan administration exercised worldwide leadership on this question. It did so in part because a careful analysis by the Council of Economic Advisers showed that the benefits of such protection greatly outweighed the costs.[7] The Montreal Protocol has been a terrific success story, and cost-benefit analysis helped to make it happen. But there are some important and revealing wrinkles.

Some ozone-depleting chemicals, including chlorofluorocarbons (CFCs), are emitted by devices that administer asthma medicines. These emissions are small, even trivial, and so regulating asthma medicines is far from the most important step toward protecting the ozone layer. On the other hand, the regulation does not create big problems, because CFC-free substitutes are available for asthmatics, or can be made available with a little lead time. In such cases, compliance with the Montreal Protocol does not cause health problems. So far, so good.

In 2008, however, the Bush administration banned the product Primatene Mist. This was a controversial step, because Primatene Mist was the only over-the-counter asthma medicine, and it did not, at the time, have a CFC-free substitute. The Bush administration instituted the ban with the understanding that an over-the-counter substitute would be made available by the end of 2011, when the ban was to go into effect. As 2011 drew to a close, however, no such substitute was available. Somewhere between two million and three million people used Primatene Mist, and all of them were left without an over-the-counter medicine.

This was a problem in light of two facts. First, the prescription alternatives were more expensive. Second, many people who used Primatene Mist (perhaps as many as 20 percent) did not have health insurance. A number of people, including Primatene Mist users, complained vigorously. Why on earth, they asked, is the government banning their preferred asthma medicine when the alternatives are more expensive and require a visit to the doctor's office? It is a lot simpler, after all, just to go to the pharmacy.

In the Obama administration, some of us struggled a lot with the question whether to extend the deadline for the phaseout of Primatene Mist. I confess that I believed that the deadline should have been extended. But ultimately the Food and Drug Administration declined to give an extension, in part on the ground that asthma sufferers would do better to find doctors and to use the prescription medicine that really was right for them.

Whatever the best answer to this particular question, the general problem is clear. Efforts to reduce some risks (such as those associated with depletion of the ozone layer) can increase other risks (such as those associated with asthma). We are often dealing with *health-health trade-offs*, which arise when risk-reduction initiatives create health risks of their own.

There are many examples. A decision to ban asbestos may cause manufacturers to use less safe substitutes. A decision to increase restrictions on nuclear power may increase the demand for coal-fired power plants, with potentially harmful environmental consequences. Strict regulation of air pollution may increase electricity prices, and because higher electricity prices can affect people's ability to afford air-conditioning and heating, such regulation may impose harm. Here, then, is a real virtue of cost-benefit analysis. It helps to overcome people's tendency to focus on mere parts of problems by requiring them to look broadly at the consequences, often indirect, of apparently isolated actions.

It is important to see that while regulation of some risks can *increase* other risks, it is also true that regulation of some risks can simultaneously *decrease* other risks. In the Obama administration, we issued an important air pollution regulation whose principal goal was to reduce emissions of mercury. The same technologies that would reduce those emissions would reduce emissions of particulate matter, another air pollutant. It turns out that the "cobenefits" produced by reductions in particulate matter were, in terms of human health, by far the biggest quantifiable gains from the mercury rule, preventing thousands of premature deaths and tens of thousands of illnesses each year.

Some critics of the mercury rule objected that the largest benefits did not involve mercury at all. In their view, the rule was a kind of fake, because the largest gains came from reductions in particulate matter. But this criticism was misplaced. There was no fakery here. For any rule, what is needed is a full accounting. If a rule creates incidental harm, that harm should be taken into account; the same is true if a rule creates incidental benefits.

Playing Regulatory Moneyball

We can now identify the ingredients of a behaviorally informed argument for cost-benefit analysis. But serious questions remain.

Suppose that the monetized benefits of a food safety rule are $200 million, while the monetized costs are $300 million. Is it so clear that the rule should not be issued? Don't we have to know what those figures represent, exactly? Does the $200 million in benefits represent money in the form of strictly economic savings for consumers? Or does it represent some effort to monetize lives saved or illnesses averted? And who would enjoy those benefits and bear those costs? Would children gain? Would big food processors lose? For that matter, suppose that the monetized benefits of a food safety rule are $300 million and that the monetized costs are $200 million. Is it so clear that the rule should be issued? We could ask exactly the same questions.

The best defense of cost-benefit analysis is that government should try to promote social welfare, broadly understood, and that cost-benefit analysis is a nudge toward achieving that goal—imperfect to be sure, but valuable nonetheless. To see why this might be so, let us consider some stylized examples.

1. The Department of Energy is considering a rule to make refrigerators more energy efficient. The rule would add an average of $200 to the initial price of a refrigerator, but because the refrigerators are more energy efficient, the average consumer would save money— $100 over the life of the refrigerator. Suppose that eight million refrigerators are sold in the United States every year, so that the cost of the rule is $1.6 billion and the benefits are $800 million. If the goal is to help consumers, the rule sounds pretty hard to defend. The rule would make consumers lose money! Cost-benefit analysis shows why. Without an accounting, we would not be in a good position to know whether this rule is a sensible idea.

2. Same as Case 1, but the average consumer would save $400 over the life of the refrigerator. If so, the rule seems to make a lot of sense; it would help consumers a lot. Its benefits are $3.2 billion, exactly

double its costs, which is really good. To be sure, there are some important questions to ask. We need to know whether the new, energy-efficient refrigerators are as good as the current ones. If they don't refrigerate as well, then the rule is imposing a separate cost, and we need to consider that cost in our assessment. If we make refrigerators lousy, that's a big problem. We also need to know whether the rule would make consumers less or more likely to buy new refrigerators. If consumers bought fewer refrigerators, the rule would impose a cost (on consumers and the economy) that we have not yet considered. (If consumers bought more refrigerators, however, the rule would confer benefits that we have not yet considered.) We also need to know whether consumers would increase their use of the refrigerator simply because it is cheaper to operate (the so-called rebound effect). A big increase may not force us to reach a different conclusion, but it might be relevant. Finally, we have to explain why the market is not already producing more energy-efficient refrigerators. If consumers would benefit, why aren't they buying them? (The answer may have something to do with salience and myopia.) All of these questions are part of the standard cost-benefit analysis. If they have good answers, and if the benefits remain far higher than the costs, it makes sense to proceed.

3. Same as Case 1, but the rule would also produce significant reductions in air pollution. Those reductions would prevent one thousand premature deaths every year (and a large number of illnesses, of varying degrees of seriousness, and missed workdays). Suppose that federal agencies value a human life at around $8 million (as they typically do). The rule is easily justified, even if we put to one side illnesses and missed workdays. The costs are $1.6 billion, but the benefits are $8.6 billion. Here too we have to answer some questions: Why is a human life valued at $8 million? Where does this figure come from? For the moment, let's assume that the question has a good answer. If so, the benefits easily exceed the costs.

4. Same as Case 1, but the rule would also produce only modest reductions in air pollution. Those reductions would prevent fifty pre-

mature deaths every year (and a very small number of illnesses and missed workdays). The rule is not easy to justify; the costs are $1.6 billion, which is far higher than the $1.2 billion in benefits.

Cases 1 and 2 are easy. Cases 3 and 4 also seem straightforward, but as noted, it is natural to ask how we translate premature deaths into monetary equivalents. The literature on that question is large and highly technical,[8] and I can only scratch the surface here. The key point is that in engaging in cost-benefit analysis, regulators do not really try to identify the monetary value of a human life. Instead they ask about *the value of eliminating a statistical risk of death*. That question, while hardly easy, is far more tractable.

Suppose that the question is whether to eliminate a risk of death of 1 in 100,000. How much is it worth to eliminate that risk? There are many ways to answer that question. One way is simply to ask people, "How much would you pay to eliminate such a risk?" If you answer "As little as $0" or "As much as $500," you are pretty unusual. A standard answer is $50.

Of course, there are problems with posing abstract, hypothetical questions of this sort; maybe the answers are not meaningful. If you say that you are willing to pay $500 to eliminate a mortality risk of 1 in 100,000, you might want to think about what else you could buy with $500. (Maybe you could buy a television. Maybe you could eliminate a far more serious mortality risk—say, a risk of 1 in 10,000!)

Another way to answer the question is to look at the evidence of the market. Suppose that we know, across large populations, that if workers are subject to a risk of 1 in 100,000, they receive a wage bonus, or premium, of $50. If so, the conclusion would be that the value of a statistical life (VSL) is $5 million. It should be clear that this conclusion really means that when the government is eliminating risks of 1 in 100,000, it will spend no more and no less than $50 to do so.

The current technical literature suggests that the appropriate VSL is around $9 million (in 2012 dollars).[9] In the Obama administration, agencies made some modest increases in VSL, largely to take account of national income growth. As nations become wealthier, VSL naturally increases, because people have more money to spend on reducing risks. We also worked hard to ensure that the actual practice of government agencies is well within the range of the technical literature, and that they avoid large or puzzling inconsistencies.[10] It would not be good if the Environmental Protection Agency values a life at $9 million, the Department of Transportation values a life at $3 million, and the Department of Human Services values a life at $1 million. The current numbers are not uniform across agencies, but they are generally within the range of $7 million to $9 million. The relatively small current differences do not appear to be affecting decisions about whether to issue regulations and about how stringent regulations should be.

So much for current practice; of course, many questions remain.

- *Age*. Should children's lives be valued more, less, or the same as the lives of adults? More precisely, how should we treat statistical risks faced by children? On the one hand, small children don't have a lot of money to pay to eliminate risks; but should that even matter? On the other hand, children have a lot of life left (at least if we take care of them); shouldn't that matter? Should we look at the number of years of life saved rather than simply the number of lives? Parents would be willing to spend a lot to reduce risks to their children; shouldn't their wishes count?[11] Or suppose that a rule would mostly extend the lives of the elderly by a short time, as, for example, with an air pollution rule whose main effect would be to add a few months to the lives of people over the age of eighty. Should agencies give a lower value to the lives of old people because we may be speaking of a matter of months? Is it really worth $8 million to extend a life by a few months, if we are also willing to spend $8 million to extend a life by decades? Or is that difference irrelevant?

- *Context*. Perhaps it is obtuse, even ridiculous, to ignore context. Perhaps the value of a mortality risk of 1 in 100,000 varies depending on whether the risk involves cancer, heart disease, or a sudden unanticipated death. There is some evidence that people would pay an extra amount to avoid a risk of cancer death;[12] should that evidence figure into official government policy? Perhaps it matters whether the risk involves a death in an automobile accident, a terrorist attack, or an airplane crash. If people are willing to pay an extra amount to prevent a risk of death in an airline crash, because they especially abhor that kind of death, should that be part of official policy as well?

- *Who?* We might want to ask about who, exactly, would be helped and hurt by regulation. Suppose that a workplace safety rule would cost $400 million and produce benefits of $350 million. At first glance the rule fails a cost-benefit test. But suppose that the costs would be incurred by those who sell and use a luxury good (say, expensive cars) and that the benefits would be enjoyed by those who are near the bottom of the economic ladder (say, those who do manual work in producing such cars). Or suppose that a rule reducing air pollution would cost $900 million but produce benefits of $800 million, with the costs imposed on polluters (and those who work for them and purchase their products, perhaps including energy) and the benefits enjoyed mostly by people who are poor or close to it. We might be interested not just in the monetary equivalents but in what those figures represent. In terms of human welfare, the two rules described above might be producing big gains, among other things by saving lives and preventing accidents and illnesses. And in terms of human welfare, the two rules might not be producing big losses; they might just mean that people have to pay a bit more for certain goods, which may not be the worst thing in the world. Here is one reason that the monetized cost and benefit figures should not produce an arithmetic straitjacket. If the benefits are $300 million and the costs $400 million, the issue may not be at an end. We might need to ask more questions. And in fact, President Obama's executive order on federal regulation, issued in 2011, allows for consideration of "equity" and "distributive impacts" in deciding whether and how to proceed.

All of these are difficult issues in and about cost-benefit analysis, and definitive answers have yet to emerge. Economists, social scientists, and others continue to work on them, and no consensus has been reached. My own impression is that, in general, they have more theoretical than practical importance. Different answers to these questions would not often have led to a different conclusion with respect to the rules that I saw. Here is why. We saw many draft rules for which the benefits were far higher than the costs, and technical adjustments, driving the benefits significantly up or down, would not have affected the ultimate judgment. We had some draft rules for which the costs were significantly higher than the benefits, and even significant technical judgments, driving benefits up, would not have made a difference. In short, there were few draft rules for which technical adjustments, resolving the questions I have just outlined, would make a rule look a lot better or a lot worse.

In the Obama administration, we did not venture novel or complex answers to the hardest questions. Following long-standing practice, agencies continue to use a single value for a statistical life, without making distinctions for age, context, or wealth. In some cases, however, we took account of qualitative considerations, some of which did respond to the questions raised above (as we shall shortly see).

Let's bracket the tough issues and return to the central point. Careful consideration of costs and benefits is a method for testing the question of whether a regulation is a good idea. If a rule would impose high costs but deliver small benefits, it almost certainly makes sense to put it on a not-to-do list. (Compare Billy Beane's similar list.) And if a rule would save a lot of lives, it probably makes sense to do it unless the cost would be very high indeed. I hope that enough has been said to explain why cost-benefit analysis has been endorsed by both Democratic and Republican administrations and why efforts to catalogue benefits and costs have provided a strong nudge toward better policies.

In fact we should make a distinction here. On one view, analysis of costs and benefits really is just a nudge. Agencies have to produce such an analysis, but they do not need to be constrained by it. If the costs outweigh the benefits, they remain entitled to go forward. On another view, the analysis of costs and benefits is not merely a nudge; it is a rule of decision. On this view, agencies cannot proceed unless the benefits justify the costs. In the Obama administration we took the stronger view: Agencies could not go forward if the benefits did not justify the costs, unless the law required them to do so. Of course, nonmonetizable, nonquantifiable benefits might turn out to be important, as we will see.

The Precautionary Principle: A Hostile Note

Many people who dislike cost-benefit analysis prefer an approach known as the *precautionary principle*. This principle can be understood in many different ways, but the basic idea is that we should maintain a margin of safety and impose a heavy burden on those who would impose risks on the public. According to strong versions of the precautionary principle, people cannot go forward with an activity or a product unless they can show that it is safe.

Yet the precautionary principle, for all its rhetorical appeal, is deeply incoherent in most of its forms,[13] and the Obama administration did not adopt it. Of course, it is true that we should take precautions against many dangers that are not likely to come to fruition. If you are faced with a 5 percent risk of dying in a car crash, you will take steps to eliminate that risk. Precautions make a lot of sense. The problem with the precautionary principle is that it bans what it simultaneously requires. The objection is not that the principle leads in bad directions; the objection is that it is paralyzing and self-defeating.

Consider the Iraq War. At times, the Bush administration justified the war on explicitly precautionary grounds. In its view, even the possibility of a nuclear-armed Iraq was so threatening that it demanded action. The very idea of "preemptive war," endorsed by President Bush, is a kind of precautionary principle. The nation went to war on the chance that Saddam Hussein had weapons of mass destruction. But this precaution imposed a heavy price. Whether a preemptive war is justified depends on a full accounting of effects, not on a general idea of precaution.

War is unique, but the same point holds in other contexts, including that of climate change, in which costly precautions inevitably create risks of one or another kind. This is not at all to say that we should decline to take action to avert the dangers posed by climate change; the fuel economy rules, which are designed in part to reduce greenhouse gas emissions, are examples of sensible regulation.[14] But no choice is risk-free. For environmental and other problems, we need to decide which risks to combat, not comfort ourselves with the pretense that there is such a thing as a risk-free choice.

Consider the case of genetically modified food. Many people fear that "tampering with nature" could produce harmful consequences for our health and for the environment. But others argue that a failure to allow genetic modification might well result in numerous deaths and a small probability of many more. The reason: Genetic modification holds out the possibility of producing food that is both cheaper and healthier, resulting in products that might have large benefits in developing countries. The point is not to take a side in these complex debates; the point is only that the precautionary principle provides no guidance.

Regulations sometimes give rise to substitute risks. DDT, for example, is often regulated in the interest of protecting birds and human health. But in poor nations, banning DDT eliminates what appears to be the most effective way of combating malaria and may significantly compromise public health. Or consider the "drug lag," produced whenever the government takes a highly precautionary approach to the introduction of new drugs. Stringent review protects people against inadequately tested drugs, but it also prevents people from receiving the benefits of new medications until those medications are deemed safe. Is it "precautionary" to require extensive testing, or to do the opposite? In the Obama administration the FDA has worked hard to strike the right balance, but it is a balance that must be struck.

If you were to try to follow the precautionary principle in the next twenty-four hours, you'd face a real challenge. Not exercising imposes risks; exercising imposes risks. Hard work can be hazardous, but if you don't work hard, you might irritate your employer. And if you do that, you'll be imposing some risks on yourself and your family. What is true for individuals is true for policymakers as well. To be sure, we should often take precautions. But we should not adopt the precautionary principle. What precautions should we take? The answer depends largely on costs and benefits.

Of Dignity, Equity, and Distribution

In his executive order on regulation, President Obama firmly embraced a form of Regulatory Moneyball, explicitly directing agencies to quantify both benefits and costs "as accurately as possible." But the same executive order acknowledges that quantification is sometimes impossible, because we don't have enough information. The executive order also recognizes that some values are not easily turned into monetary equivalents. Thus it says that agencies "may consider (and discuss qualitatively) values that are difficult or impossible to quantify, including equity, human dignity, fairness, and distributive impacts."

This provision is a frank recognition that it is acceptable to consider factors, such as dignity and equity, that cannot be easily monetized. You can even understand this provision as a nudge toward consideration of these factors—as, for example, when an agency attempts to enable wheelchair-bound veterans to have access to public bathrooms.

There is no conflict between emphasizing the importance of quantification and recognizing that some things cannot be quantified. If an expensive rule would prevent premature deaths, we should to try to see how many premature deaths it would prevent. Two? Fifty? A thousand? If a rule would impose costs, we need to know the magnitude of those costs. Would the figure be $100 million, or $200 million, or $900 million? The answer could make a big difference. You can believe deeply in quantification while recognizing its limits.

Human dignity and equity are hardly foreign to American traditions. But to say the least, the executive order's emphasis on those factors was not universally well-received. An editorial in the *Wall Street Journal* stated:[15]

> Equity and fairness can be defined to include more or less anything as a benefit. Under this calculus, a rule might pass Mr. Obama's cost-benefit test if it imposes $999 billion in hard costs but supposedly results in a $1 trillion increase in human dignity, whatever that means in bureaucratic practice. Another rule could pass muster even if it reduces work and investment, as long as it also lessens income inequality.
>
> Any cost-benefit analysis depends to some extent on matters of judgment, but typically the criteria are more economically tangible, such as how to price risk or the discount rate. No business would recognize Mr. Obama's version, since his "values" loophole boils down to a preference for bigger government. The danger is that his executive order will transform an important tool to check excessive regulation into a way to justify whatever rule the permanent bureaucracy wants. . . . This sounds more like the end of cost-benefit analysis than the beginning.

Members of Congress similarly ridiculed the references to dignity and equity, seeing those words as huge qualifiers that would enable bureaucrats to do whatever they want. Representative John Sullivan of Oklahoma objected to "this gobbledygook" and wondered what it could possibly mean. Representative Cliff Stearns of Florida stated that agencies had thrown "rational, quantitative cost-benefit analysis out the window" in favor of "amorphous, subjective language and politically correct ideology." [16]

In a way it is odd and even surreal to hear elected representatives of We the People disparaging the time-honored idea of "human dignity." And in the end, I do think that the disparagement was shameful. But for those who are concerned about the risk of excessive regulation, the concern is not entirely pointless or surprising. Certainly we should agree that agencies should not take qualitative factors as a license to do whatever they like.

In practice, however, the executive order's reference to unquantifiable factors is less original and a bit less important than it may seem. Ever since 1993, a governing executive order has authorized regulators to take account of both equity and distributive impacts. Both Democratic and Republican administrations have agreed that if a rule would impose especially serious hardship on poor people, or confer large benefits on them, regulators are allowed to take that hardship or those benefits into account.

But to date, the point has been more important in theory than in practice. Rules that make cars safer or more fuel-efficient have an assortment of effects, both good and bad, and those effects are felt by a wide range of people, rich and poor alike. The same is true of rules that make food safer. Rules that make the air cleaner will have broad consequences; they may create big health benefits for poor people, but it is not clear that environmental protection is especially or disproportionately good for those at the bottom of the economic ladder.[17] Workplace safety rules will mostly help those who are far from wealthy, but such rules may also impose costs on those very workers (if, for example, the result is to decrease employment or wages).

Assessment of distributional impacts raises an assortment of hard empirical issues. It is true that to the extent that rules increase prices, the harmful effects are especially bad for people without a lot of money. It is also true that if rules cost jobs, those who are not well-off will be particularly burdened. These issues deserve more attention. At OIRA, I asked members of the public to comment on the possibility that regulation will cost jobs, and we worked very hard to explore whether expensive rules would create jobs, sacrifice jobs, or do neither. If the best analysis suggested that a rule would eliminate a lot of jobs, I would have had real trouble with the rule, and a number of us would work together to reduce the risk that this would happen. Economists and others should be devoting careful attention to the relationship between expensive regulations and employment, especially in tough economic periods, when workers who lose their jobs may have a hard time finding another position.

President Obama's reference to human dignity is genuinely new, and dignity and related concepts have mattered in some important cases. Consider some examples:

- In 2009 the Centers for Disease Control eliminated the long-standing ban on entry of HIV-positive people into the United States. This was an extremely important decision, vindicating one of President Obama's promises in the 2008 campaign. Along with many others, I worked hard to make it happen. In supporting its decision, the CDC presented a lot of numbers in a detailed quantitative analysis of the expected benefits and costs, including economic benefits (for example, because more people would be able to enter the United States and to engage in economic activity) and health effects (some of them not so good, because we might be able to expect an increase, though a modest one, in infections as a result of the new entries). At the same time, the CDC emphasized that some of the most important benefits of the rule could not really be turned into monetary equivalents. "Although we are unable to quantify all of the benefits of this change in policy, we believe it will help reduce stigmatization of HIV-infected people; [and] bring family members together who had been barred from entry (thus strengthening families). . . . There are also ethical, humanitarian, distributional, and international benefits that are important to consider but difficult to quantify."[18] With explicit reference to these unquantifiable benefits, the CDC concluded that the benefits of the rule justified its costs.

- In 2010 the Equal Employment Opportunity Commission (EEOC) issued regulations implementing amendments to the Americans with Disabilities Act. The regulations strengthen the protection of those with physical and mental disabilities, forbidding certain forms of discrimination (including, for example, discrimination against those wrongly believed to have mental disorders, such as clinical depression) and requiring employers to accommodate people with disabilities (by, for example, giving people reasonable time off to get physical or mental therapy). In describing the benefits of the rule, the EEOC said that it "promotes inclusion and fairness in the workplace; combats second-class citizenship of individuals with disabilities; avoids humiliation and stigma; and promotes human dignity by enabling qualified individuals to participate in the workforce." [19] Here, then, is an explicit emphasis on values that are hard to monetize.

- Responding to a direction from Congress, the Department of Transportation proposed, for public comment, a new rule to increase rear visibility in cars and thus to reduce back-over deaths and injuries. The proposal, which would require rearview cameras to be placed in new cars, was expensive (over $2 billion annually). Those costs greatly exceeded the benefits that could be quantified (in terms of the prevention of deaths and injuries as well as property damage). But recall that protection of children raises special issues. Acknowledging this fact, the Department of Transportation stated, "[T]he quantitative analysis does not offer a full accounting. . . . [W]ell over 40 percent of the victims of backover crashes are very young children (under the age of five), with nearly their entire life ahead of them. . . . In addition, this regulation will, in many cases, reduce a qualitatively distinct risk, which is that of directly causing or contributing to the death or injury of one's own child." [20] Thus the Department emphasized a concern with equity, because many of the victims were children, as well as the heartbreaking and perhaps unique harm faced by those who inadvertently cause the relevant deaths and injuries.

- The Department of Justice issued a rule to reduce the incidence of prison rape. In explaining the effects of the rule, the Department described the purely monetary costs, which involve hundreds of millions of dollars in annual costs that state and local governments would have to spend on monitoring and training. The Department also described the benefits, which involve a significant reduction in the incidence of rape in prison. The Department did its best to specify that reduction—and even to say how reductions in rape could be turned into monetary equivalents. But it frankly acknowledged the limits of its effort, emphasizing that human dignity was involved and had to be taken into account: "[T]his analysis inevitably excludes benefits that are not monetizable, but still must be included in a cost-benefit analysis. These include the values of equity, human dignity, and fairness. Such non-quantifiable benefits will be received by victims who receive proper treatment after an assault. . . . [N]on-quantifiable benefits will accrue to society at large, by ensuring that inmates re-entering the community are less traumatized and better equipped to support their community."[21]

• As part of a regulation increasing building access for disabled people, the Department of Justice included a provision to protect wheelchair users by requiring new bathrooms to contain enough space for them. The cost of this provision was high. The Department acknowledged that "the monetized costs of these requirements substantially exceed the monetized benefits."[22] The Department's response to this concern is not exactly written in the plainest of language, but it is important and worth quoting at length:

> [T]he additional benefits that persons with disabilities will derive from greater safety, enhanced independence, and the avoidance of stigma and humiliation—benefits that the Department's economic model could not put in monetary terms—are, in the Department's experience and considered judgment, likely to be quite high. Wheelchair users, including veterans returning from our Nation's wars with disabilities, are taught to transfer onto toilets from the side. Side transfers are the safest, most efficient, and most independence-promoting way for wheelchair users to get onto the toilet. The opportunity to effect a side transfer will often obviate the need for a wheelchair user or individual with another type of mobility impairment to obtain the assistance of another person to engage in what is, for most people, among the most private of activities. . . . [I]t is important to recognize that the ADA [Americans with Disabilities Act] is intended to provide important benefits that are distributional and equitable in character. These water closet clearance provisions will

have non-monetized benefits that promote equal access and equal opportunity for individuals with disabilities.

In these cases, the protection of human dignity and related values have helped to inform the government's decision. Such factors will unquestionably matter in the future. This point raises a broader question: If we are really trying to play Regulatory Moneyball, how can we incorporate the nonquantifiable?

Dealing with the Nonquantifiable

Let's broaden the viewscreen a bit. It should be clear that nonquantifiable factors come in different (if sometimes overlapping) categories:

- The problem may involve *specifying the size of certain effects*. An agency may know that a rule will reduce the risk of a terrorist attack, but it may not be able to quantify the reduction and thus be unable to describe the benefits. This problem was especially challenging during the Bush administration, whose Department of Homeland Security issued a number of rules to protect against terrorism in the aftermath of the 9/11 attacks. DHS could not specify the benefits of those rules. I am told that OIRA struggled mightily with this challenge. In many cases, the direction of an effect is clear—we know that the rule will be helpful—but the magnitude is difficult or impossible to specify.

- The issue may involve *monetary equivalents*. The Department of Health and Human Services may know that a rule will promote personal privacy, by making electronic health records more secure. HHS may even know how many people and how many records will be affected. But it may not know how to turn these benefits into monetary equivalents. How much is an increase in privacy worth? Or the Environmental Protection Agency might know that a rule will have a beneficial effect on ecosystems and preserve a known number of a certain species of fish, but it might not find it easy to translate that effect into monetary equivalents.

- A rule may have significant beneficial or adverse *distributional effects on lower income groups*. Those effects may or may not themselves be quantifiable. Maybe the government knows exactly who will be affected and how much. Maybe the government is aware that poor people will be particularly affected, and helped or hurt, but maybe it is unable to say to what degree. Even when quantification of distributional effects is possible, they are not easily used as part of a standard analysis of costs and benefits.

- A rule might be designed to protect *human dignity*. As we have seen, it might reduce the incidence of rape or allow wheelchair-bound employees to have easier access to bathrooms. Or a harmful effect on human dignity may be an unintended cost of a rule. For example, a rule designed to protect homeland security might involve body searches or scans that some people consider to be an invasion of dignity or privacy.

- A rule might be designed to protect *fairness*. It might, for example, prohibit discrimination on the basis of sexual orientation with respect to certain government benefits, or it might ban sexual harassment.

- A rule might be designed to protect *equity*. It might, for example, prohibit insurance companies from refusing to issue health insurance to children with preexisting conditions, or it might eliminate annual or lifetime limits on health insurance in order to protect those facing serious and long-term problems (such as cancer or heart disease).

An effect might, of course, fall in more than one category. The line between "fairness" and "equity" is not simple or sharp; it depends on how we define these concepts. A rule may also have nonquantifiable effects that run counter to each other. A big increase in the level of the minimum wage may seem justified from the standpoint of fairness, but if it decreases employment it will probably hurt people who are already struggling.

How should these possibilities be treated? The first step is to promote accountability, and here simplicity is extremely important. When I was there, OIRA tried to do exactly that. We recommended that all significant regulations should be accompanied with, first, a simple table, placed prominently and offering a clear statement of both quantitative and qualitative benefits and costs of the proposed or final action, together with, second, a presentation of uncertainties and, third, similar information for reasonable alternatives to the proposed or final action.[23] A key advantage of this approach is that it promotes transparency for the public. If, for example, it is possible to quantify certain benefits (such as protection of water quality) but not to turn them into monetary equivalents, then the public should be made aware of that fact. At the same time, qualitative discussion of non-quantifiable benefits and costs should help both public officials and citizens to understand the goals of the regulation and how it might achieve those goals. When equity is an important goal of a rule—as it was in preventing insurance companies from denying insurance to children with preexisting conditions—we said exactly that.

In a related step, I required agencies to include, for complex or lengthy rules, a clear, simple executive summary, explaining what they were doing and why and offering a crisp account of costs and benefits, both quantitative and qualitative. This requirement was motivated by the fact that many rules are really long and complex, and it is hard for people to know what they are doing and why. Some exceed a thousand pages, including detailed tables on costs and benefits. A short executive summary can be extremely helpful to those both inside and outside government. It can also display, in an unmistakable way, the use of nonquantifiable values.

Even when agencies are transparent, it is not obvious whether and how they should proceed when important effects cannot be quantified. As we have seen, skeptics can plausibly ask, "Aren't agencies getting a blank check? Can't they exploit notions of equity and dignity to go in whatever direction they like best?" To answer these questions, many agencies have found it useful to engage in what is called *breakeven analysis*. Under this approach, agencies specify how high the unquantified or unmonetized benefits would have to be in order for the benefits to justify the costs.

Suppose, for example, that a regulation that protects water quality costs $175 million annually and that it also has significant effects in reducing pollution in rivers and streams. It is clear that the regulation would be justified if and only if those effects could reasonably be valued at $175 million or more. Imagine that the regulation would have large effects in cleaning up hundreds of thousands of streams, protecting recreational opportunities and precious ecological resources. In that case, there is a reasonable argument that the $175 million expenditure would be justified. But imagine, by contrast, that the rule would protect a small number of streams—say, two hundred—and that it would benefit them only modestly. In that event, an expenditure of $175 million is not easy to defend.

The general point is that once the nature and extent of the water quality benefits are understood, it might well be easy to see whether or not the benefits plausibly justify the costs, and if that question is difficult, at least it would be clear why it is difficult. The same technique can be applied in many areas, involving homeland security, privacy, and even dignity. Break-even analysis is an important tool, and it has a lot of value when quantification is speculative or impossible.

Let me end where I began. In sports, there has been a growing effort to downplay intuitions, anecdotes, dogmas, and impressions and to rely instead on evidence and data. System 2 is increasingly triumphing over System 1. With the help of statistical analysis, we are increasingly able to make projections about athletic performance—to see how much different players and different strategies are likely to contribute to winning. For regulatory choices, intuitions, anecdotes, dogmas, and impressions are also inadequate, and there is a pressing need for evidence and data. Recall that when people speak in a foreign language, they cease making errors that they make in their native tongue.

Cost-benefit analysis is a foreign language, and a pretty good one, It is also the closest thing we have to Regulatory Moneyball. Let's play.

8 ELIMINATING RED TAPE

What do you project that your personal expenses will be over the next year? If you are like most people, you will inevitably engage in some guesswork, and your estimate may turn out to be way off. Some of us struggle to project even a month out. The anticipated cost of a home construction project often ends up being far too low. The expense of a child's birthday party, not to mention a wedding, might run way over what you imagine. Public officials try really hard to get the numbers right, and they have both experience and expertise, but what is true for ordinary people can be true for officials as well. Undertaken in advance, projections of costs and benefits may rest on pretty speculative assumptions.

Government may not be able to specify the cost of a rule that would require reductions in air pollution or the benefits of a rule that would reduce risks of injuries in coal mines. Sometimes the most that can be done is to identify "ranges" for both benefits and costs, and those ranges can be fairly wide. Cost estimates of $200 million to $400 million are not unusual. Benefits estimates of 1,000 to 3,000 lives saved are not hard to find. In addition, the ranges themselves may be either too optimistic or too pessimistic. Costs may turn out to be far higher than anticipated; the same is true of benefits.

How concerned should we be about this? In light of those ranges of uncertainty, what are the prospects for Regulatory Moneyball?

Inconsistent Dogmas

As OIRA administrator, I was often told that regulators err in a predictable direction. The problem is that the people who told me that offered radically (and almost comically) inconsistent stories when making their point.

In the business community, not to mention conservative think tanks, most intelligent people seem to share a single view: government agencies are far too optimistic, even self-serving, about both benefits and costs. When I spoke on one occasion to a group of people engaged in small businesses, an executive asked me with complete exasperation, "How can we possibly trust cost-benefit analysis when agencies keep lowballing the costs?" Many conservatives told me (and continue to tell me) that agencies cook their numbers so as to make their rules look a lot better than they actually are. In their view, agencies are irredeemably self-interested; they want to justify their rules and so tweak or twist the numbers to provide that justification. In short, regulators cannot be trusted. Their policy preferences are driving their numbers, rather than vice versa, or so the story goes.

In the public interest community, and especially among environmentalists, most intelligent people hold precisely the opposite belief. When I was speaking on one occasion to a group of committed environmentalists, one of them asked me, with real frustration, "How can we rely on cost-benefit analysis, when the costs are always inflated?" Many progressives think that agencies underestimate the benefits and exaggerate the costs.

Time and again, environmentalists told me that the real benefits are far greater than agencies say they are and that the real costs are a lot lower. They pointed out that agencies have to depend on industry for cost estimates. (This is true; industries often have most of the relevant data, and government may have to rely on what industries tell it, at least for starters). This reliance, environmentalists contend, results in wild overstatements of what companies will actually pay after rules are placed on the books. To public interest groups, agency cost estimates are really industry scare tactics. In the real world, rules will impose only a small fraction of the projected costs, or so the story goes.

Both camps can cite apparently convincing examples. In the Obama administration, some proposed rules were withdrawn because agencies were ultimately convinced that the costs would be a lot higher than they expected. For example, the Occupational Safety and Health Administration withdrew a highly controversial rule designed to protect workers from excessive noise.[1] It did so in part on the ground that it appeared to have underestimated the costs.

On some occasions, other agencies have given unrealistically low estimates of the burdens imposed by paperwork and reporting requirements. Real people have to spend real time on those requirements,, even if they seem simple and easy to navigate to those who wrote them. I have already discussed efforts to reform FAFSA so as to increase the likelihood that students who need financial help will be able to attend college. But some specialists argue that we didn't go far enough, and that even now, the FAFSA form requires a lot more time and effort than the Department of Education projects.[2]

On the other hand, agencies have sometimes offered inflated estimates. The Clean Air Act requires companies to reduce acid rain. Originally the Environmental Protection Agency projected that this requirement would impose high costs, and industry contended that the costs would actually be much higher than the EPA projected. It turned out that the costs were a lot lower.[3] In many cases industries learn a great deal over time. The expense of a requirement today may be much higher than the expense of the same requirement tomorrow, in part because of cost-reducing innovation spurred by the regulation itself. Focusing on just this point, the Department of Energy has been rethinking its cost projections for rules requiring energy efficiency.[4] In its view, a "learning curve" analysis is needed to get the right numbers. Because industry learns how to do things more efficiently, innovation often drives anticipated costs way down.

Without a doubt, those with an incentive to oppose rules will tend to overstate the costs and perhaps even claim that if rules are finalized, the sky will fall. I saw such overstatements at least one a month. I also saw professional civil servants at agencies, working with OIRA and other offices within the government, trying to generate the right numbers. But if industry overstates costs, regulators may not have enough information to make a correction.

While the polarized positions divide most often on costs, benefits matter too. Do government agencies overstate or underestimate them? Industry representatives argue that benefits are wildly exaggerated and highly speculative. Public interest groups argue that benefits are underestimated, especially in light of the fact that many are hard to quantify and are based on evolving scientific information.

Data

Whether agencies systematically understate or overstate benefits and costs is an empirical question. In principle, the answer to that question is knowable. Researchers have started to try to answer it. Current findings do not support either of the polar positions. It turns out that both industry and the public interest community have a great deal of confidence in evidence-free dogmas.

A careful study by the economist Winston Harrington, building on previous work, explores sixty-one rules for which benefit-cost ratios could be compared before and after the fact.[5] Harrington found no systematic bias. Agencies overestimated benefits and costs with about equal frequency. Specifically, in sixteen of the sixty-one cases, the ratios were found to be pretty accurate. In twenty-four cases, the ratio was better, not worse, than the agency had anticipated. In twenty-one cases, the ratio was worse than anticipated. Harrington's general conclusion is that while both costs and benefits tend to be lower than estimated, no bias can be found in estimates of benefit-cost ratios.

Harrington's study focuses on benefit-cost ratios, and it does not specify the degree to which benefits and costs were underestimated or overestimated. Other studies explore exactly that question. One analyzed twenty-five environmental and occupational safety regulations for which retrospective estimates could be found. The basic conclusion: a modest tendency to overestimate costs (a finding in support of the progressive view). For twelve rules, agencies overestimated costs; they estimated costs accurately for five; they underestimated for two; and the costs were indeterminate for six.[6]

In 2005, the Office of Management and Budget, and in particular the OIRA staff, provided an overview of many retrospective analyses based on an examination of forty-seven case studies.[7] There were three key conclusions. First, agencies were far more likely to overestimate benefits than to underestimate them.[8] More particularly, agencies overestimated benefits

40 percent of the time, whereas they underestimated benefits only 2 percent of the time. Second, agencies tended to overestimate the cost-benefit ratio, and thus to be a bit too optimistic about the consequences of their rules. Agency estimates were accurate 23 percent of the time, while the ratio was overestimated 47 percent of the time and underestimated 30 percent of the time. Third, agencies were slightly more likely to overestimate than to underestimate costs. Agencies were accurate 26 percent of the time, overestimated costs 34 percent of the time, and underestimated costs 26 percent of the time.

The upshot? Neither of the competing dogmas can be supported by the evidence. Agencies make a lot of mistakes, but there does not appear to be a systematic bias in one or another direction.

That is useful and important to know. But it is even more important to acknowledge that we need to know a lot more than we now do. The existing studies cover only a very small fraction of rules on the books. Much more can and should be done to compare prospective estimates with what actually happens in the world. We certainly know that some rules work less well than anticipated and that others work much better. Armed with an understanding of how rules are working in fact, we should be in a much better position to decide how to proceed—and in many cases, to streamline, improve, and even eliminate existing requirements.

The Regulatory Lookback

A sensible regulatory system must go beyond the competing dogmas. It should track reality. A key question is whether particular rules should be revised, simplified, strengthened, or eliminated in light of what we learn about what those rules are actually doing. It is an astonishing fact that until very recently there has been no real effort to gather, let alone act on, that information. Such an effort might well help agencies to expand their most successful programs, and also to eliminate a lot of pointless red tape.

A special problem, and one that makes the project of simplification all the more imperative, is that agencies impose high cumulative burdens on the private sector. Requirements may be sensible taken individually, but taken as a whole, they might be redundant, inconsistent, overlapping, and immensely frustrating, even crazy-making (to use the technical term). In fact the problem of cumulative burdens may have been the most common complaint that I heard during my time in government. Why, people asked me, can't agencies coordinate with one another, or simplify their own over-lapping requirements, or work together with state and local government, so that we don't have to do the same thing twice, or five times, or ten times?

Some business groups made that complaint while focusing particularly on the need for international regulatory cooperation. They objected that just as it makes no sense to have to meet redundant requirements from the federal government and California and Georgia and New York, it is also senseless for companies to have to absorb and meet complex and overlapping requirements from the United States, Canada, Mexico, the United Kingdom, and France. If nations do not really disagree about facts or values, shouldn't they attempt to harmonize their requirements, if only to promote trade and growth? One representative of a large business organization went so far as to say to me, early on, that while domestic regulation from the Obama administration was a concern, the problem of unnecessary inter-national differences was a much larger one, and that if we could do something to reduce that problem, we would make a major contribution. We took these concerns very seriously.

In January 2011, focusing directly on the issue of simplification, Presi-dent Obama called for a government-wide "retrospective analysis" of existing rules and required agencies to produce, in short order, preliminary plans for such analysis. Motivated above all by the goal of streamlining the regulatory system, the requirement had a particular origin. Everyone knows that during the first term of the Obama administration, Congress enacted and the president signed the Affordable Care Act, which amounted to the most important social legislation since the 1960s. Also during the first term, Congress enacted and the president signed the Dodd-Frank Wall Street Reform and Consumer Protection Act, which amounted to the most important financial legislation since the 1930s. And while we focused on net benefits and tried to keep costs down, we also issued a number of im-portant rules to protect public safety, health, and the environment. Some of those rules were expensive.

At the same time that we moved forward in these ways, we believed that in a difficult economic period, there was a pressing need to eliminate unjustified requirements and to reassess rules on the books. Doing so, we knew, would be a significant step toward making the whole system simpler. We also heard this suggestion, loud and clear, from businesses both large and small. Some expensive rules, even if well-motivated when issued, probably never made a whole lot of sense. Some old rules, sensible when issued, do not make sense today. Changed circumstances can make rules ripe for reassessment and trimming, or maybe deletion. Perhaps new technologies make such rules obsolete. Maybe there is a problem of redundancy and overlap. Maybe states are also imposing requirements, and federal regulations are no longer needed. Maybe the private market is now working plenty well enough, and old regulations no longer have a point.

Retrospective analysis, measuring the actual effects of current rules, is a good way of nudging government. Consider this suggestion from the MIT economist Michael Greenstone, former chief economist at the Council of Economic Advisers: "The single greatest problem with the current system is that most regulations are subject to a cost-benefit analysis only in advance of their implementation. This is the point when the least is known and any analysis must rest on many unverifiable and potentially controversial assumptions."[9]

By contrast, retrospective analysis can help show what actually works and what does not. In the process, it can promote the repeal or streamlining of less effective rules and the strengthening or expansion of those that turn out to do more good than harm. In an important paper, which greatly influenced my thinking, Greenstone urges a series of ambitious reforms designed to promote a culture of experimentation and evaluation.[10] These reforms include an effort to ensure that regulations are written and implemented so as to facilitate reliable evaluation.

As it happens, Greenstone was a colleague of mine when he worked in the Council of Economic Advisers in 2009. He also became a good friend. We had a lot of discussions about the need for retrospective analysis. He emphasized that while regulators typically act with the best of motivations, they often don't know enough to be certain about either the benefits or the costs. Others have raised the possibility that (as happens in industry and advocacy groups of every stripe) technical people within a government agency might sometimes be seeking, even if unconsciously, to support the policy views of the agency's leadership.

In my own experience—and I know that Greenstone agrees—agencies are highly professional, and they work hard to get the analysis right. Those who do the analysis are civil servants, not political appointees. In addition, there are many checks on what they do. If an agency's estimates are doubtful, OIRA will raise questions, as will the Council of Economic Advisers, the National Economic Council, the Office of Scientific and Technology Policy, and others. On numerous occasions, the agency's draft analysis of costs and benefits gets altered because of this process of close scrutiny. And if an agency proposes a rule with an implausible or doubtful analysis, members of the public will raise questions, and those questions will get a serious hearing. Critics often neglect these safeguards, which often produce big changes in the agency's original analysis. I saw many such cases.

But Greenstone's central point remains. When agencies issue rules, they have to speculate about benefits and costs. After rules are in place, they should test those speculations, and they should use what they learn when revisiting a regulation or issuing a new one. This is a central point for the future of regulatory reform. Indeed, it is one of the most important steps imaginable, not least because it can reduce cumulative burdens and promote the goal of simplification.

The Lookback in Action

The first step was the production of preliminary plans for retrospective review, which the president required within 120 days. This was a tight timeline, especially considering the fact that public officials have a lot of things to do. Many agencies began by asking for suggestions from the public. For example, the Environmental Protection Agency and the Departments of Commerce, Transportation, the Interior, Homeland Security, State, and the Treasury posted notices in the Federal Register, asking for ideas about how the process should work and which rules should be streamlined or repealed. Several agencies held public meetings nationwide.[11]

In the early days, I encountered a lot of skepticism about the president's initiative, certainly outside government. Critics in the business community contended that this was a symbolic exercise that was unlikely to produce anything real. Those in the public interest community agreed. They added that the idea of a regulatory lookback was a distraction from what was important, which was to look forward by issuing long-overdue public safeguards. But within the government itself, President Obama's clear commitment to the project, expressed in his 2011 State of the Union Address and in highly publicized remarks to the US Chamber of Commerce, had a big impact. Throughout the federal government, agencies were energized. A number of officials had long wanted to engage in an initiative of this sort, but time is limited and officials have to set priorities. Now the president himself had directed them to act, and the lookback requirement gave real space to officials who were already excited about the basic idea. For officials who had not thought about it, the requirement spurred real creativity. In the end, every agency met the president's deadline. (True, I had to cajole one or two to make sure that they delivered precisely on time.)

In May 2011, the agencies released their preliminary plans, identifying hundreds of reforms, many of which would streamline or delete regulatory requirements. Recognizing the importance of public participation, every agency made these plans publicly available and requested comments and suggestions.[12] I issued a guidance document, binding on agencies and directing them to address the comments they received and to make their plans final within eighty days.

Twenty-six such plans were issued in August 2011. They included over 580 initiatives, filling more than eight hundred pages. The initiatives promise billions of dollars of savings and tens of millions of hours of reductions in annual paperwork and reporting requirements.[13] Within a short period, over a hundred of the initiatives were finalized or formally proposed to the public.

One of these enjoyed short-term fame, not only because it eliminated unnecessary costs but also because it had the dubious honor of being the most twittered moment of the 2012 State of the Union Address. It took a village, but I share the responsibility for that particular honor.

Since the 1970s, milk had been defined by law as an "oil" and potentially subject to costly rules designed to prevent oil spills. This was silly. While oil spills can be quite bad for the environment, milk spills are pretty innocuous, and they really shouldn't be subject to the same restrictions. (As one skeptic said, people don't confuse "Got Milk?" with "Got Oil?") The agricultural community, including many small businesses, had long asked

EPA to repeal these restrictions. As a key part of its retrospective review plan, EPA concluded that the regulatory requirements placed unjustifiable burdens on dairy farmers, and it issued a final rule to exempt them. The projected five-year savings are over $700 million.[14]

Inside the government we liked to say, a bit sheepishly (and maybe with a trace of self-loathing), that this deregulatory initiative gave new meaning to the phrase "Don't cry over spilled milk." The president made a joke in this vein in his State of the Union Address. People groaned a lot—hence the twittering.

Here are just a few other examples, none of which easily gives rise to any kind of joke, but each of which is having a real impact:

- The Department of Health and Human Services finalized several rules to remove unnecessary regulatory and reporting requirements previously imposed on hospitals and other health care providers, thus saving about $5 billion over the next five years.[15] These streamlining initiatives were received with great enthusiasm by nurses and doctors, who had long urged the government to eliminate pointless red tape.

- HHS finalized a rule to eliminate certain restrictions on the use of telemedicine, particularly helping hospitals in rural areas. This rule is a big benefit to patients as well as doctors. Because it removes an anachronistic restriction, people in rural areas can now get quality care with the aid of computers and telephones. The five-year savings are $67 million, and the dollar figure understates the benefits that doctors and patients are receiving.

- The Department of Labor finalized a rule to harmonize hazard warnings for workers with those of other nations, producing savings in excess of $2.5 billion over the next five years, most of it for employers.[16] The basic idea is that many employers do business in more than one nation, and if they have to alter their hazard warnings whenever they cross national borders, they will incur pointless costs. (Recall the importance of international regulatory cooperation.) A big advantage of this rule is that it promotes trade and exports. As a special bonus, the new warnings are simpler and easier to understand, and lives are expected to be saved as a result.

- The Department of Transportation finalized a rule to eliminate unnecessary regulation of the railroad industry, saving up to $340 million and avoiding the risk that regulatory costs will be passed on to consumers.[17]

- The Occupational Safety and Health Administration issued a final rule to remove over 1.9 million annual hours of redundant reporting burdens imposed on employers, thus saving more than $40 million in annual costs.[18] When I talked to members of the business community, this reform seemed to be the biggest winner—not because it has a massive economic impact but because OSHA is not famous for eliminating regulatory burdens.

- EPA finalized a rule to eliminate the requirement, imposed in some states, that gas stations place air pollution controls on the nozzles that people use to put gas into their tanks. Because modern cars and trucks already have effective air pollution control technologies, the required controls were redundant and could be eliminated without increasing pollution. The anticipated five-year savings are about $450 million.[19]

- The Departments of Commerce and State undertook a series of steps to eliminate barriers to exports, including duplicative and unnecessary regulatory requirements, thus reducing the cumulative burden and uncertainty faced by American companies and their trading partners.[20]

Just a few of these initiatives, already finalized or formally proposed to the public, will produce savings of more than $10 billion over the next five years. This figure is a small fraction of the eventual savings. Many of the lookback initiatives also provide benefits that are hard to monetize but likely to be significant. For example, we can't easily quantify the economic benefits, including the jobs created, of reducing restrictions on exports and simplifying the requirements imposed on those who do business across national borders. Nonetheless, those benefits are expected to be high.

Toward a Culture of Retrospective Analysis

After the plans were finalized, we did a great deal to try to create a culture of retrospective analysis rather than just a onetime endeavor. In 2012 the president issued an executive order with three key components. First, agencies are required to reach out to the public, on a continuing basis, to solicit ideas about reforms. Second, agencies must give priority to reforms that would have a significant impact—for example, those with big economic savings. New initiatives should make a real difference; they should not be symbolic measures or mere updating. Third, and perhaps most important, agencies have to report on their progress to OIRA and to the public on a continuing basis. This final step is designed to promote accountability—to ensure that if agencies are not doing much, the public will be able to see that and provide a corrective. Here, as elsewhere, we attempted to enlist sunlight as a check on drift and inaction. All of these steps can be understood as a further effort to establish a kind of choice architecture for the federal government itself.

Also in 2012, the president issued an executive order designed to reduce red tape by promoting international regulatory cooperation.[21] The executive order explicitly links the lookback to such cooperation, calling for initiatives that will reduce costs and simplify the system by eliminating unnecessary disparities across nations. There is a lot more to do in this area, removing barriers to growth and trade. Through the work of the Regulatory Cooperation Council that I cochaired, Canada and the United States have been working productively together to do exactly that,[22] and we made significant progress with Mexico too.[23] Further steps, with considerable promise, might well involve Europe, which should be engaging in a lookback of its own.

As part of the general simplification enterprise, I issued a memorandum on cumulative effects, directing agencies to take steps to reduce redundant and inconsistent requirements, in part by engaging with the private sector to explore potential interactions among rules under consideration, and also between those rules and rules now on the books.[24] International regulatory cooperation and reduction of cumulative burdens remain high priorities and major challenges for the future. We should expect bipartisan consensus on that point.

As an additional step, I directed agencies to undertake significant new initiatives to eliminate reporting and paperwork burdens. I called for simplified applications, short-form options, exemptions or streamlining for small businesses, electronic filing, and elimination of unnecessary requirements.[25] More specifically, I directed the agencies that now impose the highest paperwork burdens to identify at least one initiative, or combination of initiatives, that would eliminate two million hours or more in annual reporting burdens. I also directed all agencies to identify at least one initiative, or combination of initiatives, that would eliminate at least 50,000 hours in annual burdens. In the fullness of time, I expect to see major results from these requirements, very possibly in excess of the targets.

As it happens, the Department of the Treasury and the Internal Revenue Service in particular are responsible for well over 80 percent of the total annual paperwork burden placed on the American people. As many taxpayers reminded me while I was at OIRA, there are many opportunities here for making things easier and less frustrating. Often working with OIRA, the IRS has already done a great deal to simplify its forms—for example, with Form 1040 EZ and with the growth of electronic filing.[26] Other "EZ" forms are now available and in use, and they are greatly easing people's burdens. The Plain Writing Act of 2010, with which I was heavily involved, should help to promote clarity, because it is designed to ensure that when government communicates with citizens, it does so in a way that people can easily understand.[27]

I am confident that everyone will agree that far more should be done to make the tax system easier to navigate. Unfortunately, congressional requirements impose limits on the IRS's ability to increase simplification; a number of imaginable steps, sought by many taxpayers, would be inconsistent with the law as it now stands. I am not the first to say that we could really use a congressional lookback, focused in particular on the tax system and putting a high priority on simplification. But even within the constraints of the law, the IRS could do a lot more to achieve that goal, and my memorandum was meant to spur it to do so.

The lookback emphasized, and will continue to emphasize, the streamlining of regulations and reducing burdens and costs. In a 2012 interview with the *Des Moines Register*, outlining his highest priorities for his second term, President Obama made some brief remarks that deserve to be highlighted: "I've expressed a deep desire and taken executive action to weed out regulations that aren't contributing to the health and public safety of our people. And we've made a commitment to look back and see if there are regulations out there that aren't working, then let's get rid of them and see if we can clear out some of the underbrush on that. Again, that's something that should be nonideological."[28]

As these remarks suggest, the lookback has been focused, above all, on "weeding out," getting rid of rules that are not working and clearing out the "underbrush." The president's 2011 executive order has the same emphasis, but it also acknowledges that agencies may "expand" their regulations if retrospective analysis supports that step. We can easily imagine why this might be so—and why a careful lookback could justify expansion as well as elimination of rules. An agency might learn that a rule costs a lot less than was anticipated and that more stringency is required by cost-benefit analysis. Or an agency might learn that with new technologies—electronic rather than paper reporting, for example—compliance is cheap and easy, and an exemption of (say) small businesses is no longer warranted. Or an agency might learn that a rule really is working well, but that its coverage is too narrow, and more people should be subject to it.

All of these points are right and even important, but in the lookback process we did not emphasize them, and I do not expect that they will be the emphasis in the future. The reason is that in the Obama administration agencies were generally working diligently to fill regulatory gaps and to build on what was working. They did not need the lookback to engage in that endeavor. Gap-filling is exceedingly important, but for this initiative, we found it best to focus on streamlining and burden reduction, not on gap-filling. While expansion is not off the table, simplification has been and will continue to be the principal concern.

Experiments and Trials

To get the facts right, we need to engage in far more evaluation and experimentation. This is not a point about retrospective review, but it is closely related. It is a central part of the future of reform not only of regulation but of policymaking in general.

In the past decade there has been growing interest in the use of randomized controlled trials as a means of learning the effects of policy initiatives.[29] In medicine, of course, people rely on such trials to see if a drug is really safe and effective. For drugs, it wouldn't make a lot of sense simply to guess, to rely on informed hunches, or even to make simple "before and after" assessments. Suppose that we learn that people who use a certain asthma medicine do better after taking the medicine than before. If so, we know a lot—but we don't know nearly enough. The risk with before-and-after assessments is that they may not control for confounding variables. Maybe people are doing better because of some change in the environment that is not adequately understood by those who are making the assessment.

In the medical domain, the beauty of randomized controlled experiments is that they have the potential to provide a clear sense of the actual effects of the intervention. The MIT economist Esther Duflo, along with several others, has pioneered the use of randomized controlled trials for purposes of policy evaluation. Duflo has shown that in many cases, small measures, even nudges, can have big effects, especially in helping poor people.[30]

In the regulatory area, the use of such trials remains in a preliminary state. Analysis of costs and benefits is rarely informed by them. But it is easy to imagine serious evaluations. Consider a few examples:

- Would states really save lives by banning use of cell phones while driving? This is a disputed question. Laboratory experiments, showing that people's reaction times slow down when they are distracted, strongly suggest that the answer is yes, and indeed that driving while talking on a phone is a bit like driving while drunk, producing a fourfold increase in relative crash risk.[31] But maybe those experiments are an unreliable guide to the real world. We could test whether a ban on cell phone use would have major effects on safety by comparing similarly situated localities, one with such a ban and one without. Or we could test whether accidents increase in periods in which cell phone use goes up—for example, when rates decrease after 9 p.m.[32]

- What are the effects of different methods of increasing rear visibility in cars? If cameras are placed in the dashboard, do accidents drop? How much, and compared with what? Do improved mirrors have an effect? What about sonar devices, making beeping noises? Do they work as well as cameras?

- As I have previously noted, we need to evaluate different disclosure requirements. We might test whether different fuel economy labels have different effects on similarly situated consumers. Does one label produce different choices? How different? If labels draw attention to annual fuel costs, are people affected? Do people care about environmental factors? How much? The same kinds of questions might be asked about disclosure requirements for credit cards, mortgages, cell phones, and school loans.

In important areas, experimentation might take the form of advance testing of regulatory alternatives through randomized controlled trials. A movement in this direction would have major advantages over current approaches, such as focus groups, which are often highly artificial and which sometimes test what people like rather than what they would actually do. People might love a certain fuel economy sticker or the Food Pyramid (okay, few people love that), but it might not be helpful, and it might not lead to informed choices. A presentation might be pleasing without having much of an effect on what people understand and do.

If a randomized trial is not feasible, we might be able to design experiments that replicate actual behavior by asking people concrete questions about what they would do if provided with certain information or if given a range of options. As I have noted, the current fuel economy label was based on tests of this kind. But such experiments are second-best. Randomized controlled trials deserve pride of place.

Of course there are constraints—involving not merely law but also resources and feasibility—in using randomized controlled trials in the regulatory context. But in some cases, they would be both appropriate and useful. The agencies' retrospective review plans show an unambiguous commitment to moving in this direction. The Department of Treasury states that it will work to "develop and incorporate experimental designs into retrospective analysis, when appropriate."[33] The Department of Labor states that it "is contemplating how to incorporate the use of experimental designs to determine the impact of various regulations."[34] The Department of Interior states that it will consider the use of "experimental or quasi-experimental designs, including randomized controlled trials."[35] We should expect far more progress in the future.

For the regulatory lookback, we made an ambitious start. But there's a lot more to be done. What is needed is a genuine culture of retrospective analysis, in which agencies stand ready and willing to improve and simplify rules completed decades ago, or years ago, or months ago, or even weeks ago. Well-functioning companies are flexible and adaptive. They learn in real time. The same should be true of government.

9 THE NANNY STATE?

Suppose that you are applying to renew your driver's license. You are at the Department of Motor Vehicles, and you are having a pretty bad time. Actually, you are completely miserable. The local officials have asked you for three documents to prove your identity and three more to prove your residence. The six documents cannot overlap. You have to fill out two sets of forms, one of which is eighteen pages in length. The type is really small. You can't remember the answers to some of the questions, which ask about your parking tickets over the past three years. There are questions about your parents and your children. A false answer is a criminal offense. No one is willing to help you.

The nightmarish (and maybe not entirely unfamiliar?) example reminds us why, in countless domains, no one objects to greater simplicity. In fact many states have taken major steps to make it easier to renew your driver's license. In some states, you fill out a quick electronic application, and then (amazing!) the license comes right away by mail. For anyone renewing a license, improved choice architecture, eliminating unnecessary burdens and complexity, is welcome. What is true for the Department of Motor Vehicles is true for many government agencies, which can function far more effectively by streamlining their requirements. Choice architecture affects outcomes, but it need not be in any sense paternalistic. If the Internal Revenue Service makes it easier for you to fill out your tax return, life is a bit better, and paternalism is not involved.

Nonetheless, some forms of choice architecture, and some nudges, unquestionably count as paternalistic. Some people fear that nudges are both manipulative and invisible, and hence especially insidious. They are not comforted by the fact that nudges preserve choice, seeing the preservation of choice as an inadequate safeguard, especially in light of all we now know about the cognitive difficulties and biases explored here.

Consider, in this light, Mayor Michael Bloomberg's highly controversial decision in 2012, approved by the New York City Board of Public Health, to ban the sale (in certain places) of sodas in containers of more than sixteen ounces. Mayor Bloomberg seeks to reduce obesity, and he believes that the ban will help to achieve that result. But some people choose drinks in large containers, and Mayor Bloomberg's initiative does not allow that choice. Much of the intensely negative reaction to his initiative stems from the view that it is paternalistic and unacceptable for that reason. Why, critics asked and sometimes raged, should Mayor Bloomberg decide on the size of soft drink containers? Vitriolic reactions, including a Center for Consumer Freedom advertisement depicting Mayor Bloomberg in a nanny outfit, were a predictable result.

But self-interested industries were not the only source of criticism. Consider these revealing comments from the comedian Jon Stewart: "No! . . . I love this idea you have of banning sodas larger than sixteen ounces. It combines the draconian government overreach people love with the probable lack of results they expect."[1] With these remarks, Stewart is capturing a pervasive and general skepticism about paternalism in general and nudges in particular. If we share that skepticism, we might think that simplification is fine but that nudges that try to influence people's choices aren't. At its most extreme, that skepticism informed Glenn Beck's charge that I was "the most evil man, the most dangerous man in America." That claim does seem a bit much. (I might be biased, but still.) Nonetheless, there are convincing objections to many kinds of paternalism, and so it is important to engage the critics of paternalism in general and nudging in particular. Americans seem particularly skeptical about paternalism, and while the skepticism is sometimes excessive, it is an exceedingly valuable part of a culture that prizes liberty.

Paternalism comes in many shapes and sizes, and we need to offer a working definition. What seems to unify paternalistic approaches, however diverse, is that *government does not believe that people's choices will promote their welfare, and it is taking steps to influence or alter people's choices for their own good.* When a government is trying to prevent harm to others—for example, when it regulates polluters to protect public health—it is not acting paternalistically. Choice architecture is paternalistic if it is attempting to protect choosers from themselves.

We should immediately distinguish between paternalism about means and paternalism about ends. To appreciate the distinction, consider the GPS in your car (or smartphone). A GPS provides information about how to get from one place to another; people can ignore what the GPS says and try their own route, but if they do so, there is a serious risk that they will get lost. *Means paternalists* build on the GPS example. Suppose that most people want to save money by making a sensible trade-off between a car's up-front costs and the fuel costs incurred over the life of that car—but they often fail to do so. Means paternalists would steer them in the direction of considering all relevant costs at the time of purchase. *Ends paternalists* have more ambitious goals. They might think, for example, that chastity or living a long, healthy life is what is most important, and that even if you disagree, they should steer you toward chastity or longevity. Nudgers are focused on means paternalism; they are reluctant to question people's ends.

To get clearer on underlying concepts, we need to specify the set of tools that a paternalistic government might use. Consider some possibilities:

1. Government says that no one may smoke cigarettes and that the sanction for smoking cigarettes is a criminal penalty of $200.
2. Government says that no one may smoke cigarettes and that the sanction for smoking cigarettes is a criminal penalty of one cent.
3. Government says that no one may smoke cigarettes and that the sanction for smoking cigarettes is a civil fine of $200.
4. Government says that no one may smoke cigarettes and that the sanction for smoking is a civil fine of one cent.
5. Government doesn't say that people may not smoke cigarettes, but it imposes a tax on cigarette purchases of sixty cents per pack.
6. Government doesn't say that people may not smoke cigarettes, but it creates a program that provides a financial subsidy of $500 to smokers who quit for six months.

7. Government doesn't say that people may not smoke cigarettes, but it engages in a vivid, frightening advertising campaign, emphasizing the dangers of smoking.

8. Government doesn't say that people may not smoke cigarettes, but it requires packages to contain vivid, frightening images, emphasizing the dangers of smoking.

9. Government doesn't say that people may not smoke cigarettes, but it engages in a public education campaign designed to make smoking seem deviant, or antisocial, or uncool.

10. Government doesn't say that people may not smoke cigarettes, but it engages in a truthful, fact-filled educational campaign, disclosing the dangers of smoking.

11. Government doesn't say that people may not smoke cigarettes, but it requires packages to provide truthful information, disclosing the dangers of smoking.

12. Government doesn't say that people may not smoke cigarettes, but it requires those who sell cigarettes to place them in an inconspicuous place so that people will not happen across them and must affirmatively ask for them.

13. Government doesn't say that people may not smoke cigarettes, but it requires cigarettes to be sold in small containers, each having no more than ten cigarettes. (As of now, cigarette packs usually have twenty cigarettes.)

If we look into the paternalist's toolbox, the first thing we should acknowledge is that these cases are not all the same. Some forms of paternalism are *hard*, in the sense that they impose material costs on people's choices. For example, a jail sentence or a fine counts as a form of hard paternalism. Of course, there is a continuum here, because severe sanctions will influence choices more than lenient ones will, and we might not think of very small sanctions (say, a nominal fine) as particularly hard.[2] Other forms of paternalism are *soft*, in the sense that they do not impose material costs but nonetheless affect what people choose. Decisions to require graphic warnings and to use location to discourage people from making certain choices count as forms of soft paternalism. Nudges represent soft paternalism, because they do not impose material costs on people's choices. Approaches that impose light sanctions, or that you can get around at a low cost, are not nudges, because material costs are imposed—but they are not exactly aggressive forms of paternalism, and if the sanctions are very low, the approaches are certainly nudge-like.

Which of the thirteen approaches are paternalistic at all? Approaches 1 through 5, imposing civil and criminal penalties, clearly count as forms of paternalism, and hard forms at that, though as the sanction gets small, they are not exactly aggressive. Approach 6 is harder to characterize. Is it paternalistic to subsidize behavior? Does paternalism include not merely penalties but also subsidies? What about selective subsides, as in, for example, a decision to provide food stamps for almost everything, but not for soda or chocolate bars? (In 2011 Mayor Bloomberg petitioned the Department of Agriculture for permission to do something like that; the Department denied the petition.)

It is tempting to insist that subsidizing behavior doesn't count as paternalism. After all, someone could forgo the subsidy and buy the cigarettes (or soda, or chocolate) anyway. But I think that this answer is unhelpful and a bit of a dodge. Insofar as a subsidy is designed to influence people's choices in order to promote their own welfare, it should be counted as paternalism, whether or not of an unobjectionable kind. And because a subsidy imposes material incentives, it is a hard form as well. Of course, it would be possible to think that a subsidy, even if paternalistic, is acceptable, whereas any form of fine or punishment is not.

By contrast, disclosure of truthful information—a primary kind of nudge—is not ordinarily understood as paternalistic. Why? The answer is that disclosure requirements are meant to inform, not to displace, people's understanding of which choices will promote their welfare. But we have to be careful here. In requiring disclosure, government may not be able to avoid at least a little paternalism. We have seen that how people will respond depends on how information is disclosed—how it is framed—and any disclosure requirement will inevitably include a certain kind of framing. And what, exactly, does government choose to require people to disclose? For cars, government requires disclosure of fuel economy but not of speed, acceleration, or coolness. The very emphasis on fuel economy, rather than on other features, will affect people's choices. The example suggests that we may dispute whether a particular disclosure requirement is simply inform-ing choices, or whether it is doing so selectively in order to encourage cer-tain preferred outcomes. Some forms of disclosure can certainly fall within the category of soft paternalism.

What about approaches 7 and 8, involving the use of vivid, frightening images? We have seen that psychic costs, no less than material costs, can alter behavior. Some people might think that efforts to frighten people, and going beyond mere disclosure of facts and also grabbing the attention of their System 1, must be taken as a form of soft paternalism. That view is certainly reasonable.

Approaches 12 and 13 also involve forms of soft paternalism. If officials put a product in an inconspicuous place, and if their goal is to discourage its purchase, they are steering people in a certain direction because they distrust people's own judgments about what would promote their welfare. No monetary penalty is involved, but time and effort must be expended to find the affected goods. And if government requires a product to be sold in small containers so that people will consume less of it, it is behaving pa-ternalistically insofar as it is making it harder for them to make the choices they prefer.

I have noted that it would be possible to insist that we should have a sim-pler government and at the same time to rule paternalism out of bounds. In my view, however, this position is indefensible, a form of dogmatism, even chest-thumping, masquerading as tough-mindedness. Nonetheless, the ob-jections to paternalism have a lot of force, and they should be treated with respect.

Problems with Paternalism

The first objection to paternalism has to do with people's welfare. The sec-ond involves people's autonomy.

Suppose that we care about human welfare, understood broadly to cap-ture how well people's lives are going. Suppose that we believe that people's lives should go as well as possible. People might really enjoy running, sleep-ing, having sex, singing, jumping, smoking, drinking, gambling, or (over) eating. They might have their own views about how, exactly, to go about enjoying those activities. So long as they are not harming others, aren't their own judgments the best guide to what will make their lives go well? A central objection, applicable to any kind of paternalism, is that errors are more likely to come from public officials than from individuals. Such officials lack the information that individuals have.

It should go without saying that human beings are highly diverse in terms of their tastes and values. With respect to diet, savings, exercise, credit cards, mortgages, cell phones, health care, computers, and much more, different people have different desires and circumstances, and it is reasonable for them to trade off relevant values in different ways. Why influence or put pressure on their choices? The simple fact of human diversity suggests that if government nudges in the direction of a certain outcome, and if it departs from people's own sense of what is best, the welfare of some people might be reduced rather than increased.

We have seen that people err and that their mistakes can impair their welfare. But mistakes can be instructive. Life is a movie, not a snapshot. On one view, government should not short-circuit the valuable process of learning by doing. If people make mistakes about diets, drinks, love, or investments, they can obtain valuable lessons, and those lessons can make their lives much better.

Public officials also have their own biases and motivations. Perhaps they are under the sway of powerful interest groups. To be sure, my own experience suggests that this concern is often overstated, at least within the executive branch. Officials try to do the right thing. But no one can deny that at some times and places, official judgments can be distorted by the pressures imposed by powerful interests. And even if they are well-motivated, officials are human and hardly immune to the kinds of biases that affect ordinary people. They too have a System 1.

There is a final point. In a market economy, companies compete with one another, and people are free to choose among a wide range of options. If a refrigerator isn't great, and if it costs a lot of money to operate, people will not keep buying it. As a result, companies will produce better refrigerators. Some consumers may be fooled or tricked, but in the long run free competition and open markets will provide a solution. On this view, paternalism presents a major risk, because it may freeze the process of competition. Even if officials are armed with knowledge of behavioral market failures, and even if they are public-spirited, they will (the objection goes) do far worse than free markets.

If these concerns are put together, the central problem with paternalism is that it may, in the end, make people's lives worse, not better.[3] Sure, soft paternalism allows for greater flexibility, and that is a strong point in its favor—but all of these points might be brought to bear against paternalism of any kind.

Nudges, Increasing Human Welfare

These objections have a lot of force. But even if we are concerned about welfare, and even if we are inclined to think that individuals are generally the best judges of how to make their own lives go well, the word *generally* is important. With that qualification, we can see that the objections to paternalism depend on some empirical judgments. Those judgments might be wrong. Do people's choices always promote their welfare? That question cannot be answered with intuitions and anecdotes. The relationship between freedom of choice and welfare is testable, at least in principle, and it is being tested, with complex results. We are learning more every day. We know that good nudges can help. They might even save lives.

The findings discussed in chapters 2 and 3 provide a number of reasons that people's choices do not always promote their welfare and they help to explain why good choice architecture is important and even indispensable. If welfare is our guide, soft paternalism might be required, not forbidden. If people procrastinate, and if System 1 is the reason, then their failure to alter the status quo may be a mistake, with possibly bad and even dangerous consequences. Consider a decision not to take certain precautions against financial risks or health hazards.

True, people learn; and true, people have diverse interests and concerns. We choose certain activities not because they are fun or joyful, but because they are right, perhaps because they are meaningful. People want their lives to have purpose; they do not only want their lives to be happy in some simple sense. People sensibly, even virtuously choose things that they will not necessarily enjoy. For example, they may want to help others even when it is not a lot of fun to do so. A survey suggests that people's projected choices are *generally* based on what they believe would promote their happiness or subjective well-being—but that sometimes people are willing to make choices that would sacrifice their own happiness in favor of promoting an assortment of other goals, including promoting the happiness of their family, increasing their control over their lives, increasing their social status, or improving their sense of purpose in life.[4]

But I am speaking of the more straightforward cases, in which people, focused on what they will like, end up with a result they neither hope for nor expect. Their choices, in short, do not make them happy, and a nudge might promote their welfare rather than undermine it. The technical term here is *affective forecasting errors*.[5] The term is unlovely but hardly unintelligible; it applies in easily imagined cases in which people make a choice on the ground that they believe it is likely to produce a desired result for them—and they turn out to be wrong.

Affective forecasting errors are paralleled by many other kinds of errors. People might, for example, believe that a certain decision will increase the happiness of their family members but be entirely wrong in that belief. We can easily imagine research on the behavioral economics of birthdays, or on the behavioral economics of Christmas. Do you ever receive birthday presents, even from people who know you really well, that you don't much like? Bowls of some kind? Mysterious gadgets? Ugly ties? Unreadable books? Hideous sweaters? (There is actually some evidence here. Less than ideal Christmas presents, given with affection or even love by friends and family members, produce tens of billions of dollars in economic losses every year, in the sense that they are worth a lot less to the recipient than the gift-giver paid for them.[6]) Similarly, people might believe that a certain outcome will increase their social status or their sense of purpose or meaning, but they might be wrong in that belief as well. I am not aware of any behaviorally informed literature on "meaningfulness forecasting errors," but I forecast that there will be such literature.

Here's a simple but striking example of the possibility that paternalism can actually increase people's welfare. We would ordinarily expect people to be worse off if government makes it more expensive for them to purchase goods that they want. If government tells you that you have to spend more to buy a computer, a lamp, or a pair of shoes, your life will hardly be better. But careful empirical work suggests that there are exceptions. More specifically, *cigarettes taxes appear to make smokers happier.*[7] To the extent that this is so, it is because smokers tend to be less happy because they smoke. When they are taxed, they smoke less and might even quit, and they are better off as a result.

For various reasons, including its addictive nature, smoking is a highly unusual activity. But smoking may not be unique. It is not unimaginable that people would be happier as a result of other taxes on goods that they choose. Consider taxes on foods that cause obesity.[8] Whether or not such taxes can ultimately be justified on balance (and this is a complex question), there is an intelligible argument for them. In light of the risks of error and abuse, we have to be careful here. But the broader point is that in some cases, there can be real space between anticipated welfare and actual experience. The space suggests that if welfare is our guide, objections to paternalism, at least in the form of nudges, will run into serious problems.

No sensible person believes that public officials should be making people's choices for them. They shouldn't. Freedom of choice and free markets are great engines for prosperity and human liberty. Nothing in this book is inconsistent with that claim. On the contrary, simplification is designed to increase liberty and to help promote prosperity. Nudges maintain free choice. The only claim I am making here is that in identifiable contexts, human welfare can be promoted by approaches that count as paternalistic. If we are concerned with people's welfare, we will not always rule those approaches out of bounds.

Autonomy

Suppose that we are not so focused on welfare and that we believe that freedom of choice has a special and independent status. We might think that people have a right to choose, and that government cannot legitimately intrude on that right even if it does in fact know best. If people want to buy twenty-four-ounce sodas, energy-inefficient refrigerators, or cars that have terrible fuel economy, they are entitled to do just that. If they want to gamble or smoke, to spend their money rather than save it, or to exercise just once a year, the government has no business intervening, even if those choices cause harm. Regulatory Moneyball may be a good idea, but if it begins to intrude on people's autonomy, we might want to start playing a different game.

The thin version of this position suggests that freedom of choice is an ingredient in welfare, indeed an important one, and we need to take careful account of the welfare-reducing effects of interfering with people's freedom of choice. People dislike it when government overrides or interferes with their choices, and when it does so, they experience a loss in welfare, and possibly a serious one. If the government tells people that they have to save money for retirement, cannot eat fatty foods, must not talk on their cell phone while driving, or have to buckle their seat belts, it may make them frustrated and angry. If so, government has to give careful attention to that problem.

The thick version of this position is that freedom of choice is not merely an ingredient in welfare but an end in itself, and thus a kind of trump card. On this view, freedom of choice should be overridden or compromised rarely and if at all, only for the most compelling reasons. Many of the most deeply felt objections to paternalism, strong or weak, are based on an intuition or judgment of this kind. They often take the form of a question: By what right can government legitimately interfere with the choices of free adults? The thick version does not turn on empirical questions, and it is, in a sense, a showstopper. If people have to be treated as ends rather than as means, and if this principle means that government cannot influence private choices, there is not a lot of room for further discussion. On this view, government should be a lot simpler, but it shouldn't nudge.

Nudges, Respecting Autonomy

Suppose that freedom of choice is part of what people care about. Suppose too that if people are denied choice, they will suffer a loss in welfare, in part because they feel frustrated or mistreated. To the extent that this is so, there will be a legitimate argument against paternalism. In particular, active choosing will start to look very attractive. Suppose too that freedom matters in itself and that it is wrong for government to interfere with people's choices, not necessarily because it reduces their welfare but because it is disrespectful and insulting to do so.

It is important to emphasize that even if these points are powerful in the abstract, they may not be decisive in particular cases, and that their force is greatly reduced insofar as we are dealing with soft paternalism. In areas that are new, complex, unfamiliar, or highly technical, maybe people will actually favor a default rule and would not like to be forced to choose. Recall that many employers (both private and public) default employees into certain pension plans, and this may well be the right thing to do; employees do not seem to object or to see the default rules as insulting to their autonomy. Even for those who cherish their autonomy, nudges, preserving freedom of choice, are often acceptable and even highly desirable. In certain circumstances, active choosing is a burden rather than a benefit; it is not something that most people would prefer.

Both the thin and the thick versions of the autonomy argument ask important questions, which must be answered by hard paternalists in particular. But do those questions really raise serious problems for nudges of the kind I have endorsed here? Are warnings and default rules out of bounds? We should be able to agree that insofar as choice architects are maintaining freedom of choice, the grounds for reasonable objection are greatly weakened.

Actually, there is a deeper problem. All of us could, in principle, make far more decisions than we do. Every hour of every day, choices are made for us by both private and public institutions, and we are better off as a result. Time is limited, and some issues are complex or boring. If we were not able to benefit from an explicit or implicit delegation of choice-making from us to others, we would be far worse off. In an important sense, we would be less autonomous, if only because we would have no time to focus our attention on our real concerns. Sometimes we adopt routines for this reason. Consider these words from President Obama, explaining why he wears just a few suits: "I'm trying to pare down decisions. I don't want to make decisions about what I'm eating or wearing. Because I have too many other decisions to make. You need to focus your decision-making energy. You need to routinize yourself."[9]

This is terrific advice, and not only for national leaders; sensible people do routinize themselves. But our lives are also routinized, and made livable, by countless decisions made by others. Most of us do not, for example, have to make choices about what a refrigerator should look like, or how many rooms are in the building in which we work, or how to build a car, or how best to clean tap water, or how to fly an airplane, or what safety equipment should be on trains.

Recall Esther Duflo's emphasis on the fact that people who are well off do not have to be responsible for a wide range of things, because others are making the relevant decisions, and usually to their benefit. "If we do nothing," she writes, "we are on the right track. For most of the poor, if they do nothing, they are on the wrong track."[10] All of us need to conserve our decision-making energy, and our lives are made simpler, and in an important sense more free, because we can operate against the background of choices made by other people.

If we were asked to make choices about everything that affects us, we would immediately run out of time. If we do not appreciate this point, it is only because we are able to take the social environment for granted—so much so, in fact, that we may not even see it. Sensible choice architecture ensures that we make the right number of decisions, which is a very small fraction of the decisions that we might make in principle.

Of Transparency and Political Safeguards

A distinctive objection to certain kinds of nudging is that they may be invisible. Mandates and commands, by contrast, are highly visible, and government is accountable for them. If public officials require increases in fuel economy, forbid people to ride motorcycles without wearing helmets, or require them to buckle their seat belts, nothing is mysterious, hidden, or secret. The prohibitions may or may not be acceptable, but they lack the particular vice of insidiousness. If people object, political safeguards are triggered. The government must defend itself publicly. And if that defense is perceived as weak, the proposed mandate or ban is likely to crumble.

On this count, soft paternalism may not fare so well. Precisely because of their softness, nudges may fade into the background. They may even be self-insulating insofar as they alter the very behavior, and perhaps the beliefs and understandings, that would otherwise be brought to bear against them. Prominent critics of nudging have suggested that the lack of transparency is a serious problem. In the words of the economist Edward Glaeser, "Hard paternalism generally involves measurable instruments. The public can observe the size of sin taxes and voters can tell that certain activities have been outlawed. Rules can be set in advance about how far governments can go in pursuing their policies of hard paternalism. Effective soft paternalism must be situation specific and creative in the language of its message. This fact makes soft paternalism intrinsically difficult to control and means that it is, at least on these grounds, more subject to abuse than hard paternalism." [11]

The best response to this concern is simple: Nothing should be hidden. Soft paternalism, nudges, and other behaviorally informed approaches should be visible, scrutinized, and monitored. Consider some of the initiatives I have highlighted here: the substitution of the Food Plate for the Food Pyramid, the new fuel economy label, and other disclosure requirements; Smart Disclosure; automatic enrollment in savings and health care plans; simplification of existing requirements; salient health warnings. All of these initiatives are visible and public. None is secret. All were, and remain, subject to public scrutiny. What is the problem?

Of Easy Reversibility

In failing to impose material costs on choices, nudges differ from mandates and bans. Because of the absence of such costs, nudges are *easily reversible*.

Information designed to ensure that choices are based on fact rather than fiction counts as a nudge, and it might be designed to influence choices; but people can disregard it. Graphic warnings do not override individual choice, and while they are not neutral and are meant to influence choice, people can ignore them if they want. Those who run cafeterias and grocery stores might place fruits and vegetables at the front and cigarettes and fatty foods at the back. Even if they do so, people can always go to the back. A default rule in favor of automatic enrollment—in a savings plan or a privacy policy—greatly affects outcomes and it may be decisive for many of us. But we can always opt out.

Does this mean that no one should worry about any abuse of authority or power exercised through nudges? Hardly. We can easily identify an important problem with the idea of easy reversibility: In part because of the power of System 1, nudges may prove decisive. [12]

True, we can search for chocolate candy and cigarettes at the back of the store, and true, we might be allowed to opt out of a website policy that involves a lot of tracking (perhaps with a simple click)—but because of the influence of inertia, many of us won't do so. Graphic warnings may be exceedingly effective precisely because they target identifiable features of human cognition. The idea of easy reversibility might, in these circumstances, seem a bit of rhetoric, even a fraud—comforting, to be sure, but not a realistic response to those who are concerned about errors or bad faith on the part of nudgers.

This objection has force. It would be misleading to suggest that because of (what seems to be) easy reversibility, all risks are eliminated. If people are defaulted into exploitative savings plans (with high fees and little diversification) or costly health insurance programs, it is not adequate to say that they can go their own way if they choose to do so. How often do you click on the "unsubscribe" button when you find yourself on an unwanted email list? If you are like most people, not often enough.

It remains true, however, that because they maintain freedom of choice, nudges are less intrusive and less dangerous than mandates and bans. This is so even if people will exercise that freedom less often than they would if inertia and procrastination were not powerful forces. As we have seen, people do reject default rules that they really dislike (at least if they know about them). If people are defaulted into a health insurance plan that works out badly for them, many will switch. If people are defaulted into a retirement plan that puts a lot of their money into savings and gives them too little now, they will opt out. For that reason, liberty of choice is a real safeguard.

For the reasons outlined here, the freedom to opt out is no panacea. But it is exceedingly important.

The Legitimate Claims of System 1

Here is one way to understand one of the central claims I have made: Often because of the power of System 1, people err. We need to strengthen the hand of a well-functioning System 2, promoting self-control, counteracting biases, eliminating an undue focus on the short term. The best nudges move people in the directions that they would go if they were fully rational. Indeed that is a central point of good choice architecture.

But what of the legitimate claims of System 1? More bluntly, don't nudges disregard a lot of what is most important in human life? Most of us care a lot more about current consumption than consumption twenty years from now. Some of our favorite foods are pretty fattening. True, most people care about their health, but their health is hardly the only thing they care about. Many people like to drink and to smoke. When people enjoy their lives, it is because of System 1. The future matters, but the present matters too. Why should public officials, or anyone else, make people focus on something other than what they want to focus on, and select choice architecture that devalues, denigrates, and undermines some of our most fundamental motivations and concerns? Indeed, might not System 2, if it lacks a sense of those concerns, be paralyzed? How will it know what to do?

Consider a patient of Antonio Damasio, who suffered from brain damage that prevented him from experiencing emotions.[13] Because the patient lacked "gut reactions," he could perform some tasks well; for example, he was able to drive safely on icy roads, avoiding the natural impulse to hit the brakes during a skid. On the other hand, his ability to focus on consequences was accompanied by extreme difficulty in making decisions:

I was discussing with the same patient when his next visit to the laboratory should take place. I suggested two alternative dates, both in the coming month and just a few days apart from each other. The patient pulled out his appointment book and began consulting the calendar. . . . For the better part of a half hour, the patient enumerated reasons for and against each of the two dates: previous engagements, proximity to other engagements, possible meteorological conditions, virtually anything that one could reasonably think about concerning a single date. Just as calmly as he had driven over the ice, and recounted that episode, he was now walking us through a tiresome cost-benefit analysis, an endless outlining and fruitless comparison of options and possible consequences. [We] finally did tell him, quietly, that he should come on the second of the alternative dates. His response was equally calm and prompt. He simply said, "That's fine."

Without emotions, and without System 1, might we not be endlessly listing consequences while lacking a motivation for choosing among them?

The underlying questions here are legitimate, and they suggest the problems with some imaginable nudges. At the same time, they reflect a fundamental misunderstanding of the argument I have made and the initiatives that it supports. To see why, we need to make a distinction between two different understandings of the kinds of biases and errors that nudges might counteract.

One understanding is that choice architecture should be established to ensure that people act as they would if they were responding directly to System 2. This view should be rejected, because some of the greatest pleasures of life appeal to System 1. No sensible private or public institution would be indifferent to the fact that people take risks because that is what they like to do. They fall in love, they overeat, they stay up all night, they get drunk, they act on impulse, they run with apparently unpromising ideas, they experiment in a million and one different ways.

In a different understanding, human beings make what they themselves see as serious mistakes, or would see as serious mistakes after reflection, and choice architecture should be established to help make those errors less frequent and less damaging. If complexity and optimism are combining to cause economic harm for cell phone users, and if disclosure requirements can reduce that harm, we might welcome such requirements. If a problem of self-control is leading people to endanger their health, and if they want private and public institutions to help solve that problem (and not to exploit it), then there is no cause for complaint if they get some help. If inertia leads people not to take action that they agree is in their interest, then inertia might be enlisted to promote outcomes that are in their interest. We need not denigrate the legitimate claims of System 1 in order to accept these points.

With respect to issues of this kind, there are limits to how much progress can be made in the abstract. We have to ask concrete questions about concrete problems. We could imagine forms of choice architecture that would be objectionable because they would neglect what people really care about. Consider the Suffer Now, Celebrate Much Later Pension Plan, automatically putting 51 percent of people's salaries into savings; or the Fun-Free Wellness

Program, asking employees to commit to a grueling and unpleasant daily exercise regime; or the Joyless Cafeteria, with the tastiest foods relatively hidden. We could also imagine choice architecture that is helpful rather than harmful. The challenge is to avoid the latter and promote the former.

A Real Concern: Impermissible Motivations

The most problematic nudges reflect not unacceptable paternalism but an altogether different problem: *impermissible motivations*. Many of the strongest intuitive objections to paternalism, even in its soft form, involve examples, real or imagined, in which government is acting on the basis of illicit factors.

We would not, for example, want government to default people into voting for incumbents by saying that unless citizens explicitly indicate otherwise, or actually show up at the ballot booth, they are presumed to vote for incumbents. Or suppose it were declared that for purposes of the census, citizens are presumed to be Caucasian unless they explicitly state otherwise. Or imagine that in an educational campaign, government decided to inform people (truthfully) about all the misdeeds done by members of a particular religious faith (say, Catholics or Jews). Or suppose that government decided to use vivid images to persuade people to choose products manufactured by its favorite interest groups.

In all of these cases, the problem does not lie with paternalism. It lies in the illegitimate or illicit ends that government nudging is meant to produce. Government is not supposed to use the basic rules of voting to entrench itself, or to favor certain racial groups, or to stigmatize members of a particular faith, or to tell people to buy a favored group's products. The examples are important because they establish some limits on even minimally intrusive policies. The use of paternalism—soft or hard—for illegitimate ends is wrong because the ends are illegitimate. But these objections do not establish the central claim, which is that certain forms of nudging are objectionable as such.

No sensible person wholeheartedly embraces government paternalism. But an important part of the simplification project, as I have understood it here, enlists choice architecture and nudges to make people's lives longer, healthier, and easier. Freedom of choice is certainly a central part of a good life—hence the preference for soft paternalism. But legitimate concerns about illegitimate paternalism should not be allowed to prevent officials from seeking to identify the best ways to improve people's lives, even if they end up influencing people's choices.

10 SIMPLIFYING CHOICE ARCHITECTURE

When private institutions want to make things easy for people, they know exactly what to do. Credit card companies allow online applications and provide self-addressed stamped envelopes. Magazines renew subscriptions automatically. They know that if subscribers have to take action to renew, a lot of them won't, even if they really like what they have been reading. Candidates for public office increasingly allow people to donate to their campaigns in a matter of seconds. In competitive markets, making it easy is often the winning strategy, and that fact is becoming clearer every day. True, you might be able to make some money by enlisting complexity and confusion. In the long run, however, that's probably not the best business model, and even if it is, we can hope for, and perhaps even expect, some well-placed nudges from the government in response.

Government itself must get simpler. It is true that in countless ways, the world is getting more complex, and some of the complexity has to be mirrored by the public sector. The Affordable Care Act is helping many millions of people, but it is not exactly short and sweet. As they say, Rome was not built in a day, and the same is true of Government EZ. But we should not overlook or downplay the effects of removing tens of millions of hours in paperwork requirements, promoting plain language, eliminating outmoded requirements, promoting public participation, using sensible default rules, mandating executive summaries, and replacing incomprehensible disclosure requirements with efforts to ensure that people actually know before they owe. In countless areas, pointless red tape is being removed. The day of one-click government has not yet arrived, but in important areas, it really is on its way.

Even when it is invisible, choice architecture affects our health, our wealth, our safety, our work, and our environment. In the private and public sectors alike, it is often important to make things automatic, intuitive, and meaningful and not to strain System 2. A lot of people are alive today because of nudges. Recall the remarkable fact that in 2011, the number of deaths on the highway was the lowest in recorded history. Many nudges helped to produce that happy result; they include educational campaigns, warnings, and public-private partnerships. With respect to highway safety and in other areas, there are limitless opportunities to save money and to save lives. One advantage of nudges is that even if they don't work so well, their costs are low, and most of the time they are likely to cause little harm. They reflect humility about how much government knows, and they lack the disadvantages of large-scale government planning.

I have also emphasized the importance of empirical testing of regulations—of knowing as much as we can before the fact and of learning after the fact. We need to proceed on the path toward Regulatory Moneyball. Too much of the time, regulations have been based on intuitions and hunches. Too much of the time, regulations stay on the books even if they are doing little good and indeed even if they are causing a lot of harm. Too much of the time, we fail to build on regulations that are saving lives and money, even though they are working well and need to be strengthened. Simplification itself needs careful evaluation both before and after the fact.

No one doubts that incentives matter. People care about their money, and they certainly care about their health. If the price of gasoline goes up, people will drive less. If people are convinced that smoking will make them sick, they will become less likely to smoke. In many areas, the most important thing that we can do is to improve people's incentives (and to make those incentives salient). But outcomes are independently influenced by choice architecture—by the social environment and by prevailing social norms.

It is right to celebrate freedom of choice. But in many domains, choices are made for us. Thank goodness! If each of us had to participate in each of the decisions that affect us, we would be immediately overwhelmed by complexity. A settled background can promote our freedom, not undermine it.

In the United States, the Constitution itself makes a number of choices, and those choices, while amendable in theory, are generally fixed in reality.

We don't have to decide whether there will be a Congress or whether freedom of speech and freedom of religion should exist; these things are settled. Most of us don't have to figure out how to build brakes that actually work, or how to make salt or cement, or where streets and highways should be located, or what property and contract law should look like. When some people live lives that are long and good, it is often because the social background and existing norms enable them to take for granted, and perhaps not even to think much about, a set of practices that serve them well. When some people get obese and others do not, it is often because the latter are benefiting from good choice architecture and the former are not.

Disclosure of information is an important regulatory tool, and it can be used effectively by both private and public institutions. At the same time, disclosure must be not merely technically accurate but also simple, meaningful, and helpful. Choice architects must pay careful attention to how people process and use information. The best approaches inform people of what exactly they should do to get benefits or to avoid losses: Plate, not Pyramid.

We also need to distinguish between summary disclosure, typically provided at the point of purchase, and full disclosure, typically provided on the Internet. Summary disclosure should be clear, simple, and salient, and it should emphasize factors that actually matter to people, such as the economic value of energy-efficient choices. Are people going to save $1 or $5 or $205? It is important not merely to provide information but to do so in such a way as to enable people to compare products and services.

Full disclosure should provide information that the private sector can use in a lot of ways, making free markets work better. Return to the example of the GPS, made possible because President Clinton unscrambled the underlying data in 2000, thus allowing the private sector to use a lot of information that had previously been reserved to the military. Companies and individuals are now using that information in countless ways, many of them entirely unanticipated by the Clinton administration. Take a look, if you will, at data.gov, which we designed in order to provide a treasure trove of data that can be adapted for people to use in their daily lives as citizens and consumers.

Whenever information is released, the most important uses often come from the private sector, which creates fun and ingenious apps and promotes comparison shopping among multiple options. Some of the most important efforts, captured under the heading of Smart Disclosure, are increasingly allowing people to see the nature and effects of their own past choices and to understand the likely effects of different and better choices in the future. Companies have a ton of information about what people have chosen with respect to cell phone plans, energy, credit cards, and health care; people should be given the opportunity to learn about their own choices. In all cases, disclosure is most useful if it informs people of what, precisely, they should do in order to avoid significant risks or obtain significant goods—again, Plate, not Pyramid.

Default rules are pervasive, even when we do not notice them, and they have major effects on outcomes. Sensible defaults can serve as a complement or alternative to mandates and bans. One of the advantages of well-chosen default rules is that they simplify and ease people's choices—for example, by producing automatic enrollment in programs that are usually beneficial while also allowing people to opt out. Default rules are especially valuable in complex areas and when one size fits all (or at least most). True, choice architects do not always know which default rules are best. It is possible that they may be influenced by their own interests or by those of self-interested private groups. One size may not fit all (or even most). At least when the affected group is diverse, when people like to choose, and when the domain is familiar, active choosing is likely to be preferable to default rules. Indeed, active choosing is often an excellent way of learning what people prefer, and that learning can in turn inform the creation of sensible and perhaps personalized defaults. As we have seen, personalized default rules, based on information about what best suits individual situations, have many of the advantages of active choosing. In important areas, they are the wave of the future.

Some programs do not work because people do not participate in them. People do not participate because the requirements for participation are too challenging. Reduced paperwork and form-filling burdens can produce real gains—as, for example, through fewer questions, use of skip patterns, electronic filing, and prepopulation of forms.

Recall once more the local who, in giving directions, says, "You can't miss it!" When people say "You can't miss it," it is because they are talking about a place that is so clear in their own minds, and so salient to them, that it seems impossible that any sane, seeing person could miss it. But to someone who does not know the area, the "it" may not be recognizable, and it may be part of a perplexing, large background.

In my experience, the same is true for a lot of people in government, including those who design regulations, policies, and forms. For them, adding a few provisions, questions, or subparts just isn't a big deal, because to them, it is all so familiar. But if a student, a parent, or an owner of a small business tries to grapple with government documents, it is easy to get lost. Some people may give up entirely. The consequences can be bad and in some cases even tragic.

We need to start making gorillas more visible. People are far more likely to respond when key facts, risks, or possibilities are salient. Designers of effective warnings are alert to the problem of invisible gorillas.

Good regulations work in concert with social norms, helping to save lives and money and to increase compliance with the law. Sometimes you don't need regulation at all. Public-private partnerships, enlisting the creativity of the private sector, can be the simplest and best approach of all. All over the world, obesity and distracted driving present difficult challenges. In other areas, private-public partnerships have already produced big improvements; consider reductions in drunk driving and increases in seat belt use. If we are to make progress on obesity and distracted driving, it will be largely a result of helpful norms, smart choice architecture, and private-public partnerships.

I began this book by pointing to the best of modern technologies, which are at once unfathomably complex and extraordinarily simple. For ordinary people (including very young children), a lot of these technologies are easy and straightforward to use, and they are getting more so every day. System 1 doesn't wrangle with them. Much of the time, System 2 doesn't have to get deeply engaged. There is a model here for countless institutions and organizations, including government itself. Let's make things simpler.

EPILOGUE

The Three Most Important Things I Learned

After teaching law for over a quarter-century, I was blessed to have the opportunity to work in the federal government. I learned a great deal, and much of what I learned appears in these pages. But three points stand out above all others, and they deserve special emphasis.

Recall a remarkable fact: People stop making some important mistakes when they speak in a foreign language. If we are using a language with which we are not entirely familiar, System 1 retreats and System 2 is activated. We slow down. We think more deliberatively.

In government, I learned that cost-benefit analysis is, in a sense, a foreign language, and it works for that reason. It helps to displace intuitions and reactions that can lead us in unfortunate and potentially even dangerous directions. It helps to counteract both hysteria and neglect. Cost-benefit analysis is not itself simple, but it is a great engine of simplification.

True, we should not put public policy into an arithmetic straitjacket. I have emphasized that some values, such as human dignity, cannot easily be turned into monetary equivalents. But we need more and better cost-benefit analysis, sometimes produced with the aid of randomized controlled trials. The immense promise of nudges lies in the fact that they can confer big benefits without imposing big costs. When a disclosure policy or a default rule saves people a lot of money, improves their health, and lengthens their lives, we know that we are on the right track.

The second lesson involves the sources of unnecessary complexity. Government is full of hardworking people who have chosen to make a career of public service. They are highly professional. They are specialists; they really know their areas. Even when rules are complex, frustrating, and incomprehensible to the public, they tend to seem simple and straightforward to those who wrote them, because rule writers are experts and have a highly trained System 1. Chess masters can immediately read a board, and in a fraction of a second, professional tennis players know how to handle a blistering crosscourt backhand. So too, rule writers understand the meaning of jargon-filled terms and requirements that seem impossibly baffling to those who are subject to them. Much of what I did in government and many of the recommendations made here are meant to encourage the people who write the rules to step back and reduce the strain on the System 2 of people who are required to understand the rules.

The third lesson involves the dispersed information of the public. I have emphasized that public officials know a lot. But inevitably, they lack important information that members of the public have.

Suppose, for example, that the government is adopting a rule that will make cars safer, or that will reduce costs and red tape now imposed on those who work at hospitals, including doctors and nurses. The automobile industry knows a lot about the likely effects of safety rules. Doctors and nurses have a great deal of information about the likely effects of efforts to cut costs and red tape. Public officials need to find out what they know. They need to respect what we might call "regulatory due process."

Time and again, government officials learn from public comments on proposed rules. Greater simplification of those rules promotes informed public comments, and informed public comments promote simplification. It is not merely sensible to provide people with an opportunity to comment on rules before they are finalized; it is indispensable, a crucial safeguard against error. This is partly a point about the sovereignty of We the People—about self-government and political legitimacy. But it is even more than that. It is a point about mistakes and how to avoid them. It is a point about choice architecture for choice architects.

To be sure, rules are not improved by sloganeering, fact-free letter-writing campaigns, or special pleading from interest groups. If our goal is Regulatory Moneyball, regulations should not be designed by referendum. But crucial information often comes from people in the private sphere, which has unique access to that information—about costs, about benefits, about what works and what doesn't, about unintended bad consequences, about unintended good consequences, about what is too complex and what is too simple.

Here, then, is a final nudge. Those who have the privilege of serving the American public should listen closely to those whom they are privileged to serve.

APPENDIX

Executive Order 13563 of January 18, 2011,
Improving Regulation and Regulatory Review

By the authority vested in me as President by the Constitution and the laws of the United States of America, and in order to improve regulation and regulatory review, it is hereby ordered as follows:

Section 1. *General Principles of Regulation.* (a) Our regulatory system must protect public health, welfare, safety, and our environment while promoting economic growth, innovation, competitiveness, and job creation. It must be based on the best available science. It must allow for public participation and an open exchange of ideas. It must promote predictability and reduce uncertainty. It must identify and use the best, most innovative, and least burdensome tools for achieving regulatory ends. It must take into account benefits and costs, both quantitative and qualitative. It must ensure that regulations are accessible, consistent, written in plain language, and easy to understand. It must measure, and seek to improve, the actual results of regulatory requirements.

(b) This order is supplemental to and reaffirms the principles, structures, and definitions governing contemporary regulatory review that were established in Executive Order 12866 of September 30, 1993. As stated in that Executive Order and to the extent permitted by law, each agency must, among other things: (1) propose or adopt a regulation only upon a reasoned determination that its benefits justify its costs (recognizing that some benefits and costs are difficult to quantify); (2) tailor its regulations to impose the least burden on society, consistent with obtaining regulatory objectives, taking into account, among other things, and to the extent practicable, the costs of cumulative regulations; (3) select, in choosing among alternative regulatory approaches, those approaches that maximize net benefits (including potential economic, environmental, public health and safety, and other advantages; distributive impacts; and equity); (4) to the extent feasible, specify performance objectives, rather than specifying the behavior or manner of compliance that regulated entities must adopt; and (5) identify and assess available alternatives to direct regulation, including providing economic *incentives* to encourage the desired behavior, such as user fees or marketable permits, or providing information upon which choices can be made by the public.

(c) In applying these principles, each agency is directed to use the best available techniques to quantify anticipated present and future benefits and costs as accurately as possible. Where appropriate and permitted by law, each agency may consider (and discuss qualitatively) values that are difficult or impossible to quantify, including equity, human dignity, fairness, and distributive impacts.

SEC. 2. *Public Participation.* (a) Regulations shall be adopted through a process that involves public participation. To that end, regulations shall be based, to the extent feasible and consistent with law, on the open exchange of information and perspectives among State, local, and tribal officials, experts in relevant disciplines, affected stakeholders in the private sector, and the public as a whole.

(b) To promote that open exchange, each agency, consistent with Executive Order 12866 and other applicable legal requirements, shall endeavor to provide the public with an opportunity to participate in the regulatory process. To the extent feasible and permitted by law, each agency shall afford the public a meaningful opportunity to comment through the Internet on any proposed regulation, with a comment period that should generally be at least 60 days. To the extent feasible and permitted by law, each agency shall also provide, for both proposed and final rules, timely online access to the rulemaking docket on regulations.gov, including relevant scientific and technical findings, in an open format that can be easily searched and downloaded. For proposed rules, such access shall include, to the extent feasible and permitted by law, an opportunity for public comment on all pertinent parts of the rulemaking docket, including relevant scientific and technical findings.

(c) Before issuing a notice of proposed rulemaking, each agency, where feasible and appropriate, shall seek the views of those who are likely to be affected, including those who are likely to benefit from and those who are potentially subject to such rulemaking.

Sec. 3. *Integration and Innovation.* Some sectors and *industries* face a significant number of regulatory requirements, some of which may be redundant, inconsistent, or overlapping. Greater coordination across agencies could reduce these requirements, thus reducing costs and simplifying and harmonizing rules. In developing regulatory actions and identifying appropriate approaches, each agency shall attempt to promote such coordination, simplification, and harmonization. Each agency shall also seek to identify, as appropriate, means to achieve regulatory goals that are designed to promote innovation.

Sec. 4. *Flexible Approaches.* Where relevant, feasible, and consistent with regulatory objectives, and to the extent permitted by law, each agency shall identify and consider regulatory approaches that reduce burdens and maintain flexibility and freedom of choice for the public. These approaches include warnings, appropriate default rules, and disclosure requirements as well as provision of information to the public in a form that is clear and intelligible.

Sec. 5. *Science.* Consistent with the President's Memorandum for the Heads of Executive Departments and Agencies, "Scientific Integrity" (March 9, 2009), and its implementing guidance, each agency shall ensure the objectivity of any scientific and technological information and processes used to support the agency's regulatory actions.

Sec. 6. *Retrospective Analyses of Existing Rules.* (a) To facilitate the periodic review of existing significant regulations, agencies shall consider how best to promote retrospective analysis of rules that may be outmoded, ineffective, insufficient, or excessively burdensome, and to modify, streamline, expand, or repeal them in accordance with what has been learned. Such retrospective analyses, including supporting data, should be released online whenever possible.

(b) Within 120 days of the date of this order, each agency shall develop and submit to the Office of Information and Regulatory Affairs a preliminary plan, consistent with law and its resources and regulatory priorities, under which the agency will periodically review its existing significant regulations to determine whether any such regulations should be modified, streamlined, expanded, or repealed so as to make the agency's regulatory program more effective or less burdensome in achieving the regulatory objectives.

ACKNOWLEDGMENTS

No one in the Obama administration read the manuscript of this book, but to countless former colleagues I am more grateful than I can say. Thanks to each and every one of you. It's hazardous to single out anyone, and as a kind of self-control strategy I am limiting myself to five people with whom I worked especially closely for long periods.

Carol Browner taught me a ton, not only about the Clean Air Act but also about government, collegiality, and friendship. Larry Summers is both wise and funny about everything, and he's committed to Regulatory Moneyball, and he makes everyone around him better. If Gene Sperling likes cost-benefit analysis slightly less than I do, it's only because he has the biggest heart in the world. Jeff Zients, my suitemate for over two years, makes a cameo appearance in chapter 2; I am thankful to him for his wisdom, his generosity, his ability to run a meeting, and his willingness to spend a lot of time tossing around a football. (He throws a tight spiral.) Nancy-Ann DeParle is a national treasure, and a hero, and it was an honor, and a lot of fun, to be able to work closely with her on a dazzling array of topics (including snakes, but that's a long story, and I'm not going to tell it).

The United States has been blessed to have Barack Obama as president, and I have been particularly blessed to know him as a colleague, boss, and friend. Everyone knows that he's a pretty cool customer. What I want to add is that his personal kindness knows no bounds.

Some chapters of this book use materials from two academic papers. Chapters 3 and 4 draw on my essay "Empirically Informed Regulation," *University of Chicago Law Review* 78 (2011), available at http://papers.ssrn.com/sol3/papers.cfm?abstract_id=2128806. Chapter 10 (along with a few other passages) draws on "Behavioral Economics and Paternalism," *Yale Law Journal* 122 (2013), which was the basis for the Storrs Lectures, given at Yale Law School on November 12 and 13, 2012. I am grateful to the editors of the *University of Chicago Law Review* and the *Yale Law Journal* for their valuable comments and for permission to use the relevant materials. Interested readers might wish to consult those essays for more detailed discussion than I have provided here. Also of interest may be "Impersonal Default Rules vs. Active Choosing vs. Personalized Default Rules: A Triptych" (2012, unpublished manuscript), available at http://papers.ssrn.com/sol3/papers.cfm?abstract_id=2171343.

My friends and colleagues at Harvard Law School, and Harvard University more generally, provide an extraordinary intellectual atmosphere, and the views of many colleagues have had a large impact on this book. Special thanks to Dean Martha Minow for help of every conceivable kind. Much of the manuscript was written at the Brookings Institution, where I was provided with an office and a congenial atmosphere while I was on research leave from Harvard. I am grateful to Strobe Talbott and Darrell West for their hospitality and kindness.

For exceptional comments on the manuscript, I am thankful to Chip Heath, Christine Jolls, Daniel Kahneman, Michael Lewis, Eric Posner, Lucia Reisch, and Dick Thaler. I am truly astonished that these amazing people were willing to take the time to go through a manuscript, especially one that was a lot longer than the book you are now reading. I am acutely aware that I have not been able to respond adequately to their suggestions and advice. (But I really tried.)

My agent, Sarah Chalfant, saw some promise in this project before it started, and I am immensely grateful to her for her support, suggestions, and general wisdom. Dan Kanter provided superb substantive comments and truly extraordinary research assistance. The book is a lot better because of his boundless energy and help.

I think that I have decided to forgive Thomas LeBien for cutting about thirty thousand words from the original manuscript, because he is the best imaginable editor (and because he was right to cut them). Thomas saw a far better, cleaner, simpler book than the one I wrote, and with generosity, brilliance, and extraordinary care (and speed), he moved the manuscript in that direction. If we ended up close to what he saw, he's the reason.

A lot of other people helped in various ways, through generosity, support, perspective, wisdom, humor, lunch, dinner, and occasional silliness, which lightened the author's load, and made him smile, and produced something like background music for the writing of this book. I won't name names. You know who you are.

This book is dedicated to two people, and I thank them above all. Dick Thaler has been a treasured friend and an inspiration for many years. This book could not exist without his work and our book *Nudge*, which is the parent to everything said here. Dick does not, of course, agree with everything in this book. But he deserves shared credit for anything that might prove good or sensible.

Samantha Power happens to have the best System 1 in the history of the world. She works in the White House on foreign policy, but she has had an immeasurable impact on regulation, simplification, and nudging; what is described in this book wouldn't have happened without her. She's the one you want in your corner, because if you even start to get hurt, she'll be in the ring immediately, right there beside you. She's the kindest person I know, and the most generous, and the best listener, and she's tough, and she's (very) funny, and she has the highest standards, and sometimes she's fierce, and she crushes me on the basketball court, and she makes every day a joy.

NOTES

INTRODUCTION

1. Michael Lewis, *Moneyball: The Art of Winning an Unfair Game* (New York: W. W. Norton & Company, 2003), 31.
2. See Richard H. Thaler and Cass R. Sunstein, *Nudge: Improving Decisions About Health, Wealth, and Happiness* (New Haven, CT: Yale University Press, 2008).

CHAPTER 1

1. Cass R. Sunstein, *On Rumors: How Falsehoods Spread, Why We Believe Them, What Can Be Done* (New York: Farrar, Straus and Giroux, 2009).
2. See F. A. Hayek, *The Road to Serfdom: Text and Documents—The Definitive Edition*, ed. Bruce Caldwell (Chicago: University of Chicago Press, 1944, 2007), 88.
3. See Office of Management and Budget, *Draft 2012 Report to Congress on the Benefits and Costs of Federal Regulations and Unfunded Mandates on State, Local, and Tribal Entities*, 54, www.whitehouse.gov/sites/default/files/omb/oira/draft_2012 _cost_benefit_report.pdf.
4. See US Food and Drug Administration, "FDA: New Final Rule to Ensure Egg Safety, Reduce Salmonella Illnesses Goes into Effect," press release, July 9, 2010, www.fda.gov/NewsEvents/Newsroom/PressAnnouncements/ucm218461.htm.

CHAPTER 2

1. See Dan Ariely, *The (Honest) Truth About Dishonesty: How We Lie to Everyone—Especially Ourselves* (New York: HarperCollins Publishers, 2012).
2. See Eric Johnson et al., "Can Consumers Make Affordable Care Affordable? The Value of Choice Architecture" (unpublished manuscript, 2012).
3. Daniel Kahneman, *Thinking, Fast and Slow* (New York: Farrar, Straus and Giroux, 2011).
4. B. Keysar, S. L. Hayakawa, and S. G. An, "The Foreign-Language Effect: Thinking in a Foreign Tongue Reduces Decision Biases," *Psychological Science* 23, no. 6 (June 2012): 661–68.
5. See John E. Hunter and Ronda F. Hunter, "Validity and Utility of Alternative Predictors of Job Performance," *Psychological Bulletin* 96, no. 1 (July 1984): 72–98. For a more qualified view, see Michael A. McDaniel et al., "The Validity of Employment Interviews: A Comprehensive Review and Meta-Analysis," *Journal of Applied Psychology* 79, no. 4 (August 1994): 599–616.
6. See Paul Slovic, *The Feeling of Risk: New Perspectives on Risk Perception* (New York: Taylor & Francis, 2010).

7. Colin Camerer, George Lowenstein, and Drazen Prelec, "Neuroeconomics: How Neuroscience Can Inform Economics," *Journal of Economic Literature* 43 (March 2005): 9, 17.

8. See Jason P. Mitchell et al., "Medial Prefrontal Cortex Predicts Intertemporal Choice," *Journal of Cognitive Neuroscience* 23, no. 4 (April 2011): 857–66.

9. The quotation can be found at Susan Parker, "Esther Duflo Explains Why She Believes Randomized Controlled Trials Are So Vital," *Center for Effective Philanthropy Blog*, June 23, 2011, www.effectivephilanthropy.org/blog/2011/06/esther-duflo-explains-why-she-believes-randomized-controlled-trials-are-so-vital/.

10. See Matthew Syed, *Bounce: Mozart, Federer, Picasso, Beckham, and the Science of Success* (New York: Harper Perennial, 2011); Sian Beilock, *Choke: What the Secrets of the Brain Reveal About Getting It Right When You Have To* (New York: Free Press, 2010).

11. As reported in an extraordinary book: Jack McCallum, *Dream Team: How Michael, Magic, Larry, Charles, and the Greatest Team of All Time Conquered the World and Changed the Game of Basketball Forever* (New York: Ballantine Books, 2012), 19.

CHAPTER 3

1. The papers are collected in Richard H. Thaler, *Quasi Rational Economics* (New York: Russell Sage Foundation, 1994).

2. See generally Thomas Gilovich, Dale Griffin, and Daniel Kahneman, eds., *Heuristics and Biases: The Psychology of Intuitive Judgment* (Cambridge, UK: Cambridge University Press, 2002); Daniel Kahneman and Amos Tversky, eds., *Choices, Values, and Frames* (Cambridge, UK: Cambridge University Press, 2000). For discussion of many relevant findings, see generally Kahneman, *Thinking, Fast and Slow* (see chap. 2, n. 3).

3. Mitchell et al., "Medial Prefrontal Cortex" (see chap. 2, n. 8).

4. Ibid, 861.

5. See Ted O'Donoghue and Matthew Rabin, "Choice and Procrastination," *Quarterly Journal of Economics* 116, no. 1 (January 2001): 121, 122; Richard H. Thaler and Shlomo Benartzi, "Save More Tomorrow: Using Behavioral Economics to Increase Employee Saving," *Journal of Political Economy* 112, no. 1 (February 2004): S164, S168–69. In the context of poverty, see Abhijit V. Banerjee and Esther Duflo, *Poor Economics: A Radical Rethinking of the Way to Fight Global Poverty* (New York: Public Affairs, 2011), 64–68.

6. See Esther Duflo et al., "Nudging Farmers to Use Fertilizer: Theory and Experimental Evidence from Kenya," *American Economic Review* 101, no. 6 (October 2011): 2351–2353 (finding that farmers in western Kenya do not make economically advantageous fertilizer investments, but that a small, time-limited discount on the cost of acquiring fertilizer can increase investments, thus producing higher welfare than either a laissez-faire approach or large subsidies).

7. Hal E. Hirshfield et al., "Increasing Saving Behavior through Age-Progressed Renderings of the Future Self," *Journal of Marketing Research* 48 (November 2011): S23-S37.

8. See Shlomo Benartzi and Richard H. Thaler, "Myopic Loss Aversion and the Equity Premium Puzzle," *Quarterly Journal of Economics* 110, no. 1 (February 1995): 73, 88.

9. See David Laibson, "Golden Eggs and Hyperbolic Discounting," *Quarterly Journal of Economics* 112, no. 2 (1997): 443, 445.

10. See Raj Chetty et al., "Active vs. Passive Decisions and Crowdout in Retirement Savings Accounts: Evidence from Denmark" (unpublished manuscript, December 2012), http://obs.rc.fas.harvard.edu/chetty/crowdout.pdf. For more evidence on automatic enrollment and savings, see Brigitte C. Madrian and Dennis F. Shea, "The Power of Suggestion: Inertia in 401(k) Participation and Savings Behavior," *Quarterly Journal of Economics* 116, no. 4 (2001): 1149, 1184. For a discussion of the effect of inertia on choice of travel modes, see Alessandro Innocenti, Patrizia Lattarulo, and Maria Grazia Pazienza, "Heuristics and Biases in Travel Mode Choice" (working paper 27, University of Siena Experimental Economics Laboratory, Siena, Italy, 2009), 20, http://papers.ssrn.com/sol3/papers.cfm?abstract_id=1522168.

11. See Eric J. Johnson and Daniel G. Goldstein, "Do Defaults Save Lives?" *Science* 302 (November 21, 2003): 1338, http://papers.ssrn.com/sol3/papers.cfm?abstract_id=1324774; Duncan J. Watts, *Everything Is Obvious: How Common Sense Fails Us* (New York: Crown Business, 2011), 30–31; Eric J. Johnson and Daniel G. Goldstein, "Decisions by Default," in *The Behavioral Foundations of Public Policy*, ed. Eldar Shafir (Princeton, NJ: Princeton University Press, 2013), 417.

12. See Daniel Pichert and Konstantinos V. Katsikopoulos, "Green Defaults: Information Presentation and Pro-Environmental Behaviour," *Journal of Environmental Psychology* 28, no. 1 (March 2008): 63–73.

13. See Howard Leventhal, Robert Singer, and Susan Jones, "Effects of Fear and Specificity of Recommendation upon Attitudes and Behavior," *Journal of Personality and Social Psychology* 2, no. 1 (July 1965): 20, 27–28.

14. Chip Heath and Dan Heath, *Switch: How to Change When Change Is Hard* (New York: Broadway Books, 2010), 15–17 (describing the effects of a targeted milk marketing campaign in West Virginia, which changed the local market share of low-fat milk from 18 percent to 35 percent over a six-month period).

15. Ibid., 27; David W. Nickerson and Todd Rogers, "Do You Have a Voting Plan? Implementation Intentions, Voter Turnout, and Organic Plan Making," *Psychological Science* 21, no. 2 (2010): 194, 198 (showing that people are significantly more likely to vote if asked to identify when and where they will vote). For a popular treatment with citations of the academic literature, see Heath and Heath, *Switch*, 15–17.

16. See Jason Riis and Rebecca Ratner, "Simplified Nutrition Guidelines to Fight Obesity," in *Leveraging Consumer Psychology for Effective Health Communications: The Obesity Challenge*, eds. Rajeev Batra, Punam Anand Keller, and Victor J. Strecher (Armonk, NY: M. E. Sharpe, 2010), 334 (discussing the importance of simplicity for health-related communications). For examples of relevant advice in connection with dietary guidelines, see U.S. Department of Agriculture, "Dietary Guidelines 2010" (January 2011), www.cnpp.usda.gov/Publications/DietaryGuidelines/2010/PolicyDoc/SelectedMessages.pdf. These take the form of relatively specific guidance, such as "Make half your plate fruits and vegetables," "Switch to fat-free or low-fat (1%) milk," and "Drink water instead of sugary drinks." See also Katherine L. Milkman et al., "Using Implementation Intentions Prompts to Enhance Influenza Vaccination Rates," *Proceedings of the National Academy of Sciences of the United*

States of America 108, no. 26 (June 28, 2011): 10415–420, www.pnas.org/content/ 108/26/10415 (finding that people are significantly more likely to be vaccinated if they are given a prompt asking them to write down the date and time when they will do so, but that a prompt asking them simply to write down the date has no such effect). See also the discussion of the replacement of the food pyramid with the food plate in chapter 4.

17. David Pogue, "A Tablet to Rival the Leader," *New York Times*, July 5, 2012, B1, www .nytimes.com/2012/07/05/technology/personaltech/nexus-7-googles-new-tablet -seriously-challenges-the-ipad-state-of-the-art.html.

18. Elli Stuhler, "Lost and Confused at Ikea? It's All Part of Their Plan," *Globe and Mail* (Canada), September 10, 2012, www.theglobeandmail.com/life/the-hot-button/ lost-and-confused-at-ikea-its-all-part-of-their-plan/article613259/.

19. See Irwin P. Levin, Sandra L. Schneider, and Gary J. Gaeth, "All Frames Are Not Created Equal: A Typology and Critical Analysis of Framing Effects," *Organizational Behavior and Human Decision Processes* 76, no. 2 (November 1998): 149, 150.

20. See Marti Hope Gonzales, Elliot Aronson, and Mark A. Costanzo, "Using Social Cognition and Persuasion to Promote Energy Conservation: A Quasi-Experiment," *Journal of Applied Social Psychology* 18, no. 12 (September 1988): 1049, 1062. For a demonstration that people's decisions about when to claim Social Security benefits are affected by framing, see Jeffrey R. Brown, Arie Kapteyn, and Olivia S. Mitchell, "Framing Effects and Expected Social Security Claiming Behavior" (working paper 17018, National Bureau of Economic Research, Cambridge, MA, May 2011), 4, 5, http://papers.ssrn.com/sol3/papers.cfm?abstract_id=1833155 (finding that use of "breakeven analysis" leads people to claim early and that people are more likely to delay claiming when later claiming is framed as a gain rather than a loss).

21. See Donald A. Redelmeier, Paul Rozin, and Daniel Kahneman, "Understanding Patients' Decisions: Cognitive and Emotional Perspectives," *Journal of the American Medical Association* 270, no. 1 (July 7, 1993): 72, 73.

22. See John W. Payne et al., "Life Expectancy as a Constructed Belief: Evidence of a Live-to or Die-by Framing Effect" (working paper 12-10, Columbia Business School, New York, January 18, 2012), http://papers.ssrn.com/sol3/papers.cfm ?abstract_id=1987618.

23. See Richard E. Nisbett et al., "Popular Induction: Information Is Not Necessarily Informative," in *Judgment under Uncertainty: Heuristics and Biases,* eds. Daniel Kahneman, Paul Slovic, and Amos Tversky (Cambridge, UK: Cambridge University Press, 1982).

24. Eric J. Johnson et al., "Framing, Probability Distortions, and Insurance Decisions," *Journal of Risk and Uncertainty* 7, no. 1 (August 1993): 35–51.

25. See Ximena Cadena and Antoinette Schoar, "Remembering to Pay? Reminders vs. Financial Incentives for Loan Payments" (working paper 17020, National Bureau of Economic Research, Cambridge, MA, May 2011), http://papers.ssrn.com/sol3/ papers.cfm?abstract_id=1833157.

26. See Victor Stango and Jonathan Zinman, "Limited and Varying Consumer Attention: Evidence from Shocks to the Salience of Bank Overdraft Fees" (working paper 11-17, Federal Reserve Bank of Philadelphia, Philadelphia, April 1, 2011), 27, 28, http://papers.ssrn.com/sol3/papers.cfm?abstract_id=1817916.

27. Nicola Lacetera et al., "Heuristic Thinking and Limited Attention in the Car Market," *American Economic Review* 102, no. 5 (August 2012).

28. See Devin G. Pope and Maurice E. Schweitzer, "Is Tiger Woods Loss Averse? Persistent Bias in the Face of Experience, Competition, and High Stakes," *American Economic Review* 101, no. 1 (February 2011): 129, 132 (concluding that loss aversion costs the top twenty golfers in the world $640,000 a year on average); see Tom M. Sabrina et al., "The Neural Basis of Loss Aversion in Decision-Making Under Risk," *Science* 315, no. 5811 (January 26, 2007): 515.

29. See M. Keith Chen, Venkat Lakshminarayanan, and Laurie R. Santos, "How Basic Are Behavioral Biases? Evidence from Capuchin Monkey Trading Behavior," *Journal of Political Economy* 114, no. 3 (2006): 516.

30. See Roland Fryer Jr. et al., "Enhancing the Efficacy of Teacher Incentives Through Loss Aversion: A Field Experiment" (working paper 18237, National Bureau of Economic Research, Cambridge, MA, 2012), www.nber.org/papers/w18237.pdf.

31. For a valuable and important study, see Tatiana A. Homonoff, "Can Small Incentives Have Large Effects? The Impact of Taxes Versus Bonuses on Small Bag Use" (job market paper, Princeton University, Princeton, NJ, October 26, 2012), www .princeton.edu/~homonoff/THomonoff_JobMarketPaper.

32. See David Hirshleifer, "The Blind Leading the Blind: Social Influence, Fads, and Informational Cascades," in *The New Economics of Human Behavior*, ed. Mariano Tommasi and Kathryn Ierulli (Cambridge, UK: Cambridge University Press, 1995), 188–89 ("When people can observe one another's behavior, they very often end up making the same choices"); Esther Duflo and Emmanuel Saez, "The Role of Information and Social Interactions in Retirement Plan Decisions: Evidence from a Randomized Experiment," *Quarterly Journal of Economics* 118, no. 3 (August 2003): 815, 839 (discussing retirement plan decisions); Hunt Allcott, "Social Norms and Energy Conservation," *Journal of Public Economics* 95, nos. 9–10 (October 2011): 1082 (discussing energy conservation); Scott E. Carrell et al., "Is Poor Fitness Contagious? Evidence from Randomly Assigned Friends," *Journal of Public Economics* 95, nos. 7–8 (August 2011), 657–63 (concluding that peers influence personal fitness and the likelihood of failing fitness requirements); Banerjee and Duflo, *Poor Economics*, 68 (see above, n. 5) (noting that "knowledge travels" and that friends and neighbors of those given a free bed net "were also more likely to buy a net themselves"). For a treatment with a wide range of examples, see generally Nicholas A. Christakis and James H. Fowler, *Connected: The Surprising Power of Our Social Networks and How They Shape Our Lives* (New York: Little, Brown and Company, 2009). "Is Fitness Contagious?" was later published.

33. See Hirshleifer, "Blind Leading the Blind," 188, 189 (attributing patterns of alcohol, cigarette, and illegal drug consumption to "localized conformity"). For a finding of significant effects from social comparison on water consumption, see generally Paul J. Ferraro and Michael K. Price, "Using Non-Pecuniary Strategies to Influence Behavior: Evidence from a Large-Scale Field Experiment" (working paper 17189, National Bureau of Economic Research, Cambridge, MA, July 2011), www.nber.org/papers/w17189.pdf.

34. See Brent McFerran et al., "How the Body Type of Others Impacts Our Food Consumption," in *Leveraging Consumer Psychology*, 151, 161–63 (see above, n. 16).

35. See, e.g., James Surowiecki, *The Wisdom of Crowds* (New York: Anchor Books, 2005); Scott E. Page, *The Difference: How the Power of Diversity Creates Better Groups, Firms, Schools, and Societies* (Princeton, NJ: Princeton University Press, 2007); Cass R. Sunstein, *Infotopia: How Many Minds Produce Knowledge* (New York: Oxford University Press, 2006).

36. See Jan Lorenz et al., "How Social Influence Can Undermine the Wisdom of Crowd Effect," *Proceedings of the National Academy of Sciences of the United States of America* 108, no. 22 (May 31, 2011): 9020–25.

37. See Geoffrey Cohen, "Party over Policy: The Dominating Effect of Group Influence on Political Beliefs," *Journal of Personality and Social Psychology* 85, no. 5 (November 2003): 808–22.

38. For an outline, see Thaler and Sunstein, *Nudge* (see Introduction, n. 2)

39. See Hirshleifer, "Blind Leading the Blind" (above, n. 31), 19 ("[A]n *informational cascade* occurs when the information implicit in predecessors' actions—or resulting payoffs—is so conclusive that a rational follower will *unconditionally* imitate them, without regard to information from other sources"). For an interesting application, see Brian Knight and Nathan Schiff, "Momentum and Social Learning in Presidential Primaries" (working paper 13637, National Bureau of Economic Research, Cambridge, MA, November 2007), 13, 14, 15, 16, www.nber.org/papers/w13637 .pdf (exploring social learning in the context of presidential primaries and finding that early voters have a disproportionate influence in the selection of candidates compared with late voters).

40. See Timur Kuran, *Private Truths, Public Lies: The Social Consequences of Preference Falsification* (Cambridge, MA: Harvard University Press, 1997) , 35–38.

41. See Robert A. Kagan and Jerome H. Skolnick, "Banning Smoking: Compliance Without Enforcement," in *Smoking Policy: Law, Politics, and Culture*, ed. Robert L. Rabin and Stephen D. Sugarman (New York: Oxford University Press, 1993), 69, 72 (finding that a source of compliance with a law prohibiting smoking indoors was public support); Tho Bella Dinh-Zarr et al., "Reviews of Evidence Regarding Interventions to Increase the Use of Safety Belts," *American Journal of Preventive Medicine* 21, no. 4 (supplement) (November 2001): 48, 49 (suggesting that efforts to enforce safety belt use are effective in large part because they help to make safety belt use a social norm); Maggie Wittlin, "Buckling Under Pressure: An Empirical Test of the Expressive Effects of Law," *Yale Journal on Regulation* 28, no. 2 (February 11, 2011): 419, 443–47 (finding that laws requiring seat belt use have significant effects even when researchers control for citations issued), http://papers.ssrn .com/sol3/papers.cfm?abstract_id=1759993.

42. See Neil D. Weinstein, "Unrealistic Optimism about Susceptibility to Health Problems: Conclusions from a Community-Wide Sample," *Journal of Behavioral Medicine* 10, no. 5 (October 1987): 481, 494. For an interesting complication, showing that people sometimes tend to see themselves as below average for difficult or unusual tasks, see Don Moore and Deborah Small, "Error and Bias in Comparative Judgment: On Being Both Better and Worse Than We Think We Are," *Journal of Personality and Social Psychology* 92, no. 6 (June 2007): 972.

43. See Heather Mahar, "Why Are There So Few Prenuptial Agreements?" (discussion paper 436, Harvard Law School John M. Olin Center for Law, Economics, and

Business, Cambridge, MA, September 2003), 2, www.law.harvard.edu/programs/olin_center/papers/pdf/436.pdf.

44. See Paul Slovic, "Do Adolescent Smokers Know the Risks?" *Duke Law Journal* 47, no. 6 (April 1998): 1133, 1136–37 (1998).

45 See Joshua Tasoff and Robert Letzler, *Everyone Believes in Redemption: Overoptimism and Nudges* (unpublished manuscript, November 9, 2012), http://papers.ssrn.com/sol3/papers.cfm?abstract_id=2066930.

46. See Amos Tversky and Daniel Kahneman, "Availability: A Heuristic for Judging Frequency and Probability," *Cognitive Psychology* 5, no. 2 (September 1973): 207, 221.

47. See Elke U. Weber, "Experience-Based and Description-Based Perceptions of Long-Term Risk: Why Global Warming Does Not Scare Us (Yet)," *Climatic Change* 77, nos. 1–2 (2006) 103, 107–8.

48. See Paul Slovic, Baruch Fischhoff, and Sarah Lichtenstein, "Cognitive Processes and Societal Risk Taking," in *The Perception of Risk,* ed. Paul Slovic (London: Earthscan, 2000), 32, 37–38; Laurette Dubé-Rioux and J. Edward Russo, "An Availability Bias in Professional Judgment," *Journal of Behavioral Decision Making* 1, no. 4 (October–December 1988): 223, 234

49. Ye Li, Eric J. Johnson, and Lisa Zaval, "Local Warming: Daily Temperature Change Influences Belief in Global Warming," *Psychological Science* 22, no. 4 (April 2011): 454–59.

50. For a vivid presentation, see Brian Wansink, David R. Just, and Joe McKendry, "Lunch Line Redesign," *New York Times,* October 21, 2010, A35, www.nytimes.com/interactive/2010/10/21/opinion/20101021_Oplunch.html, and, in particular, this suggestion: "A smarter lunchroom wouldn't be draconian. Rather, it would nudge students toward making better choices on their own by changing the way their options are presented. One school we have observed in upstate New York, for instance, tripled the number of salads students bought simply by moving the salad bar away from the wall and placing it in front of the cash registers." For related evidence, see generally Anne N. Thorndike et al., "A 2-Phase Labeling and Choice Architecture Intervention to Improve Healthy Food and Vending Choices," *American Journal of Public Health* 102, no. 3 (March 2012): 527, http://javeriana.edu.co/redcups/Thorndike.pdf (finding that a color-coded labeling intervention increased healthy choices and that increased visibility and convenience of healthy choices also had a significant effect).

51. See Paul Rozin et al., "Nudge to Nobesity I: Minor Changes in Accessibility Decrease Food Intake," *Judgment and Decision Making* 6, no. 4 (June 2011): 323, 329.

52. Banerjee and Duflo, *Poor Economics,* 269 (see above, n. 5).

53. National Highway Traffic Administration, US Department of Transportation, *Corporate Average Fuel Economy for MY 2017-MY 2025 Passenger Cars and Light Trucks: Final Regulatory Impact Analysis,* August 2012, 983. www.nhtsa.gov/static files/rulemaking/pdf/cafe/FRIA_2017-2025.pdf. For a valuable overview, showing the complexity of the underlying issues and the amount that remains to be learned, see Hunt Allcott and Michael Greenstone, "Is There an Energy Efficiency Gap?" *Journal of Economic Perspectives* 26, no. 1 (Winter 2012): 3.

54. See Daniel J. Benjamin, Sebastian A. Brown, and Jesse M. Shapiro, "Who Is 'Be-

havioral'? Cognitive Ability and Anomalous Preferences" (unpublished manuscript, March 2012), http://faculty.chicagobooth.edu/jesse.shapiro/research/iq.pdf.

55. See Hans-Martin von Gaudecker, Arthur van Soest, and Erik Wengström, "Heterogeneity in Risky Choice Behavior in a Broad Population," *American Economic Review* 101, no. 2 (April 2011): 664–94.

CHAPTER 4

1. See Heath and Heath, *Switch*, 61–62 (see chap. 3, n. 15).
2. www.ChooseMyPlate.gov.
3. See Archon Fung, Mary Graham, and David Weil, *Full Disclosure: The Perils and Promise of Transparency* (New York: Cambridge University Press, 2008), 5–6; Brian Wansink and Matthew M. Cheney, "Leveraging FDA Health Claims," *Journal of Consumer Affairs* 39, no. 2 (Winter 2006): 386, 393, 396.
4. See Amartya Sen, *Poverty and Famines: An Essay on Entitlement and Deprivation* (New York: Oxford University Press, 1983).
5. See US Environmental Protection Agency, "Greenhouse Gas (GHG) Data," www.epa.gov/ghgreporting/ghgdata/index.html.
6. Chris Hamby, Center for Public Integrity, "EPA Hopes Disclosure Leads to Greenhouse Gas Reductions," news release, January 11, 2012, 4:35 p.m., www.publicintegrity.org/2012/01/11/7850/epa-hopes-disclosure-leads-greenhouse-gas-reductions.
7. See Marty Makary, *Unaccountable: What Hospitals Won't Tell You and How Transparency Can Revolutionize Health Care* (New York: Bloomsbury Press, 2012).
8. See Friedrich A. Hayek, "The Uses of Knowledge in Society," *American Economic Review* 35, no. 4 (September 1945): 519–30.
9. See Jeffrey R. Kling et al., "Comparison Friction: Experimental Evidence from Medicare Drug Plans," *Quarterly Journal of Economics* 127, no. 1 (February 2012): 199–235.
10. Fuel Economy Label Format Requirements, 40 C.F.R. § 600.302-08 (2011).
11. See Fuel Economy Regulations for Automobiles: Technical Amendments and Corrections, 74 Fed. Reg. 61,537, 61,542, 61,550–53 (November 25, 2009) (to be codified at 40 C.F.R. pts. 86, 600).
12. See Richard P. Larrick and Jack B. Soll, "The MPG Illusion," *Science* 320, no. 5883 (June 20, 2008): 1593.
13. Ibid., 1594.
14. Hunt Allcott, "Consumers' Perceptions and Misperceptions of Energy Costs," *American Economic Review* 101, no. 3 (May 2011): 98, 102.
15. For one view, see Carolyn Fischer, "Let's Turn CAFE Regulation on Its Head," 1, 2 (issue brief 09-06, Resources for the Future, Washington, DC, May 2009), www.rff.org/RFF/Documents/RFF-IB-09-06.pdf.
16. See generally Fuel Economy Regulations for Automobiles, 74 Fed. Reg. at 61,537.
17. See Kling et al., "Comparison Friction" (see above, n. 9).
18. Revisions and Additions to Motor Vehicle Fuel Economy Label, 76 Fed. Reg. 39,478, 39,480 fig.I-1 (July 6, 2011) (to be codified at 40 C.F.R. pts. 85, 86, and 600).
19. See Oren Bar-Gill, *Seduction by Contract: Law, Economics, and Psychology in Consumer Markets* (Oxford, UK: Oxford University Press, 2012).

20. Credit Card Accountability Responsibility and Disclosure Act of 2009, Pub. L. No. 111-24, 123 Stat. 1734 (2009) (codified in various sections of Titles 15 and 16).

21. See Credit CARD Act § 203, 15 USC § 1632 (2009).

22. See Nutrition Label Content, 9 C.F.R. § 317.309 (2012).

23. Ibid.

24. For one example, see US Department of Health and Human Services, HealthCare .gov, www.healthcare.gov, (last visited November 16, 2012), designed to increase transparency and to promote comparison shopping. See also Patient Protection and Affordable Care Act § 6401(a), 42 USC § 1395cc(j) (2010).

25. Patient Protection and Affordable Care Act § 1103, 42 USC § 18003 (2010).

26. Ibid., (b)(1) (2010).

27. Patient Protection and Affordable Care Act; Exchange Function in the Individual Market: Eligibility Determinations; Exchange Standards for Employers, 76 Fed. Reg. 51,202, 51,210 (August 17, 2011) (to be codified at 45 C.F.R. pts. 155, 157).

28. See Patient Protection and Affordable Care Act § 4205(b), 21 USC § 343(q)(5)(H) (2010). See also 21 USC 343(q)(1)(C)–(D) (2010).

29. See Riis and Ratner, "Simplified Nutrition Guidelines," 334 (see chap. 3, n. 17) (emphasizing the importance of simplicity to promote effective communication of health messages); Jessica Wisdom, Julie S. Downs, and George Loewenstein, "Promoting Healthy Choices: Information versus Convenience," *American Economic Journal: Applied Economics* 2, no. 2 (April 2010): 164, 175–76; Julie S. Downs, George Loewenstein, and Jessica Wisdom, "Strategies for Promoting Healthier Food Choices," *American Economic Review* 99, no. 2 (May 2009): 159, 162; Wansink and Cheney, "Leveraging" (see above, n. 3), 394.

30. See Susanna Kim Ripken, "The Dangers and Drawbacks of the Disclosure Antidote: Toward a More Substantive Approach to Securities Regulation," *Baylor Law Review* 58, no. 1 (January 2006): 139, 160–63.

31. Dodd-Frank Wall Street Reform and Consumer Protection Act § 1032, 12 U.S.C § 5532 (2010).

32. Ibid. See also Riis and Ratner, "Simplified Nutrition Guidelines," 334 (see above, n. 29) (emphasizing importance of simplicity).

33. Dodd-Frank Wall Street Reform and Consumer Protection Act § 1013, 12 USC § 5493 (2010) (describing the tasks of the bureau's research unit). For a relevant discussion, see John Y. Campbell et al., "Consumer Financial Protection," *Journal of Economic Perspectives* 25, no. 1 (Winter 2011): 91, 92.

34. Fiduciary Requirements for Disclosure in Participant-Directed Individual Account Plans, 29 C.F.R. § 2550.404a-5 (2011). For a summary of the rule, see US Department of Labor, *Fact Sheet: Final Rule to Improve Transparency of Fees and Expenses to Workers in 401(k)-Type Retirement Plans,* February 2012, www.dol.gov/ebsa/news room/fsparticipantfeerule.html. For a model chart that companies may use to help their employees to compare retirement plan options under the new rule, see US Department of Labor, *Model Comparative Chart*, www.dol.gov/ebsa/participant feerulemodelchart.doc (last visited November 16, 2012).

35. Program Integrity Issues, 75 Fed. Reg. 66,832 (October 29, 2010) (to be codified at various parts of 34 C.F.R.).

36. Reporting and Disclosure Requirements for Programs That Prepare Students for Gainful Employment in a Recognized Occupation, 34 C.F.R. § 668.6 (2010). For

a summary of the rule, see US Department of Education, "Department of Education Establishes New Student Aid Rules to Protect Borrowers and Taxpayers," press release, October 28, 2010, www.ed.gov/news/press-releases/department-education-establishes-new-student-aid-rules-protect-borrowers-and-tax.

37. See US Department of Agriculture, Nutrition.gov, www.nutrition.gov (last visited January 3, 2013); see also US Department of Agriculture, ChooseMyPlate.gov, www.choosemyplate.gov (last visited November 16, 2012).

38. Pub. L. No. 99-499, 100 Stat. 1728 (1986) (codified at 42 USC § 11001 et seq.).

39. See Archon Fung and Dara O'Rourke, "Reinventing Environmental Regulation from the Grassroots Up: Explaining and Expanding the Success of the Toxics Release Inventory," *Environmental Management* 25, no. 2 (2000): 115, 116.

40. See James T. Hamilton, *Regulation Through Revelation: The Origin, Politics, and Impacts of the Toxics Release Inventory Program* (New York: Cambridge University Press, 2005), 248.

41. See US Department of Labor, Occupational Safety and Health Administration, "Workplace Injury, Illness and Fatality Statistics," www.osha.gov/oshstats/work.html (last visited January 3, 2013).

42. See US Department of Justice, "Data," October 2012, www.justice.gov/open/data.html; Data.gov, www.data.gov (last visited January 3, 2013).

43. See US Department of Labor, "Enforcement Data," http://ogesdw.dol.gov/search php (last visited November 16, 2012).

44. See US Environmental Protection Agency, "Enforcement and Compliance History Online (ECHO)," www.epa-echo.gov (last visited on November 13, 2012).

45. See Peter R. Orszag, director, Office of Management and Budget, Memorandum for the Heads of Executive Departments and Agencies, on the Open Government Directive, December 8, 2009, 2, 7, www.whitehouse.gov/omb/assets/memoranda_2010/m10-06.pdf. For the 2011 National Action Plan of the United States Government, developed as part of the international Open Government Partnership, see *The Open Government Partnership: National Action Plan for the United States of America*, September 20, 2011, www.whitehouse.gov/sites/default/files/us_national_action_plan_final_2.pdf. For material on the international Open Government Partnership, see Open Government Partnership, www.opengovpartnership.org/, last visited January 3, 2013.

46. Interactive Data to Improve Financial Reporting, 74 Fed. Reg. 6776 (February 10, 2009) (to be codified at various parts of 17 C.F.R.).

47. Ibid., 6776.

48. See Katrina Jessoe and David Rapson, "Knowledge Is (Less) Power: Experimental Evidence from Residential Energy Use" (working paper 18344, National Bureau of Economic Research, Cambridge, MA, 2012), www.nber.org/papers/w18344.pdf.

CHAPTER 5

1. See Constanca Esteves-Sorenson and Fabrizio Perretti, "Micro-Costs: Inertia in Television Viewing" *Economic Journal* 122, no. 563 (September 2012): 867–902.

2. On the effects of the credit card tip defaults, see Michael M. Grynbaum, "New York's Cabbies Like Credit Cards? Go Figure," *New York Times*, November 7, 2009, A1, http://www.nytimes.com/2009/11/08/nyregion/08taxi.html. For the admittedly very rough assessment of total additional tips collected, see Joshua Gross, "The

$144,146,165 Button," Unwieldy.net, May 13, 2012, http://notes.unwieldy.net/post/22958656041/the-144-146-165-button. The number is an informal calculation, and should of course be taken with many grains of salt.

3. Richard H. Thaler and Will Tucker, "Smarter Information, Smarter Consumers," *Harvard Business Review* (January/February 2013), http://hbr.org/2013/01/smarter-information-smarter-consumers/ar/1.

4. See Eric J. Johnson, Steven Bellman, and Gerald L. Lohse, "Defaults, Framing and Privacy: Why Opting In-Opting Out," *Marketing Letters* 13, no. 1 (2002): 5–15.

5. Eric J. Johnson and Daniel G. Goldstein, "Do Defaults Save Lives?" *Science* 302 (2003): 1338–39, http://papers.ssrn.com/sol3/papers.cfm?abstract_id=1324774; Watts, *Everything Is Obvious*, 30–31 (see chap. 3, n. 11); Johnson and Goldstein, "Decisions by Default," 417 (see chap. 3, n. 11). For a summary, see Thaler and Sunstein, *Nudge* (see Introduction, n. 2).

6. Arlene C. Chua et al., "Opt-Out of Voluntary HIV Testing: A Singapore Hospital's Experience," *PLoS ONE* 7, no. 4 (April 2012): e34663.

7. Daniel Pichert and Konstantinos V. Katsikopoulos, "Green Defaults: Information Presentation and Pro-Environmental Behaviour," *Journal of Environmental Psychology* 28, no. 1 (March 2008): 63–73.

8. See Madrian and Shea, "Power of Suggestion," 1149, 1158–60 (see chap. 3, n. 11). See also William G. Gale et al., Introduction, in *Automatic: Changing the Way America Saves,* eds. William G. Gale et al. (Washington, DC: Brookings Institution Press, 2009), 1.

9. See Gale et al., *Automatic*, 13.

10. See Peter R. Orszag and Eric Rodriguez, "Retirement Security for Latinos: Bolstering Coverage, Savings, and Adequacy," in *Automatic*, 173, 182; Leslie E. Papke, Lina Walker, and Michael Dworsky, "Retirement Savings for Women: Progress to Date and Policies for Tomorrow," in *Automatic*, 199, 216; Ngina Chiteji and Lina Walker, "Strategies to Increase the Retirement Savings of African American Households," in *Automatic*, 231, 248–49.

11. Pub. L. No. 109-280, 120 Stat. 780 (2006) (codified in various sections of Titles 26 and 29).

12. Pension Protection Act § 902, 26 USC §§ 401, 411, 416 (2006).

13. See WhiteHouse.gov, "Weekly Address: President Obama Announces New Initiatives for Retirement Savings," news release and transcript, September 5, 2009, www.whitehouse.gov/the-press-office/weekly-address-president-obama-announces-new-initiatives-retirement-savings (announcing initiatives to increase participation in IRAs and match retirement savings). For an example of the response by the IRS to this request, see generally Internal Revenue Service, "Retirement & Savings Initiatives: Helping Americans Save for the Future," *Retirement News for Employees*, September 2009, www.irs.gov/pub/irs-tege/rne_se0909.pdf (discussing four notices and three rulings designed to improve retirement saving programs).

14. See Tom Coburn, "Individual Auto-Enrollment: An Alternative to the Individual Mandate" (2009), www.coburn.senate.gov/public/index.cfm?a=Files.Serve&File_id=e87f06bf-d429-4eac-8e7e-ade046b8b882.

15. Congress of the United States, Congressional Budget Office, *Key Issues in Analyzing Major Health Insurance Proposals* (December 2008), 54, www.cbo.gov/sites/default/files/cbofiles/ftpdocs/99xx/doc9924/12-18-keyissues.pdf.

16. See Pension Protection Act § 1511, 29 USC § 218(a) (2006).

17. Department of Health and Human Services, Centers for Medicare and Medicaid Services, *Re: Express Lane Eligibility Option* (February 4, 2010), http://downloads .cms.gov/cmsgov/archived-downloads/SMDL/downloads/SHO10003.pdf.

18. Healthy, Hunger-Free Kids Act of 2012, Pub. L. No. 111-296, 124 Stat. 3183 (2012).

19. Ibid., § 101, 42 USC § 1758(b)(4) (2012).

20. "SAVEings," *OMBlog*, blog entry by Peter Orszag, March 29, 2010, 3:00 p.m., www.whitehouse.gov/omb/blog/10/03/29/SAVEings/.

21. For an overview, see US Department of Labor, "Fact Sheet: Final Regulation Relating to Service Provider Disclosures under Section 408(b)(2)," February 2012, www.dol.gov/ebsa/newsroom/fs408b2finalreg.html.

22. See Rozin et al., "Nudge to Nobesity I," 323–24, 329–30 (see chap. 3, n. 51). For a brief, vivid summary, see Wansink, Just, and McKendry, "Lunch Line Redesign" (see chap. 3, n. 50).

23. See Janet Currie et al., "The Effect of Fast Food Restaurants on Obesity and Weight Gain," *American Economic Journal: Economic Policy* 2, no. 3 (August 2010): 60, 61.

24. See Rozin et al., "Nudge to Nobesity I," 324, 329–30 (see chap. 3, n. 51). For more on the general point, see Brian Wansink, *Mindless Eating: Why We Eat More Than We Think* (New York: Bantam Books, 2007), 58–68, 83–88. For a discussion of the importance of convenience and (in a sense) default choices, see Jessica Wisdom, Julie S. Downs, and George Loewenstein, "Promoting Healthy Choices: Information versus Convenience," *American Economic Journal: Applied Economics* 2, no. 2 (April 2010): 164, 166. For a discussion of the effect of menu positions, see Eran Dayan and Maya Bar-Hillel, "Nudge to Nobesity II: Menu Positions Influence Food Orders," *Judgment and Decision Making* 6, no. 4 (June 2011): 333, 339–40 (finding, on the basis of both laboratory and real-world studies, that items placed at the beginning or the end of the list in their category are only 20 percent as popular as when they are placed in the center of the list).

25. See Wansink, *Mindless Eating*. For a detailed discussion, on which I draw here, see Cass R. Sunstein and Richard Thaler, "The Survival of the Fattest," *New Republic*, March 19, 2007, 59–63, www.tnr.com/article/books-and-arts/the-survival-the -fattest.

26. Paul Rozin et al., "The Ecology of Eating: Smaller Portion Sizes in France Than in the United States Help Explain the French Paradox," *Psychological Science* 14, no. 5 (September 2003): 450–54.

27. US Centers for Disease Control and Prevention, "The New (Ab)Normal," Making-HealthEasier.org, http://makinghealtheasier.org/newabnormal (last visited January 3, 2013).

28. See generally Janet Schwartz et al., "Inviting Consumers to Downsize Fast-Food Portions Significantly Reduces Calorie Consumption," *Health Affairs* 31, no. 2 (February 2012): 399–407.

29. See "Nudge, Nudge: New Tools to Encourage Sensible Behaviour," *Economist*, December 15, 2012, www.economist.com/news/special-report/21568072-new-tools -encourage-sensible-behaviour-nudge-nudge.

30. See, e.g., William G. Gale, J. Mark Iwry, and Spencer Walters, "Retirement Sav-

ings for Middle- and Lower-Income Households: The Pension Protection Act of 2006 and the Unfinished Agenda," in *Automatic* (see above, n. 8), 11, 13–14; Isaac M. Dinner et al., "Partitioning Default Effects: Why People Choose Not to Choose" (unpublished manuscript, November 28, 2010), http://ssrn.com/abstract =1352488; Gabriel D. Carroll et al., "Optimal Defaults and Active Choices," *Quarterly Journal of Economics* 124, no. 4 (November 2009): 1639, 1641–43.

31. See Craig R. M. McKenzie, Michael J. Liersch, and Stacey R. Finkelstein, "Recommendations Implicit in Policy Defaults," *Psychological Science* 17, no. 5 (May 2006): 414, 418–19; Madrian and Shea, "Power of Suggestion," 1182 (see chap. 3, n. 10). Of course, it is not true that all defaults are chosen because they produce the best outcomes for people. Note the important finding that while automatic enrollment carries with it an implicit suggestion, nonenrollment does not, apparently because people do not think that a nonenrollment default means that the choice architect favors nonenrollment. See David Tannenbaum and Peter H. Ditto, "Information Asymmetries in Default Options" (unpublished manuscript, (2012), https://webfiles.uci.edu/dtannenb/www/documents/default%20information%20 asymmetries.pdf.

32. See Dinner et al., "Partitioning Default Effects," 5, 6 (see above, n. 30), http://ssrn .com/abstract=1352488.

33. Ibid., 12–14; Thaler and Sunstein, *Nudge* (see Introduction, n. 2).

34. See N. Craig Smith, Daniel G. Goldstein, and Eric J. Johnson, "Smart Defaults: From Hidden Persuaders to Adaptive Helpers" (INSEAD working paper 2009/03/ ISIC, 2009), 15, 16, http://ssrn.com/abstract=1116650.

35. See 16 C.F.R. § 425 (2012); Federal Trade Commission, *Negative Options: A Report by the Staff of the FTC's Division of Enforcement* (January 2009), 5, www.ftc.gov/os/ 2009/02/P064202negativeoptionreport.pdf.

36. FTC, *Negative Options*.

37. See Gopi Shah Goda and Colleen Flaherty Manchester, "Incorporating Employee Heterogeneity into Default Rules for Retirement Plan Selection" (working paper 16099, National Bureau of Economic Research, Cambridge, MA, July 2010), www.nber.org/papers/w16099.

38. See Elizabeth F. Emens, "Changing Name Changing: Framing Rules and the Future of Marital Names," *University of Chicago Law Review* 74, no. 3 (Summer 2007): 761–863.

39. To be sure, the word *want* elides some important issues. In many cases, social norms exert a high degree of pressure, and some husbands undoubtedly make their own preferences clear, thus affecting the choices of wives. Social norms can operate as the equivalent of a default rule and overcome the legal default. It is likely that this account is, for many wives, the underlying story here.

40. See John Beshears et al., "The Limitations of Defaults" (paper prepared for the Twelfth Annual Joint conference of the Retirement Research Consortium, September 15, 2010, 8), www.nber.org/programs/ag/rrc/NB10-02,%20Beshears,%20 Choi,%20Laibson,%20Madrian.pdf.

41. An important and highly relevant discussion is Anuj K. Shah, Sendhil Mullainathan, and Eldar Shafir, "Some Consequences of Having Too Little," *Science* 338, no. 6107 (November 2, 2012): 682–85.

42. See Erin Todd Bronchetti et al., "When a Nudge Isn't Enough: Defaults and Saving Among Low-Income Tax Filers" (working paper 16887, National Bureau of Economic Research, Cambridge, MA, March 2011), 4, 11, www.nber.org/papers/w16887. Note, however, that the "default" in this study consisted of a mere statement on a form. The line between the use of such a "default" and active choosing is relatively thin.

43. See Lauren E. Willis, "When Nudges Fail: Slippery Defaults," *University of Chicago Law Review* 80 (forthcoming 2013), http://papers.ssrn.com/sol3/papers.cfm?abstract_id=2142989.

44. Ibid.

45. For a valuable discussion, see Steffan Altmann, Armin Falk, and Andreas Grunewald, "Incentives and Information as Driving Forces of Default Effects" (unpublished manuscript, April 4, 2012), www.ewi-ssl.pitt.edu/econ/files/seminars/120404_sem924_Steffen%20Altman.pdf.

46. For detailed discussion, see Cass R. Sunstein, "Impersonal Default Rules vs. Active Choosing vs. Personalized Default Rules: A Triptych" (unpublished manuscript, November 5, 2012), http://papers.ssrn.com/sol3/papers.cfm?abstract_id=2171343.

47. See Susan Dynarski and Mark Wiederspan, "Student Aid Simplification" (working paper 17834, National Bureau of Economic Research, Cambridge, MA, February 2012), www.nber.org/papers/w17834. I draw on this helpful paper for the discussion.

48. See Eric P. Bettinger et al., "The Role of Simplification and Information in College Decisions: Results from the H&R Block FAFSA Experiment" (working paper 15361, National Bureau of Economic Research, Cambridge, MA, September 2009), www.nber.org/papers/w15361.

49. See Office of Information and Regulatory Affairs, Office of Management and Budget, *Information Collection Budget of the United States Government* (2010), 22, 32–33, www.whitehouse.gov/sites/default/files/omb/inforeg/icb/icb_2010.pdf.

50. For discussion of the importance of such steps, see Bettinger et al., "Role of Simplification," 26–29 (see above, n. 48); Council of Economic Advisers and National Economic Council, *Simplifying Student Aid: The Case for an Easier, Faster, and More Accurate FAFSA* (September 2009), www.whitehouse.gov/assets/documents/FAFSA_Report.pdf.

51. See Dynarski and Wiederspan, "Student Aid Simplification" (see above, n. 47).

52. 29 C.F.R. § 1926 (2003).

53. See 31 C.F.R. § 208 (2004); US Department of Treasury, "Treasury Goes Green, Saves Green: Broad New Initiative Will Increase Electronic Transactions, Save More Than $400 Million, 12 Million Pounds of Paper in First Five Years Alone," press release, April 19, 2010, www.treasury.gov/press-center/press-releases/Pages/tg644.aspx.

54. See Cass R. Sunstein, administrator, Office of Information and Regulatory Affairs, Memorandum to Chief Information Officers, on Data Call for the 2010 Information Collection Budget, April 20, 2010, 1, 2, www.whitehouse.gov/omb/assets/inforeg/2010_icb_datacall.pdf.

55. For a list of these initiatives, see Office of Information and Regulatory Affairs, *Information Collection Budget*, 23–123 (see above, n. 49). For a subsequent list in

the 2011 report, including reduced burdens on small businesses and simplification efforts for federal benefits programs, see Office of Information and Regulatory Affairs, Office of Management and Budget, *Information Collection Budget of the United States Government* (2011), 16–79, www.whitehouse.gov/sites/default/files/omb/inforeg/icb/2011_icb.pdf.

56. See Cass R. Sunstein, administrator, Office of Information and Regulatory Affairs, Memorandum to Chief Information Officers, on Minimizing Paperwork and Reporting Burdens, February 23, 2011, 1, www.whitehouse.gov/sites/default/files/omb/inforeg/icb/2011_ICB_Data_Call.pdf. For the results of this request, see generally Office of Information and Regulatory Affairs, *Information Collection Budget* (see above, n. 49).

57. Sunstein, Memorandum on Minimizing Paperwork and Reporting Burdens.

58. See 31 C.F.R. § 208.6 (2004); Direct Express, www.usdirectexpress.com/ (last visited January 3, 2013).

59. ARA Content, "Social Security Recipients Embrace Electronic Payments, Give High Marks to Treasury-Recommended Prepaid Card," *Dallas Weekly*, August 14, 2012, http://www.dallasweekly.com/online_features/senior_living/article_f5e968 23-2c4e-5732-a603-4ab1cfaad4a1.html.

60. See Michael S. Barr, "Financial Services, Saving, and Borrowing Among Low- and Moderate-Income Households: Evidence from the Detroit Area Household Financial Services Survey," in *Insufficient Funds: Savings, Assets, Credit, and Banking Among Low-Income Households*, eds. Rebecca M. Blank and Michael S. Barr (New York: Russell Sage Foundation, 2009), 66, 76–77.

61. See Sheena Sethi-Iyengar, Gur Huberman, and Wei Jiang, "How Much Choice Is Too Much? Contributions to 401(k) Retirement Plans," in *Pension Design and Structure: New Lessons from Behavioral Finance*, eds. Olivia S. Mitchell and Stephen P. Utkus (New York: Oxford University Press, 2004), 83, 84–87.

62. Ibid., 88–91.

63. See Sheena S. Iyengar and Emir Kamenica, "Choice Proliferation, Simplicity Seeking, and Asset Allocation," *Journal of Public Economics* 94, nos. 7-8 (2010): 530, 536–38.

64. Florian Heiss, Daniel McFadden, and Joachim Winter, "Mind the Gap! Consumer Perceptions and Choices of Medicare Part D Prescription Drug Plans" (working paper 13627, National Bureau of Economic Research, Cambridge, MA, November 2007), www.nber.org/papers/w13627.

65. For a discussion of the underlying problem, see Jonathan Gruber and Jason T. Abaluck, "Choice Inconsistencies among the Elderly: Evidence from Plan Choice in the Medicare Part D Program," *American Economic Review* 101, no. 4 (June 1, 2011): 1180–1210.

66. See 42 C.F.R. § 422.506(b)(1)(iv). For a related discussion, with particular emphasis on the abilities of those who create menus, see David Goldreich and Hanna Hałaburda, "When Smaller Menus Are Better: Variability in Menu-Setting Ability" (working paper 11-086, Harvard Business School, December 12, 2011), www.hbs.edu/research/pdf/11-086.pdf.

CHAPTER 6

1. See Christopher Chabris and Daniel Simons, *The Invisible Gorilla: How Our Intuitions Deceive Us* (New York: Crown Publishers, 2010).

2. Daniel Kahneman, *Thinking, Fast and Slow*, 23 (see chap. 2, note 3).

3. David Copperfield, Foreword, in Michael S. Sweeney, *Brainworks: The Mind-Bending Science of How You See, What You Think, and Who You Are* (Washington, DC: National Geographic, 2012), 5, 9. On magic and the brain, see Stephen MacKnic and Susana Martinez-Conde, *Sleights of Mind: What the Neuroscience of Magic Reveals About Our Everyday Deceptions* (New York: Macmillan, 2010).

4. See US Centers for Disease Control and Prevention, "Tobacco Use: Targeting the Nation's Leading Killer at a Glance 2011," page last updated November 16, 2012, www.cdc.gov/chronicdisease/resources/publications/aag/osh.htm.

5. See US Centers for Disease Control and Prevention, "Videos," September 26, 2012, www.cdc.gov/tobacco/campaign/tips/resources/videos/.

6. See *R. J. Reynolds Tobacco Co. v. FDA*, 845 F. Supp. 2d 266, 275 (D.D.C. 2012).

7. Compare *R. J. Reynolds Tobacco Co. v. FDA*, 696 F.3d 1205 (D.C. Cir. 2012) (striking down the FDA regulation) with *Discount Tobacco City & Lottery, Inc. v. U.S.*, 674 F.3d 509 (6th Cir. 2012) (upholding the regulation).

8. See Hunt Allcott and Sendhil Mullainathan, "Behavior and Energy Policy," *Science* 327, no. 5970 (March 5, 2010): 1204–05; Paul J. Ferraro and Michael K. Price, "Using Non-Pecuniary Strategies to Influence Behavior: Evidence from a Large Scale Field Experiment" (working paper 17189, National Bureau of Economic Research, Cambridge, MA, July 2011), www.nber.org/papers/w17189.pdf (finding that social comparison information significantly decreased water consumption). For a discussion of the importance of reminders in increasing savings, with particular emphasis on salience, see Dean Karlan et al., "Getting to the Top of Mind: How Reminders Increase Saving" (working paper, Department of Economics, Yale University, New Haven, CT, April 23, 2010), 23, http://karlan.yale.edu/p/Top-of -Mind-April2010.pdf. For a discussion of the policy implications of consumer inattention in the context of energy savings, see Hunt Allcott, Sendhil Mullainathan, and Dmitry Taubinsky, "Externalizing the Internality" (unpublished manuscript, July 24, 2011, 5, 6, 7), www.ncsu.edu/cenrep/workshops/TREE/documents/AMT July2011.pdf.

9. Ian Ayres, Sophie Raseman, and Alice Shih, "Evidence from Two Large Field Experiments That Peer Comparison Feedback Can Reduce Energy Use" (working paper 15386, National Bureau of Economic Research, September 2009), www .nber.org/papers/w15386.pdf.

10. See Allcott, Mullainathan and Taubinsky, "Externalizing" (see above, n. 8); Richard B. Howarth, Brent M. Haddad, and Bruce Paton, "The Economics of Energy Efficiency: Insights from Voluntary Participation Programs," *Energy Policy* 28, no. 6-7 (June 2000): 477, 484–85.

11. See Tatiana A. Homonoff, "Can Small Incentives Have Large Effects? The Impact of Taxes Versus Bonuses on Disposable Bag Use" (unpublished manuscript, Princeton University, Princeton, NJ, October 26, 2012), www.princeton.edu/~homonoff/ THomonoff_JobMarketPaper.

12. See Claudia R. Sahm, Matthew D. Shapiro, and Joel Slemrod, "Check in the

Mail or More in the Paycheck: Does the Effectiveness of Fiscal Stimulus Depend on How It Is Delivered?" (working paper 2010-40, Finance and Economic Discussion Series, Divisions of Research & Statistics and Monetary Affairs, Federal Reserve Board, Washington, DC, 2011), 20–22, www.federalreserve.gov/pubs/feds/2010/201040/201040pap.pdf.

13. Ibid., 20, 21.

14. See Raj Chetty, Adam Looney, and Kory Kroft, "Salience and Taxation: Theory and Evidence," *American Economic Review* 99, no. 4 (September 2009): 1145, 1163; Jacob Goldin and Tatiana Homonoff, "Smoke Gets in Your Eyes: Cigarette Tax Salience and Tax Regressivity," *American Economic Journal: Economic Policy* (forthcoming), http://dataspace.princeton.edu/jspui/bitstream/88435/dsp 01wm117n980/1/561.pdf. Interestingly, Goldin and Homonoff find that low-income people do pay attention to taxes at the register. For a discussion of tax salience in a broadly similar vein, see Amy Finkelstein, "E-ZTAX: Tax Salience and Tax Rates," *Quarterly Journal of Economics* 124, no. 3 (August 2009): 969, 1008–09. Finkelstein finds that electronic toll collection makes rates far less salient and hence that toll rates are 20 percent to 40 percent higher than they would be without electronic collection.

15. For relevant discussion, see Lawrence Lessig, "The Regulation of Social Meaning," *University of Chicago Law Review* 62, no. 3 (Summer 1995): 943–1045.

16. See Micah Edelson et al., "Following the Crowd: Brain Substrates of Long-Term Memory Conformity," *Science* 333, no. 6038 (July 1, 2011): 108–111.

17. See Robert B. Cialdini et al., "Managing Social Norms for Persuasive Impact," *Social Influence* 1, no. 1 (2006): 3, 10–12.

18. See Watts, *Everything Is Obvious*, 54–59 (see chap. 3, n. 11).

19. See Matthew J. Salganik, Peter Sheridan Dodds, and Duncan J. Watts, "Experimental Study of Inequality and Unpredictability in an Artificial Cultural Market," *Science* 311, no. 5762 (February 10, 2006): 584; see also Matthew J. Salganik and Duncan J. Watts, "Leading the Herd Astray: An Experimental Study of Self-Fulfilling Prophecies in an Artificial Cultural Market," *Social Psychology Quarterly* 71, no. 4 (December 2008): 338–55; Matthew J. Salganik and Duncan J. Watts, "Web-Based Experiments for the Study of Collective Social Dynamics in Cultural Markets," *Topics in Cognitive Science* 1, no. 3 (July 2009): 439–68.

20. Salganik and Watts, "Leading the Herd Astray."

21. *See* Sinan Aral, "Poked to Vote," *Nature* 489, no. 7415 (September 13, 2012): 212–14.

22. See Timur Kuran, *Private Truths, Public Lies: The Social Consequences of Preference Falsification* (Cambridge, MA: Harvard University Press, 1997); Susanne Lohmann, "The Dynamics of Informational Cascades: The Monday Demonstrations in Leipzig, East Germany, 1989–91," *World Politics* 47, no. 1 (October 1994): 42.

23. See Tho Bella Dinh-Zarr et al., "Reviews of Evidence Regarding Interventions to Increase the Use of Safety Belts," *American Journal of Preventive Medicine* 21, supplement 1 (November 2001): 48 (documenting an increase in safety belt use from 14 percent in 1983 to 71 percent in 2000).

24. Federal Leadership on Reducing Text Messaging While Driving, Exec. Order 13,513, 74 Fed. Reg. 51,225, 51,225 (October 1, 2009): "Federal employees shall not engage in text messaging (a) when driving [government-owned vehicles], or

when driving [privately owned vehicles] while on official Government business, or (b) when using electronic equipment supplied by the Government while driving."

25. See Saurabh Bhargava and Vikram Pathania, "Driving Under the (Cellular) Influence: The Link Between Cell Phone Use and Vehicle Crashes," *American Economic Journal: Economic Policy* 5 (forthcoming), www.aeaweb.org/aea/2011conference/program/retrieve.php?pdfid=182.

26. See US Department of Transportation, "DOT Releases Distraction Guidelines for Automakers," news release, February 16, 2012, http://fastlane.dot.gov/2012/02/distracted-driving-guidelines.html.

27. Anne M. Wolf and Graham A. Colditz, "Current Estimates of the Economic Cost of Obesity in the United States," *Obesity Research* 6, no. 2 (March 1998): 97–106, http://onlinelibrary.wiley.com/doi/10.1002/j.1550-8528.1998.tb00322.x/abstract.

28. See Dean Karlan et al., "Candy or Fruit? Measuring the Impact of Michelle Obama on Healthy Eating Choices" (unpublished manuscript, Yale University, New Haven, CT, November 1, 2012), http://karlan.yale.edu/p/Michelle-2012.pdf.

29. See Jamie Mulligan, "First Lady Michelle Obama Announces Collaboration with Walmart in Support of Let's Move Campaign," *Let's Move Blog*, January 26, 2011, www.letsmove.gov/blog/2011/01/25/first-lady-michelle-obama-announces-collaboration-walmart-support-lets-move-campaign.

30. Walmart, "Walmart Launches Major Initiative to Make Food Healthier and Healthier Food More Affordable," press release, January 20, 2011, http://walmartstores.com/pressroom/news/10514.aspx.

31. Ibid. See also Sheryl Gay Stolberg, "Wal-Mart Shifts Strategy to Promote Healthy Foods," *New York Times*, January 20, 2011, B1.

32. See "Food Giants Pledge to Cut 1.5 Trillion Calories Out of Products," *USA Today* (May 21, 2010), www.usatoday.com/money/industries/food/2010-05-17-cutting-calories_N.htm.

33. See Grocery Manufacturers Association, "Food and Beverage Industry Launches Nutrition Keys Front-of-Pack Nutrition Labeling Initiative to Inform Consumers and Combat Obesity," press release, January 24, 2011, www.gmaonline.org/news-events/newsroom/food-and-beverage-industry-launches-nutrition-keys-front-of-pack-nutrition-/.

34. McDonald's USA, "McDonald's USA Adding Calorie Counts to Menu Boards, Innovating with Recommended Food Groups, Publishes Nutrition Progress Report," press release, September 12, 2012, www.aboutmcdonalds.com/content/dam/AboutMcDonalds/Newsroom/Electronic%20Press%20Kits/Nutrition%20EPK/McDonalds%20USA%20Adding%20Calorie%20Counts%20to%20Menu%20Boards.pdf.

CHAPTER 7

1. Dan Kahan and his coauthors have done a great deal of valuable work on this topic. See the Cultural Cognition Project at Yale Law School, www.culturalcognition.net/kahan/ (last visited January 3, 2012).

2. See Russell Hardin, "The Crippled Epistemology of Extremism," in *Political Extremism and Rationality*, eds. Albert Breton et al. (Cambridge, UK: Cambridge University Press, 2002), 3.

3. I draw here on arguments that I have made elsewhere. See Cass R. Sunstein, "Cognition and Cost-Benefit Analysis," *Journal of Legal Studies* 29, no. S2 (June 2000):

1059–1103; Cass R. Sunstein, *Risk and Reason: Safety, Law, and Reason* (New York: Cambridge University Press, 2002); Cass R. Sunstein, *Laws of Fear: Beyond the Precautionary Principle* (Cambridge, UK: Cambridge University Press, 2005).

4. See Thaler and Sunstein, *Nudge*, 25 (see Introduction, n. 2).

5. See W. Kip Viscusi, "Alarmist Decisions with Divergent Risk Information," *Economic Journal* 107, no. 445 (November 1997): 1657–58 (studying situations under which "[n]ew information about risks may generate alarmist actions that are not commensurate with the magnitude of the risks").

6. See Paul Slovic, "Informing and Educating the Public about Risk," in *Perception of Risk*, ed. Paul Slovic, 184–85 (see chap. 3, n. 48).

7. See Richard Elliot Benedict, *Ozone Diplomacy: New Directions in Safeguarding the Planet* (Cambridge, MA: Harvard University Press, 1998), for the fascinating tale.

8. See, e.g., W. Kip Viscusi, *Fatal Tradeoffs* (New York: Oxford University Press, 1995); Sunstein, *Risk and Reason* (see above, n. 3).

9. See W. Kip Viscusi and Joseph E. Aldy, "The Value of a Statistical Life," *Journal of Risk and Uncertainty* 27, no. 1 (August 2003): 5–76.

10. Two federal agencies—the Environment Protection Agency and the Department of Transportation—have developed official guidance on VSL. In its 2011 update, DOT adopted a value of $6.2 million (2011 dollars) and required all the components of the department to use that value in their Regulatory Impact Analyses. See Polly Trottenberg, assistant secretary for transportation policy, and Robert Rivkin, general counsel, US Department of Transportation, Memorandum to Secretarial Officers and Modal Administrators, on Treatment of the Economic Value of a Statistical Life in Departmental Analyses—2011 Interim Adjustment, July 29, 2011, www.dot.gov/sites/dot.dev/files/docs/Value_of_Life_Guidance_2011_Update_07-29-2011.pdf. EPA has changed its VSL to an older value of $6.3 million (2000 dollars) and adjusts this value for real income growth to later years. In its Regulatory Impact Analysis for a new primary standard for nitrogen dioxide, for example, EPA adjusted this VSL to account for a different currency year (2006) and for income growth to 2020; the adjustment yielded a VSL of $8.9 million. US Environmental Protection Agency, *Final Regulatory Impact Analysis (RIA) for the NO2 National Ambient Air Quality Standards (NAAQS)*, 4-8 n.11 (January 2010), www.epa.gov/ttn/ecas/regdata/RIAs/FinalNO2RIAfulldocument.pdf. Although the Department of Homeland Security has no official policy on VSL, it sponsored a report through its US Customs and Border Protection and has used the recommendations of this report to inform VSL values for several recent rulemakings. This report recommends $6.3 million (2008 dollars) and also recommends that DHS adjust this value upward over time for real income growth (in a manner similar to EPA's adjustment approach). Lisa A. Robinson, *Valuing Mortality Risk Reductions in Homeland Security Regulatory Analyses* (June 2008), www.regulatory-analysis.com/robinson-dhs-mortality-risk-2008.pdf.

Other regulatory agencies that have used a VSL in individual rulemakings include the Department of Labor's Occupational Safety and Health Administration and Health and Human Services's Food and Drug Administration. In OSHA's rulemaking setting a permissible exposure limit for hexavalent chromium, it specifically referred to EPA guidance to justify a VSL of $6.8 million (2003 dollars), as the types of air exposure risks regulated in this rulemaking were similar to those in EPA rulemakings. See 71 Fed. Reg. 10,100, 10,305 (February 28, 2006) (to be codified at various parts of 29 C.F.R.). The FDA has consistently used values of $5 million and $6.5 million (2002 dollars) in several of its rulemakings to monetize mortality risks. See 68 Fed. Reg. 41,434, 41,490 (July 11, 2003) (to be codified at 21 C.F.R. pt. 101); 68 Fed. Reg. 6062, 6076 (February 6, 2003) (to be codified at 21 C.F.R. pt. 201). But it also uses a monetary value of the remaining life-years saved by alternative policies. This is sometimes referred to as "Value of a Statistical Life Year," or VSLY. See Lisa A. Robinson, "How US Government Agencies Value Mortality Risk Reductions," *Review of Environmental Economics and Policy* 1, no. 2 (Summer 2007): 283, 293.

11. See Sean Hannon Williams, "Statistical Children," *Yale Journal on Regulation* (forthcoming), http://ssrn.com/abstract=2176463.

12. See Cass R. Sunstein, "Valuing Life: A Plea for Disaggregation," *Duke Law Journal* 54 (2004): 385–45.

13. I have explored this problem in many places, including *Laws of Fear* (2008).

14. An important issue for valuation of the benefits of greenhouse gas reductions is the "social cost of carbon." For the position of the Obama administration on that issue, see Interagency Working Group on Social Cost of Carbon, *Technical Support Document: Social Cost of Carbon for Regulatory Impact Analysis Under Executive Order 12866* (February 2010), www.epa.gov/oms/climate/regulations/scc-tsd.pdf. For an illuminating critique, see William Nordhaus, "Estimates of the Social Cost of Carbon: Background and Results from the RICE-2011 Model" (discussion paper, Cowles Foundation for Research in Economics, Yale University, New Haven, CT, October 18, 2011), http://dido.econ.yale.edu/P/cd/d18a/d1826.pdf.

15. "Obama's Rule-Making Loophole," *Wall Street Journal*, January 24, 2011, http://online.wsj.com/article/SB10001424052748704881304576094132896862582.html.

16. Charles S. Clark, "Obama Regulatory Chief Draws Skepticism from GOP House Members," *Government Executive*, January 26, 2011, www.govexec.com/oversight/2011/01/obama-regulatory-chief-draws-skepticism-from-gop-house-members/33169/.

17. One study does, however, suggest that poor people may be the principal beneficiaries of clean air regulation. See Matthew E. Kahn, "The Beneficiaries of Clean Air Act Regulation," *Regulation* 24, no. 1 (Spring 2001): 34–38, www.cato.org/sites/cato.org/files/serials/files/regulation/2001/4/kahn.pdf.

18. Medical Examination of Aliens—Removal of Human Immunodeficiency Virus (HIV) Infection from Definition of Communicable Disease of Public Health Significance, 74 Fed. Reg. 56,547, 56,559 (November 2, 2009) (to be codified at 42 C.F.R. pt. 34).

19. Regulations to Implement the Equal Employment Provisions of the Americans with Disabilities Act, as Amended, 76 Fed. Reg. 16,977, 16,986 (March 25, 2011) (to be codified at 29 C.F.R. pt. 1630).

20. Federal Motor Vehicle Safety Standard, Rearview Mirrors; Federal Motor Vehicle Safety Standard, Low-Speed Vehicles Phase-In Reporting Requirements; Proposed Rule, 75 Fed. Reg. 76,185, 76,238 (December 7, 2010) (as codified at 49 C.F.R. pts. 571, 585).

21. National Standards to Prevent, Detect, and Respond to Prison Rape, 77 Fed. Reg. 37,105, 37,111 (June 20, 2012) (to be codified at 28 C.F.R. pt. 115).

22. Nondiscrimination on the Basis of Disability in State and Local Government Services; Final Rules, 75 Fed. Reg. 56,163, 56,170 (September 15, 2010) (to be codified at 28 C.F.R. pts. 35, 36).

23. See Office of Information and Regulatory Affairs, Office of Management and Budget, *2009 Report to Congress on the Benefits and Costs of Federal Regulations and Unfunded Mandates on State, Local, and Tribal Entities* (2009), 42, www.white house.gov/sites/default/files/omb/assets/legislative_reports/2009_final_BC_Report _01272010.pdf.

CHAPTER 8

1. See US Department of Labor, "US Department of Labor's OSHA Withdraws Proposed Interpretation on Occupational Noise," news release, January 19, 2011, www .osha.gov/pls/oshaweb/owadisp.show_document?p_table=NEWS_RELEASES &p_id=19119.

2. See Dynarski and Wiederspan, "Student Aid Simplification" (see chap. 5, n. 47).

3. See A. Denny Ellerman et al., *Markets for Clean Air: The U.S. Acid Rain Program* (Cambridge, UK: Cambridge University Press, 2000).

4. See Paul Voosen, "For Energy Efficiency, Chu's Law Is on the Way," *Greenwire*, June 14, 2012, http://eenews.net/public/Greenwire/2012/06/14/1; Energy Conservation Program: Energy Conservation Standards for Residential Refrigerators, Refrigerator-Freezers, and Freezers, 76 Fed. Reg. 57,516 (September 15, 2011) (to be codified at 10 C.F.R. pt. 430).

5. Winston Harrington, "Grading Estimates of the Benefits and Costs of Federal Regulation" (discussion paper 06-39, Resources for the Future, Washington, DC, September 1, 2006), http://papers.ssrn.com/sol3/papers.cfm?abstract_id=937357.

6. Winston Harrington, Richard Morgenstern, and Peter Nelson, "How Accurate Are Regulatory Cost Estimates?" (Resources for the Future, Washington, DC, March 5, 2010), http://grist.files.wordpress.com/2010/10/harringtonmorgen sternnelson_regulatory_estimates.pdf.

7. See Office of Information and Regulatory Affairs, Office of Management and Budget, *Validating Regulatory Analysis: 2005 Report to Congress on the Costs and Benefits of Federal Regulations and Unfunded Mandates on State, Local, and Tribal Entities* (2005), 46, 47, www.whitehouse.gov/sites/default/files/omb/assets/omb/ inforeg/2005_cb/final_2005_cb_report.pdf.

8. Office of Management and Budget, *Validating Regulatory Analysis: 2005 Report*, 42. As in the Harrington study (see above, n. 6), OMB's 2005 report used the term *accurate* to mean "that the post-regulation estimate is within +/− 25 percent of the pre-regulation estimate."

9. Michael Greenstone, "Toward a Culture of Persistent Regulatory Experimentation and Evaluation," in *New Perspectives on Regulation,* eds. David Moss and John Cisterno (Cambridge, MA: Tobin Project, 2009), 113.

10. Ibid.

11. See, e.g., US Environmental Protection Agency, *Improving Our Regulations: A Preliminary Plan for Periodic Retrospective Reviews of Existing Regulations* (May 24, 2011), 34, www.whitehouse.gov/files/documents/2011-regulatory-action-plans/ EnvironmentalProtectionAgencyPreliminaryRegulatoryReformPlan.pdf ("Verbal comments were solicited at a series of twenty public meetings. . . . Additionally,

EPA held nineteen more town halls and listening sessions targeting specific program areas [e.g., solid waste and emergency response] and EPA Regions").

12. See Cass R. Sunstein, administrator, Office of Information and Regulatory Affairs,
Memorandum to the Heads of Executive Departments and Agencies, on Retrospective Analysis of Existing Significant Regulations, April 25, 2011, www.white
house.gov/sites/default/files/omb/memoranda/2011/m11-19.pdf.

13. The final plans can be viewed on the White House's website, Whitehouse.gov.
See "Regulation Reform," www.whitehouse.gov/21stcenturygov/actions/21st
-century-regulatory-system (last visited January 3, 2013).

14. US Environmental Protection Agency, *Improving Our Regulations*, 5, 14 (see above,
n. 11).

15. US Department of Health and Human Services, *Plan for Retrospective Review of
Existing Rules* (August 22, 2011), 3, 8–17, www.whitehouse.gov/sites/default/files/
other/2011-regulatory-action-plans/healthandhumanservicesregulatoryreformplan
august2011.pdf.

16. US Department of Labor, *Preliminary Plan for Retrospective Analysis of Existing
Rules* (May 2011), 10, 11, www.whitehouse.gov/files/documents/2011-regulatory
-action-plans/DepartmentofLaborPreliminaryRegulatoryReformPlan.pdf.

17. The plan to propose this rule is described in US Department of Transportation,
*Plan for Implementation of Executive Order 13563: Retrospective Review and Analy-
sis of Existing Rules* (August 2011), 2, 21, www.whitehouse.gov/sites/default/files/
other/2011-regulatory-action-plans/departmentoftransportationregulatoryreform
planaugust2011.pdf.

18. US Department of Labor, *Preliminary Plan*, 9, 10 (see above, n. 16).

19. Ibid., 32, 33.

20. US Department of Commerce, *Plan for Retrospective Analysis of Existing Rules*
(August 18, 2011), 3, 4, 5, 6, www.whitehouse.gov/sites/default/files/other/2011
-regulatory-action-plans/departmentofcommerceregulatoryreformplanaugust2011a
.pdf.

21. Exec. Order 13,563, 76 Fed. Reg. 3821 (January 18, 2011).

22. See Regulatory Cooperation Council (Canada), *Joint Action Plan for the
Canada-United States Regulatory Cooperation Council* (2011), http://actionplan
.gc.ca/en/page/rcc-ccr/joint-action-plan-canada-united-states-regulatory; see also
"North America," Office of Management and Budget, www.whitehouse.gov/omb/
oira_irc_north_america (last visited January 3, 2013).

23. Relevant documents can be found at "North America," Office of Management and
Budget, www.whitehouse.gov/omb/oira_irc_north_america#mexico (last visited
January 3, 2013).

24. See Cass R. Sunstein, administrator, Office of Information and Regulatory Affairs,
Memorandum to the Heads of Executive Departments and Agencies, on Cumulative Effects of Regulations, March 20, 2012, www.whitehouse.gov/sites/default/
files/omb/assets/inforeg/cumulative-effects-guidance.pdf.

25. See Cass R. Sunstein, administrator, Office of Information and Regulatory Affairs, Memorandum to the Heads of Executive Departments and Agencies, on Reducing Reporting and Paperwork Burdens, June 22, 2012, www.whitehouse.gov/
sites/default/files/omb/inforeg/memos/reducing-reporting-and-paperwork-burdens
.pdf.

26. See Internal Revenue Service, "Choose the Simplest Tax Form for Your Situation," January 5, 2011, www.irs.gov/uac/Choose-the-Simplest-Tax-Form-for-Your-Situation.

27. See Cass R. Sunstein, administrator, Office of Information and Regulatory Affairs, Memorandum to the Heads of Executive Departments and Agencies, on Final Guidance on Implementing the Plain Writing Act of 2010, April 13, 2011, www.whitehouse.gov/sites/default/files/omb/memoranda/2011/m11-15.pdf.

28. Ezra Klein, "President Obama Lays Out His Second Term," *Wonkblog*, October 24, 2012, 4:09 p.m., www.washingtonpost.com/blogs/wonkblog/wp/2012/10/24/president-obama-lays-out-his-second-term/.

29. See generally Banerjee and Duflo, *Poor Economics* (see chap. 3, n. 5).

30. Ibid.

31. See Charlotte L. Brace, Kristie L. Young, and Michael A. Regan, "Analysis of the Literature: The Use of Mobile Phones While Driving" (publication 2007:35, Monash University Accident Research Centre, Victoria, Australia, April 17, 2007), www.nsc.org/news_resources/Resources/Documents/Analysis%20of%20the%20Literature,%20The%20Use%20of%20Mobile%20Phones%20While%20Driving.pdf.

32. See Bhargava and Pathania, "Driving under the (Cellular) Influence" (see chap. 6, n. 25).

33. US Department of the Treasury, *Plan for Retrospective Analysis of Existing Rules* (August 22, 2011), 20, www.treasury.gov/about/budget-performance/annual-performance-plan/Documents/lookback%20plan%20final%208%2018%2011%20clean.pdf.

34. US Department of Labor, *Preliminary Plan* (see above, n. 16), 22.

35. US Department of the Interior, *Preliminary Plan for Retrospective Regulatory Review* (2011), 19, www.whitehouse.gov/files/documents/2011-regulatory-action-plans/DepartmentoftheInteriorPreliminaryRegulatoryReformPlan.pdf. See also US Department of Agriculture, *Final Plan for Retrospective Analysis Pursuant to Executive Order 13563* (August 18, 2011), 23, www.whitehouse.gov/sites/default/files/other/2011-regulatory-action-plans/departmentofagricultureregulatoryreformplanaugust2011.pdf ("[The USDA] may consider the use of experimental or quasi-experimental designs, including randomized controlled trials, when promoting the empirical testing of the effects of rules").

CHAPTER 9

1. Frances Martel, "Jon Stewart Rails against Bloomberg's 'Draconian' Soda Ban with Piles of Gross 'Legal' Food," *Mediaite*, May 31, 2012, 11:24 p.m., www.mediaite.com/tv/jon-stewart-rails-against-bloombergs-draconian-soda-ban-with-piles-of-gross-legal-food/.

2. For a more detailed discussion of the distinction between hard and soft paternalism, and, indeed, of many of the questions discussed in this chapter, see Cass R. Sunstein, "Behavioral Economics and Paternalism," *Yale Law Journal* 122 (forthcoming, 2013).

3. There are many spirited and useful discussions. See Riccardo Rebonato, *Taking Liberties: A Critical Examination of Libertarian Paternalism* (New York: Palgrave Macmillan, 2012); Joshua Wright and Douglas H. Ginsburg, "Behavioral Law and Economics: Its Origins, Fatal Flaws, and Implications for Liberty," *Northwestern*

University Law Review 106, no. 3 (Summer 2012): 1033–90; Edward Glaeser, "Paternalism and Psychology," *University of Chicago Law Review* 73, no. 1 (Winter 2006): 133.

4. David Benjamin et al., "What Do You Think Would Make You Happier? What Do You Think You Would Choose?" *American Economic Review* 102, no. 5. (August 2012): 2083–2110.

5. See, e.g., Daniel T. Gilbert et al., "Immune Neglect: A Source of Durability Bias in Affective Forecasting," *Journal of Personality and Social Psychology* 75, no. 3 (September 1998): 617–38, www.wjh.harvard.edu/~dtg/Gilbert%20et%20al%20(IM MUNE)t.pdf.

6. See Joel Waldfogel, *Scroogenomics: Why You Shouldn't Buy Presents for the Holidays* (Princeton, NJ: Princeton University Press, 2009). On the behavioral economics, see George Loewenstein and Cass R. Sunstein, "Commerce Claus: The Behavioral Economics of Christmas," *New Republic*, December 20, 2012, www.tnr.com/article/politics/magazine/110860/commerce-claus.

7. See Jonathan H. Gruber and Sendhil Mullainathan, "Do Cigarette Taxes Make Smokers Happier?" *Advances in Economic Analysis and Policy* 5, no. 1 (2005).

8. See Jeff Strnad, "Conceptualizing the 'Fat Tax': The Role of Food Taxes in Developed Economies" (working paper 286, John M. Olin Program in Law and Economics at Stanford Law School, Stanford, CA, July 2004), http://papers.ssrn.com/sol3/papers.cfm?abstract_id=561321.

9. See Michael Lewis, "Obama's Way," *Vanity Fair*, October 2012, www.vanityfair.com/politics/2012/10/michael-lewis-profile-barack-obama.

10. The quotation can be found at Parker, "Esther Duflo Explains" (see chap. 2, n. 9). Duflo develops these ideas in detail in her 2012 Tanner Lectures, http://economics.mit.edu/files/7904. See also the important discussion in Shah et al., "Some Consequences of Having Too Little" (see chap. 5, n. 41).

11. Glaeser, "Paternalism and Psychology" (above, n. 3), 133, 151.

12. The point is discussed illuminatingly in Rebonato, *Taking Liberties* (above, n. 3).

13. Antonio Damasio, *Descartes' Error: Emotion, Reason, and the Human Brain* (New York: Penguin Books, 2006), 37, 193–94.

INDEX